DIVERSITY AND MARGINALISATION IN CHILDHOOD

SAGE was founded in 1965 by Sara Miller McCune to support the dissemination of usable knowledge by publishing innovative and high-quality research and teaching content. Today, we publish over 900 journals, including those of more than 400 learned societies, more than 800 new books per year, and a growing range of library products including archives, data, case studies, reports, and video. SAGE remains majority-owned by our founder, and after Sara's lifetime will become owned by a charitable trust that secures our continued independence.

Los Angeles | London | New Delhi | Singapore | Washington DC | Melbourne

DIVERSITY AND MARGINALISATION
IN CHILDHOOD
A GUIDE FOR INCLUSIVE THINKING 0–11
PAULA HAMILTON

Los Angeles | London | New Delhi
Singapore | Washington DC | Melbourne

Los Angeles | London | New Delhi
Singapore | Washington DC | Melbourne

SAGE Publications Ltd
1 Oliver's Yard
55 City Road
London EC1Y 1SP

SAGE Publications Inc.
2455 Teller Road
Thousand Oaks, California 91320

SAGE Publications India Pvt Ltd
B 1/I 1 Mohan Cooperative Industrial Area
Mathura Road
New Delhi 110 044

SAGE Publications Asia-Pacific Pte Ltd
3 Church Street
#10-04 Samsung Hub
Singapore 049483

Editor: Delayna Spencer
Assistant editor: Catriona McMullen
Production editor: Martin Fox
Marketing manager: Lorna Patkai
Cover design: Wendy Scott
Typeset by: KnowledgeWorks Global Ltd.

Library of Congress Control Number: 2020942350

British Library Cataloguing in Publication data

A catalogue record for this book is available from the British Library

ISBN 978-1-5297-3322-8
ISBN 978-1-5297-3321-1 (pbk)

I would like to dedicate this book in memory of my mother – Shirley Scott

CONTENTS

ABOUT THE AUTHOR

Paula Hamilton is a senior lecturer at the University of Chester. After completing a teacher training degree in the early 1990s, Paula worked on a European research project which focused on health promoting schools. She then spent 10 years within further education, teaching on early childhood studies and health and social care courses. Since 2007, she has worked as a senior lecturer in higher education, lecturing on programmes relating to early childhood, family, youth and primary education studies. Her PhD, completed in 2011, focused on the inclusion of migrant worker children into primary schools in North Wales. Paula's research and publications lie in the field of social justice, inclusion, diversity and the health and well-being of children, young people and families.

ACKNOWLEDGEMENTS

I would like to express my sincere thanks to my family, Mark, Holly and Ella, for the personal encouragement and proofreading.

I would also like to thank the team at SAGE, particularly Delayna Spencer and Catriona McMullen, for their invaluable support in the production of this book.

I would additionally like to thank all childhood and education studies students whom I have taught over the years for contributing to invaluable discussion around topics of diversity and marginalisation, as well as participants who have been involved in my prior research studies: they have given me the inspiration to write this book.

INTRODUCTION

Understanding Marginalisation

Marginalisation (also known as social exclusion) is a multifaceted concept, which may be understood in diverse ways. However, what all explanations have in common is that the term 'marginal' designates a position or location that is 'situated on a border, edge, or fringe' (Pelc 2017). Thus, with regard to individuals or social groups, marginalisation refers to the relegation to the fringes of society, where a person or a group might be partly or completely excluded due to a lack of rights, resources and opportunities. Marginalisation is a major cause of vulnerability, which exposes individuals and groups to a range of disadvantages, inequalities and possible harm, and often renders those affected unable or restricted in their ability to deal with the adversity experienced.

Marginalisation can be understood as both a process, and a condition, that prevents individuals or groups from full participation in social, economic and political life (Daniels 2017). Complex overlays of social and economic discrimination, political exclusion, displacement and conflict unfortunately remain features of the world, leading to disadvantage and inequitable life opportunities for certain groups of the population (Chand et al. 2017). In the past two centuries, marginality has been perceived as a response to the socio-economic and political changes and complexities created by globalisation. Many countries have undergone, and continue to undergo, structural and demographic changes, with both positive and negative consequences, which is resulting in new cultural tensions and different issues of marginality emerging in communities (Hamilton 2013a, 2013b, 2013c; Chand et al. 2017).

For many decades, the UK Government has enforced various legislation and policy which public bodies are expected to comply with, including schools and early years settings, in an attempt to redress the balance for marginalised and disadvantaged groups by reducing or eliminating exclusionary barriers. However, we appear to be living in a time and space where differences and inequality levels are escalating and 'where concerns over the marginalization of people and places have yet to be fully understood and addressed' (Chand et al. 2017: v). There are varied populations of marginalised children across the UK, as any child, young person or family can be marginalised based on their circumstances, experiences or perceived differences. There are core factors that determine who or what groups are marginalised within society; this includes but is not exclusive to the following issues a child living in deprivation or in care, or due to their socio-economic status, gender, ethnicity, language, religion, sexual orientation, or any mental or physical impairment.

Considering the numerous government initiatives over the last couple of decades, spearheading the inclusion and diversity movement, one would think that few groups are now marginalised within the UK. Unfortunately, this is far from the case, as the groups contained within this book remain disadvantaged and face many discriminatory and exclusionary barriers. Thus, this book seeks to add to the existing literature base relating to inclusion, diversity and social justice in early childhood and school settings. It aims to contribute to the academic debate on issues by encouraging early years practitioners and primary school teachers to adopt a more critical lens through:

- Examining how their own social positioning, beliefs, values, experiences and actions may negatively impact on the children and families in their care.
- Being familiar with sociological theories underpinning inclusion, diversity and marginalisation.
- An analytical appraisal of the impact of mass media through generating damaging and restrictive dominant discourses.
- An awareness of how wider social issues and tensions which exist within society and communities can filter into early years settings.
- Understanding the concept of intersectionality – how different types of marginalisation intersect to multiply inequality and disadvantage, in particular, how social deprivation and mental health commonly overlap with other aspects of social identity.
- Acknowledging the complexities of inclusive ideology and social justice in practice.
- Delivering critical inclusion, social inclusion and diversity education, where children explore core factors (social, economic, political) which serve to disadvantage and marginalise and where the marginalised can be empowered.

The stigma, prejudice, inequalities and discrimination encountered as a result of being marginalised, together with a lack of support from knowledgeable, skilled and empathic practitioners, can have serious consequences on many aspects of children's lives. Social isolation and psychological and behavioural disruption as responses to marginalisation can lead to negative self-regard, long-term health consequences (Rigby and Starbuck 2018), poor educational attainment and overall lower life chances. Thinking more critically and holistically about a child's life – their learning and social spaces, their health and well-being, their family background and community factors – is central to better understanding the inequalities and adversity faced, and responding to their needs, including identifying ways to empower the marginalised.

1

CRITICAL INCLUSION: CONCEPTS, THEORIES, CHALLENGES AND PRACTICE

CONTENTS

CHAPTER OVERVIEW

This chapter considers key concepts of social justice, inclusion and equality. It outlines some of the sociological perspectives and influential theorists underpinning the issues considered within this book, to help develop a critical understanding of the social inequalities faced by marginalised groups within early childhood and primary school settings and society in general, and to inform the delivery of social justice and inclusive education.

This chapter considers:

1   Explores concepts of social justice, equality, human rights and inclusive ideology.
2   Examines principles of inclusive education, including complexities in practice.
3   Considers influential theorists, whose views are central to understanding social inequality.
4   Outlines sociological perspectives useful for exploring social inequalities (interactionalism, functionalism, conflict theory, feminism, postmodernism and critical theory/pedagogy).
5   Examines the need for critical inclusion: non-judgemental, empathetic and reflective practitioners who educate children critically about issues of diversity and social injustice and who aim to empower the marginalised.

CONCEPTS OF SOCIAL JUSTICE, INCLUSION, EQUALITY AND HUMAN RIGHTS

What is inclusion?

Inclusion, a concept which has diverse origins, draws upon a range of perspectives. Influenced by different international governments, non-government agencies, professional groups, communities and activists, over many decades, means the concept of inclusion is often interpreted in various ways by individuals and organisations (Devarakonda 2013). Many advocates of inclusion locate their philosophy on arguments of social justice, where 'commitments to equality and diversity are not just respected ideas but enacted practices' (Gibson 2009: 1). However, doing inclusion in practice is not always straightforward and it is often loaded with tensions and complexities.

 **ACTIVITY**

Thinking about inclusion

When you consider the term 'inclusion' with regards to children and families, what do you think about?

You may have identified some of the principles below. Working with a peer, select three principles and explain why each is essential in the work undertaken with young children.

Principles of inclusion (not an exhaustive list)

Values (equality, respect, tolerance, fairness); justice; human rights; individual needs; diversity; participation; empowerment; including marginalised groups; challenging stereotypes, prejudice, discrimination and barriers; policies and practices.

It is important that early years practitioners and teachers are aware of the broader picture which influences inclusive ideology underpinning policy, practice and provision within their settings. Inclusive education, which is centred around issues of difference and identity, and has led to a 'unified drive towards minimal exclusion ... through the removal of exclusionary factors' (Nutbrown and Clough 2013: 8) within schools and early years provision, is a sub-set of the wider area of social inclusion.

Social exclusion describes the phenomenon where certain individuals or groups 'have no recognition by, or voice or stake in, the society in which they live' (Charity Commission 2001: 2). The causes are often multiple and connected to various social factors, frequently including financial hardship, and lead to many marginalised families struggling with social, economic and political aspects in their lives. Social inclusion results from positive action taken to change the factors that have led to social exclusion, enabling individuals or communities to fully participate in society (Charity Commission 2001).

Human rights and social justice

The United Nations Convention on the Rights of the Child (UNCRC) was established in 1989 and consists of 54 articles that 'set out the civil, political, economic, social and cultural rights' that governments should make available to all children (UNICEF UK, 2020). Central to this is the acknowledgement that every child under the age of 18 has basic rights, which include: the right to life, survival and development; protection from violence, abuse or neglect; health care; education; being raised by, or have a relationship with, their parents; and having their views acknowledged (Save the Children 2020). Globally, many governments have signed the Convention, agreeing that they will meet the rights outlined and help all children to reach their full potential. Although the UNCRC itself is not legally binding, many of its articles are covered by legislation in the UK, which if breached can lead to penalties.

Despite the UK having signed up to the UNCRC, many children in the country experience living conditions which impact on their basic rights. In 2016, the committee reporting back on the UK's implementation of the UNCRC expressed concern that many children with disabilities are still placed in special schools or special units in mainstream schools and that bullying remains a widespread problem, particularly against lesbian, gay, bisexual, transgender and intersex children, children with disabilities and children belonging to minority groups, including Roma, Gypsy and Traveller children. It recommended that sexual and reproductive health education should be made part of the mandatory school curriculum; that increased investment is needed to reduce child poverty, support children's mental health and strengthen the rights of asylum-seeking, refugee and migrant children; and that the UK should implement comprehensive measures to further develop inclusive education (Centre for Studies on Inclusive Education [CSIE] 2018a; Equality and Human Rights Commission [EHRC] 2019a).

Human rights and social justice, which underpin policy and practice within schools and early years provision in the UK, are essential to the care and education of children and young people. However, it is not always easy for practitioners to translate rights policy into effective practice. Rights and values underpinning social justice are complex as different principles may apply in different situations (Smith 2012) and individuals will have different opinions as to what they consider to be fair and just. Ruitenberg and Vokey (2010 cited in Smith 2012) conceptualise three principles of justice:

- *Justice as harmony* – asserts that people have different talents which, when combined, strengthen a community and society. Therefore, practitioners should treat children *differently* to support individual talents, enabling children to reach their own potential.
- *Justice as equity* – based on the belief that children need to be treated *differently* according to what they need to enable them to reach a certain level of achievement or outcome.
- *Justice as equality* – the belief that although children are not the same, they are equally deserving, so should be treated the *same*. Criticisms against this

principle are that children are individuals with different needs and therefore need to be treated differently; and treating everyone the same will mean children with difficulties will struggle and capable children will be unable to excel.

Equality of opportunity

The Equality Act 2010 replaced nine major pieces of legislation and numerous regulations relating to various forms of discrimination. It provides a single law, covering all the types of discrimination that are unlawful. The Act places a legal duty on public bodies (including schools and early years settings) to promote equality of opportunity and to protect the rights of individuals, including protection against discrimination. It highlights nine protected characteristics: sex, race, religion or belief, sexual orientation, disability, age, gender reassignment, pregnancy and maternity, and marriage and civil partnership. The Act also states there must be protection for people discriminated against because they are 'perceived' to have, or are 'associated' with someone who has, a protected characteristic. The Public Sector Equality Duty places an extra duty on public bodies, to consider how they can: eliminate discrimination and other conduct that is prohibited by the Act; advance equality of opportunity between people who share a protected characteristic and people who do not share it; and foster good relations between people who share a protected characteristic and people who do not share it (EHRC 2020a).

The Act makes it unlawful for a school to discriminate against, harass or victimise a pupil or potential pupil in relation to admissions, or the way it provides education and access to any benefit, facility or service, or by excluding a pupil or subjecting them to detriment. Schools are permitted to treat disabled pupils more favourably than pupils without disabilities and are expected to make 'reasonable adjustments' to meet the needs of pupils with special educational needs and disabilities (SEND) (Department for Education 2014a). Unlawful behaviour defined by the Act include:

- *Direct discrimination*: When a person treats one person less favourably than they would another because they have a protected characteristic.
- *Indirect discrimination*: When a provision, criterion or practice appears neutral, but its impact disadvantages people with a protected characteristic. For example banning all headwear would indirectly discriminate against people who wear headwear for religious reasons.
- *Harassment*: Unwanted conduct that creates an intimidating, hostile, degrading, humiliating or offensive environment for the complainant, or violates their dignity.
- *Victimisation*: Treating someone unfavourably because they have taken (or might be taking) action under the Equality Act, or supporting somebody who is doing so.

(EqualiTeach 2018, p. 7)

PRINCIPLES AND COMPLEXITIES
OF INCLUSIVE EDUCATION

The principles underpinning inclusive education have been evolving since the 1980s, with global and national commitments to the movement (see the Salamanca Statement [UNESCO 1994] and the Dakar Framework [UNESCO 2000]). Stemming from the concern relating to the educational provision available to children with special educational needs and disabilities (SEND), there has historically been a narrow view of inclusion – as specifically related to special educational needs (SEN). The concept of inclusive education has since widened and is based upon a 'moral position which values and respects all individuals and which welcomes diversity as a rich learning resource' (CSIE 2018b). Diversity can be understood as:

> All the ways we are unique and different from others. Dimensions of diversity include but are not limited to ... ethnicity, religion and spiritual beliefs, cultural orientation, colour, physical appearance, gender, sexual orientation, ability, education, age, ancestry, place of origin, marital status, family status, socio-economic circumstance, profession, language, health status, geographic location, group history, upbringing and life experiences. (Calgary Board of Health 2008 cited in Loreman et al. 2010: 23)

Inclusion is not optional. In the UK there is a legal duty on schools and early years settings to provide social and learning spaces which all pupils can access and where the needs and backgrounds of all children are catered for and valued. The key perspectives of inclusive education which are outlined in Table 1.1 are not exclusive of each other nor are they chronologically sequential. Instead, there is a 'dynamic relationship between the various perspectives' and they should be considered as occupying 'the same ground with different (sometimes competing) emphases and popularity' (Clough 2006: 9). The 'Index for Inclusion' (Booth and Ainscow 2011) provides a useful overview of ideas relating to the philosophy of inclusive education.

Table 1.1   Key perspectives of inclusive education

Special educational needs and disability	Educational policy for children with SEND falls into three broad periods of segregation, integration and inclusion. Until the 1970s, a 'medical model' of disability was used to categorise and segregate children with 'impairments' into special schools. Increased political pressure from disability groups in the 1980s resulted in a movement away from the psycho-medical model towards social models. During this period more children were integrated into mainstream education, but they were expected to adapt to meet the requirements of the school. In the decades which have followed, inclusive ideology has increasingly placed the onus on settings to adapt to meet the needs of individuals. See Chapter 5 for further detail.

Table 1.1 (Continued)

Disciplinary exclusion	Based on behavioural difficulties, this perspective reflects a medical model in that attention is placed on the child rather than on school systems and practices (Ekins and Grimes 2009).
Social inclusion and vulnerable groups	Educational inclusion became set in the wider context of social inclusion which expressed concern about all children who were disadvantaged in society and likely to experience barriers to education, health, future employment opportunities and community participation. With this perspective there can be a tendency to develop isolated strategies and segregated practices for vulnerable groups, which may unintentionally stigmatise (Ekins and Grimes 2009).
Human rights	Inclusion may be set within a rights-based concept focused on the idea of full participation of all children and young people in educational settings, on equal terms and without discrimination (Topping 2012). This approach sometimes involves complexities in practice. For example, rights-based ideology in the education of children with SEND is not universally accepted, even within the disabled community, and there remains disagreement as to what an inclusive education system should be (Boronski and Hassan 2015).

 **ACTIVITY**

Debating inclusive education

Debate the following statements, justifying why you agree or disagree. Try to draw on the experience you have had in practice.

- 'Inclusive education is easy to achieve.'
- 'A practitioner can be trained to meet the needs of all pupils.'
- 'Inclusive education can sometimes be detrimental.'
- 'A practitioner will realise if they have any biased ideas or discriminatory attitudes about the children and families in their settings.'

Translating inclusion into practice

It has long been acknowledged that inclusion is complex and is at risk of remaining idealistic, as principles contained within policies are not always easily translated into practice (Gibson 2009). It is essential therefore to acknowledge the realities, tensions and dilemmas which may confront practitioners. Similarly, it is important that practitioners recognise that inclusion is an ongoing process which may never be fully achieved due to multifaceted exclusionary factors and newly emerging challenges.

CASE STUDY

Inclusion in practice

Mr Jones is a teacher at St Mary's Roman Catholic school. A number of the children have diverse and complex family/social backgrounds including: a Traveller boy; a young girl who lives with same-sex foster parents; a child who has refugee status; a young boy who has Down's syndrome; a child who lives in extreme poverty; a boy who is experiencing gender dysphoria; and a highly able child.

Task

Working with a small group of peers, decide whether Mr Jones works within the early years or Key Stage 2 (7–11 years) and consider the following questions.

1   Identify two children and discuss how each might be disadvantaged or vulnerable in the setting.
2   Discuss the challenges that Mr Jones might face when trying to be inclusive for these children.
3   Mr Jones is struggling to address the needs of all of the children and feels he will have to prioritise in terms of his time and the resources available. What advice would you give to him? Do any of the children require priority? If so, on what basis?
4   What strategies could Mr Jones put into place to support these children with regard to both their learning and social spaces?

The idea of catering to the needs of all, particularly for children with high levels of diversity and need, can be a daunting task, which is not without its challenges. The adoption of inclusive attitudes and practices will be largely dependent on the personal values of the individual; the quality of continuing professional development available; the level of support offered by senior teachers/managers; and competing pressures for time, funding and resources (Loreman et al. 2010; Topping 2012).

Eradicating prejudice, discrimination and inequality is a difficult task. Practitioners need to be committed and skilled. Positive attitudes are critical to the success of inclusion. It is therefore essential that measures are put into place which call upon practitioners to critically reflect on their own attitudes and practices towards difference and diversity (Department for Children, Schools and Families [DCSF] 2009a; Nutbrown and Clough 2013). Histories, cultures and traditions hold deep-seated stereotypes that should be openly explored and acknowledged in a safe and confidential space (DCSF 2009a).

Intersectionality

It is also important that child practitioners appreciate how elements of identity frequently interact. Intersectionality, a concept introduced by Kimberlé Crenshaw (1989), is useful for understanding the multiple, intersecting aspects of identity (gender, class, economic, race, sexuality, age, language, religion, disability) which can lead to individuals being oppressed and marginalised within society. Routinely used within the field of sociology to examine social inequalities, it is a perspective that has more recently been applied to education (Bei 2019). For example, special educational needs legislation has traditionally ignored interaction with socio-economic disadvantage, despite half of the variance in attainment between schools and children being accounted for by poverty (Topping 2012).

Inclusive education has come to be viewed as a positive 'good for all' ideology. However, addressing the needs of diverse children often involves various complexities and ambiguities (Hamilton 2018a, 2018b). At the root of many tensions are differences in assumptions about the purposes of early years provision, education, the family and society. The preoccupation with a performance-driven culture, where the accomplishment of middle-class white children is typically used to set the benchmark against which all 'others' are measured, is problematic (Banks 2016). Concepts arising from the culture of performativity (school engagement, attainment, outcomes, aspirations) contribute to stigmatising certain children rather than focusing on the problems stemming from inequity in the education system and wider society (Banks 2016).

Inclusive ideology, while promoting equity for marginalised individuals and groups, may also present serious complexities and repercussions and may not be what the child (or their family) wants or needs. Hamilton's (2018a, 2018b) work revealed how some Gypsy and Traveller children were ostracised by their family and community for remaining in secondary education. Unless there is a shift in society, where young Gypsies/Roma/Travellers have unrestricted access to mainstream careers, they risk becoming socially isolated from two communities. Furthermore, some young Gypy, Roma and Traveller people are proud of their heritage, including their gendered roles, and regard mainstream education as infringement of their rights. Inclusive ideology may also be problematic for children with SEND. If a child or parent prefers a special school rather than mainstream education, should they not have a right to it (Boronski and Hassan 2015)? A final example is the historical practice of segregated English language tuition for children who had English as an additional language, and limiting the use of their mother tongue in schools and early years settings (Rutter 2006) in an attempt to advance their English to promote access to learning and social spaces. Inclusion therefore has the potential to be a double-edged sword.

Norwich (2013) stresses the importance of seeing connections between opposing positions, recognising that there may be tensions where final solutions are not found, only resolutions which may involve some balancing between principles. There needs to be acknowledgement that rights-based discourse and inclusive values and practices, which are often based on middle-class Anglo-Saxon culture, may be irrelevant, in conflict or even disadvantage some individuals/groups. Critical thinking regarding seeing and doing inclusion is essential, where tensions arising from addressing difference are carefully considered, the notion of intersectionality reflected upon, limits and possible consequences acknowledged and what is 'truly inclusive' for individuals questioned. Intersectionality is considered in further detail in Chapter 4 (pp. 68–72) and Chapter 5 (pp. 91–93).

INFLUENTIAL THEORISTS AND SOCIOLOGICAL PERSPECTIVES

A more radical understanding now underpins the inclusion movement. Sociological perspectives and empirical studies have demonstrated the significance of structural inequalities in the child's environment as being both the root cause of, and solution to, exclusive practices which marginalise certain individuals and groups. Consideration will now be given to some of the influential theorists and sociological perspectives which help to examine the inequalities that exist within early years settings, schools, communities and society in general.

Influential theorists

Karl Marx (1818–1883) –
The *Communist Manifesto*; Das Kapital

Marx was a German philosopher, political economist and journalist. Marx's work was a response to the changes caused by the Industrial Revolution of the nineteenth century. Marx focused on capitalism, a system which involves the unequal distribution of wealth and access to resources. Marxism has had a significant impact on the world's politics, particularly in terms of understanding social inequalities and social change (Robinson and Jones Diaz 2006). Social class is viewed as the organising principle in societies and the primary context in which relations of power and inequality function.

Marx suggested that social equality could be attained through a workers' revolution in which the capitalist state would be replaced by a communist social and economic system run by the ordinary people. Marxism, an economically based social theory, is regarded as a 'grand narrative' in which a particular perspective provides a universal explanation – that human thoughts, actions and institutions are influenced by their relationship to how one makes a living (Robinson and Jones Diaz 2006).

Marx contended that conflict between the ruling class or 'bourgeoisie' (those who own and control land, factories, businesses) and the ruled workers or 'proletariat' (wage earners) shaped society. This relationship is deemed to be one founded within conflict and exploitation, where the bourgeoisie exploit workers to gain profit from the resources and/or the goods they produce. Social power is linked to those who have access to, and control of, production in a capitalist society. Marxism views power as being repressive and generated by the state through institutions, such as the education system, which reproduce the values and practices of the ruling class to keep them in power (Robinson and Jones Diaz 2006).

Marxist sociologists explain child poverty as being a consequence of the capitalist economic system, which places capital (land, industry and money) in the hands of a few dominant individuals. However there is some question as to how adequate the Marxist perspective is for explaining social inequalities within modern societies (Robinson and Jones Diaz 2006).

Paulo Freire (1921–1997) – Pedagogy of the Oppressed

Freire was a Brazilian educator, social activist and education theorist. In Brazil, he developed ways to address widespread illiteracy. Working for UNESCO, Freire became involved in various programmes, in different countries, aimed at improving the education and life chances of disadvantaged groups. For Freire, education was political and intrinsically linked to culture (Pound 2005). He regarded literacy – the ability to read and write – as being essential to social change.

Freire believed education should endeavour to make the individual a morally responsible and intellectually and politically engaged activist. His work focused on the development of 'critical consciousness', a process by which individuals (especially the oppressed) are made aware of their ability to participate in their own learning and in the transformation of society (Boronski and Hassan 2015). Freire's idea of 'praxis' relates to the action required to bring about social change, informed by a critical reflection of existing practices, rules, traditions and understandings (Pound 2005).

According to Freire, the classroom should involve children exploring ideas with the teacher rather than the teacher depositing knowledge. Freire strived to promote equality and social justice, by encouraging children to analyse their lives and to deal with the just and unjust. He aimed to create learning environments where young people showed respect for each other, developed social action skills and cooperated to create a democracy (Pound 2005).

For Friere, the development of self-esteem and collective confidence, alongside the desire to change, not only for one's self but also to improve the conditions of one's social group, 'bring together the principles of freedom, democracy and equality' (Boronski and Hassan 2015: 72). His theories have been influential in tackling social inequalities and for promoting an understanding of the power needed to transform society. However, his ideas have received criticism for being simplistic, as social reconstruction relies on cooperation and a genuine desire for change (Pound 2005), and for his use of complex language, which is contrary to his aspiration to communicate with uneducated people (Boronski and Hassan 2015).

Urie Bronfenbrenner (1917–2005) –
The Ecology of Human Development

Bronfenbrenner was born in Russia but emigrated to the United States when he was a child. A developmental psychologist, he is known for formulating the Ecological Systems Theory (Bronfenbrenner 1979). Bronfenbrenner proposed that a child's development is shaped by a complex system of relationships that interact and influence each other.

> *Microsystem*: The innermost layer refers to the child's immediate surroundings and the individuals, objects and activities they interact with daily. A child's development is influenced by their parents, family, teachers, friends and their own biological and social characteristics (Crowley 2017). How a child reacts to people in their microsystem will determine how others treat them. The relationships between individuals in the microsystem will also have an impact on the developing child, such as a child being adversely affected by parental conflict.

> *Mesosystem*: This layer is concerned with how the different elements of the microsystem work together to impact the child. This can include the partnership between a child's parents and nursery setting, school or extended family. The mesosystem needs to have a positive influence on the child if they are to have the best start in life (Conkbayir and Pascal 2014).

> *Exosystem*: This consists of people or settings that the child does not interact with directly, but which can still affect the child. The structures in the exosystem which interact with the microsystem, having a positive or negative impact on the child, include parents' work settings and policies, community resources and mass media (Conkbayir and Pascal 2014).

> *Macrosystem*: The outermost layer refers to the wider social and political environment in which a child develops, such as government laws, resources, cultural values and customs. Government policy and cultural values influence all layers of the model (Conkbayir and Pascal 2014).

> *Chronosystem*: This is not a layer; instead it relates to the transitions the child makes during the life course. This includes internal factors such as a child maturing, and external factors (for example a period of economic difficulty or events such as parental divorce).

Bronfenbrenner's model enables understanding of the power of different environments, and the relationships between children and their caregivers and the wider community. However, it has received criticism for failing to consider genetics and the role of the child in their own development (Conkbayir and Pascal 2014).

Michel Foucault (1926–1984) – Discipline and Punish; The History of Sexuality

Foucault was a French philosopher and social theorist. He is known for his critiques of social institutions, most notably psychiatry, medicine and the prison service, and for his theories on sexuality. Foucault's work explored the relationship between knowledge and power, and how they are used as a form of social control through societal institutions. Foucault viewed power as being a complex relationship between economics, social structures and 'discourses' (conversations) (Robinson and Jones Diaz 2006).

Foucault's 'regimes of truth' provide understanding as to how certain discourses become dominant over others. Regimes of truth are presented through discourses that exist within the contexts and structures (family, education, religion, medicine, law) that we live in; when they are mutually reinforcing, they maintain particular truths and current power relations (Robinson and Jones Diaz 2006). The knowledges contained within these discourses are created by dominant others or 'experts', and influence the ways individuals think about and understand something. It is in the interest of dominant groups that some discourses are promoted, while others are discredited. Within this perspective, individuals become 'normalised', not just because of the surveillance of institutions, but also because they learn to self-scrutinise and normalise their own behaviours (Robinson and Jones Diaz 2006).

For Foucault institutions are places of control through the power that is supported by systems of knowledge held by experts. Knowledge is often used to problematise the behaviour of individuals who do not compare well to the 'norm'. According to Foucault, problematic groups (which may be perceived as a threat) include the sexually deviant, individuals with impairments and certain racial groups. In education, this can be seen through the historic practice of segregating 'impaired children' (Boronski and Hassan 2015). Foucault asserted that power relationships depend upon current interpretations of social space and that, as interpretations of power change, influenced by political and economic factors, so does understanding of what is symbolic of 'best practice' (Ingleby 2013).

The appeal of Foucault's work rests in his combination of exploring the impact of social institutions on individuals but also how individuals with power can influence institutions (Ingleby 2013). His early work is criticised for not adequately dealing with individual agency or for fully explaining individuals who resist power (Robinson and Jones Diaz 2006).

Pierre Bourdieu (1930–2002) – *La Distinction*

Bourdieu, a French sociologist and cultural theorist, was born into a working-class family. Bourdieu supported the rights of the unemployed, the homeless and immigrants. He is known for developing the 'cultural deprivation' theory and the concept 'habitus'. His work explained how social practices, which lead to inequalities particularly for working-class children in education, and are informed by power, politics and self-interest, are developed through the conventions of culture. Bourdieu asserted that different types of 'cultural capital' (economic, cultural, social, symbolic) combine to create different forms of power in different social contexts (Robinson and Jones Diaz 2006).

Bourdieu believed that the primary role of the education system to be the cultural reproduction of the culture of the dominant (upper and middle) classes. He argued that individuals with high social and cultural capital define their own culture as worthy of being possessed and establish it as the basis for knowledge in the education system (Bryant 2020). Thus, children from upper- and middle-class families are more likely to experience success in education as they possess a higher level of cultural capital, because their cultural values and practices are compatible with those rooted within the education setting (Robinson and Jones Diaz 2006).

Bourdieu's concept of habitus focused on the socially acquired dispositions (values, expressions, actions) produced through one's culture that enable or inhibit the effective exchange of one's capital (Robinson and Jones Diaz 2006). Bourdieu believed that success in life relies on the accomplishments of children in the primary years; according to his theory, this will depend on whether children can internalise the skills and knowledge in line with the dominant culture, which disadvantages many working-class children due to their historically and socially situated conditions (Bryant 2020).

Bourdieu claimed that teachers are influenced more by the way a child presents themselves (speech, appearance, behaviour, manners) than by the academic content of their work. Since most teachers will have a middle-class perspective and vocabulary, this creates an obstacle for children from working-class backgrounds as they are often unable to grasp the context of the range of meanings delivered (Bryant 2020).

Bourdieu's theory of social capital has been criticised for relying on observational interactions of individuals in a confined social space, questioning the generalisability some of his ideas may have on a wider scale (Claridge 2015). Furthermore, as his concept of social capital is substantiated by such a rich set of sociological theories that embrace the complexity of the social environment, many of his ideas may remain beyond the reach of most people outside of sociology (Claridge 2015).

Judith Butler (b. 1956) –
Gender Trouble: Feminism and the Subversion of Identity

Butler is an American gender theorist whose work relating to gender, sex and sexuality has been influential within cultural theory, queer theory and philosophical feminism. Butler challenges strands of feminism that are based on the concept of female and male binary categories, asserting that gender should be viewed as an attribute that shifts and changes rather than remaining fixed. She contends that grouping women together limits their unique identities (Duignan 2020). Butler extends the theory that gender is a social construct, and that conventional notions of gender perpetuate the domination of women by men, through her concept of 'performativity'; she also applies this theory to sexuality to explain the construct of heterosexuality and the oppression of lesbian, gay and transgender people.

Performativity is a socially constructed process which involves linguistic descriptors and social practices and rituals. Butler asserts that the gendering process starts from birth with the expression 'It's a girl!', or 'It's a boy!' which continues through a person's lifetime. The individual then proceeds (or is expected to proceed) to 'perform' and construct their gender in line with socially endorsed conventions, constituted in dominant discourses, of what it means to be female or male (Robinson and Jones Diaz 2006). These performances are repeated so frequently, it results in the perception that gender is biologically determined. In most cultures, the repeated performance of the male/female binary also serves to impose a heterosexual normativity (Duignan 2020).

Butler proposes that consciously 'deviant' gendered behaviour disturbs traditional roles and conformities between gender, sex and sexuality – opening up new ways of doing gender that operate outside the boundaries of the male/female binaries (Duignan 2020). Butler's theory offers a critical space in which individuals can take up different ways of being gendered and sexualised beings (Robinson and Jones Diaz 2006). Queer theorists assert that it is the visibility of the 'other' that troubles the normative culture which is underpinned by rigid cultural binaries.

Critics of Butler's work assert that her feminism is heavily based on American culture, she presents numerous contradictory concepts without suggesting how such contradictions can be resolved (Nussbaum 1999), her ideas are solely theoretical and have not been sufficiently tested empirically (Morgenroth & Ryan 2018), that any notion of the 'natural' is threatening and so must be 'cured' (Bordo 2003, p. 290), the 'performative' concept oversimplifies gender theory and fails to offer a reasoned account of individual agency (Duignan 2020) and, her jargon-style language and abstract, nonlinear argument mask a lack of original ideas (Duignan 2020).

ACTIVITY

Linking theory to practice

Refer to the case study of Mr Jones (p. 12). Select two children and establish links to some of the concepts provided by influential theorists. For example, you might use the Ecological Systems Theory (Bronfenbrenner) to identify some of the factors which may lead to exclusionary barriers and inequalities that the Traveller boy might encounter, and discuss how his 'cultural capital' (Bourdieu) might be received by the school. Also, think about any intersectionality that could present a more complex picture for these children with regard to risks of prejudice, inequality and marginalisation.

Sociological theories

Interactionalism

Rather than explaining human behaviour in the context of large social structures, interactionalism recognises the influence of small-scale interactions and social structures. It views society as the product of human interactions and focuses on how individuals interpret the social world as a result of those interactions, acknowledging that people have agency to negotiate and construct their own meanings. This perspective underpins the philosophy of the individual child. However, it is criticised for failing to consider the implications of wider social structures and trends in generating social meanings (Ingleby 2013).

Functionalism

Functionalism considers that all societies are based on the need to maintain and reproduce themselves. Functionalists believe that a successful society is grounded in a set of shared norms and values, as this allows individuals to cooperate to achieve common goals, preventing societal breakdown. This perspective is concerned with how social systems maintain consensus and how they regulate conflict and deviant behaviour. Functionalists regard different institutions (the family, education, media, economic, political, religious) as performing their own unique function that contributes to the maintenance of a stable society. The family is regarded as the immediate building block for educating its young members on basic norms and values, and the purpose of education is viewed as being to prepare young people for roles in society, through the development of the skills needed by the economic system and allocating positions most suited to an individual's abilities (Ingleby 2013; Boronski and Hassan 2015). Functionalism is criticised for neglecting the individual who negotiates their own social meanings (Ingleby 2013).

Conflict theory

Conflict theory is mainly applied to explain conflict between social class groups, and is based on the principle of competition for limited resources. It investigates the conflict that exists within social systems and takes a critical review of power differentials and dominant ideologies which are considered to support the values of the rich and powerful, as opposed to the poor and powerless (Ingleby 2013). Conflict theory is relevant to young children because of the link that exists between differences in economic wealth and children's educational attainment and well-being. However, conflict theory is criticised for focusing on economic variables and failing to consider other social factors (Ingleby 2013).

Feminism

Feminism is a broad set of ideologies that focus on explaining how gender differences and inequalities (family, social, economic, political) are products of role socialisation rather than being determined by essentialist biological explanations. Most strands, except for feminist poststructuralism, view power as operating through a patriarchal social system (Robinson and Jones Diaz 2006) which is established and reinforced in the traditional family unit. Early feminism ideology has been criticised for focusing primarily on upper-class white women. A feminist poststructuralist perspective provides a more critical lens through which to examine contemporary society – to understand the way in which individuals build their own identities, to explore power relations and normalising discourses that exist within society and personal interactions, and to determine how individuals can both contribute to and counteract social inequalities (Robinson and Jones Diaz 2006).

Postmodernism

Postmodernism seeks to deconstruct, disrupt and replace existing theories and assumptions to explain human behaviour, particularly those which underpin developmental psychology. Foucault's work, which opposed the idea that there are permanent truths (the sense of certainty and order, and that there is one right way), has been influential in challenging conventional thinking; deemed to be necessary because it has been produced by, and benefits, dominant groups in society (Pound 2009). Postmodernism aims to reconceptualise how identity, the self, power and difference are theorised. It has been used to understand factors affecting the equality and rights of children, through examining where dominant ideas have come from and what they might mean for children in different social, political and geographical locations. Postmodernism is criticised for the constant challenging of ideas, as this may lead to a lack of coherent theories (Pound 2009).

Key concepts underpinning postmodernism include discourses, lenses and other-ing. 'Discourse' concerns the way in which individuals view and construct the social world. A discourse creates a 'framework which is made up of our sense of self in relation to others; our feelings about ourselves and others; the words and images we use to think about and communicate these ideas; and the actions we take as a result' (Pound 2009: 81). Dominant discourses in society frequently function to privilege certain individuals and make their success more likely. Dominant, normalising dis-courses mean that children who differ often become seen as difficult, problematic or in 'deficit' (Yarrow and Fane 2018). The term 'lenses' is used to represent the idea that any situation can be understood in various ways, so different individuals know different truths. Because of this, it is essential that practitioners think carefully about what they see and hear, going beyond simple explanations by critically questioning their views and behaviours (Pound 2009). Finally, 'othering', which is used to under-stand power differentials, refers to the way in which dominant groups treat individu-als whom they regard as being different to themselves (Pound 2009). Othering tends to involve stereotypical expectations of individuals, which can be limiting and often serves to marginalise.

CRITICAL INCLUSION: THEORY, PEDAGOGY AND PRACTICE

Critical theory has its roots in the work of Freire and is based on the notion that education has the power to challenge social inequalities and bring about positive change. Pedagogies are centred on a moral principle that enables children to develop critical awareness of social issues, the dominant structures and discourses that exist within social institutions, and their potential as agents of change, to bring equality and justice in their immediate settings and wider community.

Paramount to the effective development of inclusive learning and social spaces is that of empowering the voices of children and families, particularly individuals who are deemed to be the 'other' and those who are undervalued or excluded. It is impor-tant that empowerment is included in practitioners' thinking and teaching, so that oppressed groups can be enabled to describe their own problems and arrive at pos-sible solutions (Gibson 2009). Although there are likely to be complexities and sen-sitivities associated with this approach, there must be time allocated to engaging in discussions, where the voices of the marginalised can be listened to and understood. Meaningful inclusion and diversity education can only take place when children (and adults) have an opportunity to openly 'think, talk and reflect in a critical envi-ronment' (Gibson 2009: 17), facilitated by skilled and caring practitioners. Children at a very young age can develop social, cultural and political biases which can lead to exclusionary attitudes and behaviours (Nutbrown and Clough 2013). Moreover, conflict is an inevitable part of relationships, and helping children to acquire the skills to manage their own conflicts is important and empowering (Yarrow and Fane 2018).

One critical theory intervention which could be used in practice to consider a broad range of social and diversity topics is 'Philosophy for Children' (P4C), founded by Matthew Lipman in the 1970s. Part of a worldwide critical thinking movement, the Society for Advancing of Philosophical Enquiry and Reflection in Education (SAPERE) was established in 1992 to promote the use of P4C in schools in the UK. In addition to improved cognitive outcomes at primary school, especially for disadvantaged pupils, P4C can be effective in promoting cooperation, empathy and tolerance for others (Siddiqui et al. 2017). There are different versions of P4C but all are aimed at promoting critical thinking, where children are encouraged to voice their opinion about topics, exchange alternative perspectives, challenge each other through the use of appropriate argumentation and negotiation, question the validity of their own ideas, and listen to and respect the views of others (Di Masi and Santi 2016). Griffin (2018) advises that for P4C to be effective in delivering social issues, children need to be provided with counter-stereotypical information, alternative role models, historical and global contexts, and stories to challenge dominant discourses and restrictive norms, through an interactive approach using practical activities and real-life scenarios. There are no set materials, so practitioners can use various items (videos, stories, pictures, persona dolls, curriculum materials) which they feel will stimulate discussion. Usually sitting in a circle the discussion should follow its own path guided by the children's thoughts, but the children must always justify their opinions (Siddiqui et al. 2017). As the practitioner acts as a facilitator only, it is important that rules of engagement are established and understood by the children before dialogue begins, to ensure these remain 'safe spaces' in which to discuss sensitive topics.

There is much evidence which demonstrates the effectiveness of persona dolls for addressing issues of diversity and prejudice with young children (Brown 2001; Smith 2013). Scenarios could be developed to reflect all of the marginalised groups presented within this book, highlighting the detrimental impact of stereotypes and binaries and promoting discussion around ways in which the dolls could be empowered. 'Difference is of interest to children, and the recognition of difference as positive rather than negative', and children recognising similarities shared by individuals and groups: both are important aims for childhood practitioners (Nutbrown and Clough 2013: 13). Additionally, children can be introduced to the social constructionist framework through 'critical media literacy' (McQueeney 2014) which could involve them critiquing media headlines, images or statements. This will help children to realise that issues which become defined as social problems, and why certain groups become 'othered', are a consequence of individuals constructing meanings, and thus definitions of social problems change over time and place.

 **REFLECTION**

Critical practitioner 'evaluating attitudes and actions in practice'

1   Consider the impact of your own values and background on the children and families that you work with. Do your beliefs and interactions normalise or disrupt dominant discourses? Do you have any conscious or unconscious biases regarding the children and families in your setting?

2   Reflect upon your last placement within an early years or primary school setting and consider the following questions:

Which children and families were most at risk of being disadvantaged or marginalised? Explain the ways in which they were at risk.

Were power relations balanced? Who appeared to hold the most power and in what way? For example, which children dominated play spaces, classrooms and interactions with practitioners? Whose voices dominated? What are the consequences of unequal power relations?

What messages were portrayed through toys, resources, the curriculum and play areas? Did any of these reflect stereotypical binaries?

Did you observe practitioners challenging stereotypical assumptions? Did you see structured activities where children explored issues of social justice and diversity?

KEY POINTS

- Inclusion is a concept which draws upon a range of perspectives. Many attach it to a philosophy of social justice, where all individuals are viewed as of equal worth and have the right to participate in social, educational, economic and political life.
- Inclusive education sits within the broader area of social inclusion and although it includes SEND, this is just one aspect of diversity it is concerned with.
- Inclusion is an ongoing process which requires a critical review of values, policies and practices.
- Inclusion is not optional; schools and early years settings in the UK have a legal and professional obligation to commit to principles of equality, inclusion and social justice.
- Inclusion is not always straightforward and can involve complexities in practice. Practitioners should adopt a critical view of inclusion, where issues of difference are carefully considered.
- It is important that practitioners develop a radical understanding about inclusive ideology which influences policy, practice and provision within their school/early years

settings. This should include knowledge of sociological perspectives, the powerful discourses that exist to marginalise individuals and groups, and the role they have as agents of positive change, empowering children through critical inclusion and social justice education.

FURTHER READING

Booth, T. and Ainsocw, M. (2011) *Index for Inclusion: Developing Learning and Participation in Schools*. Third edition. Bristol: Centre for Studies on Inclusive Education.

A practical resource which presents a principled approach to developing inclusive education, focusing on school cultures, policies and practices.

Bowles, M. (2004) *The Little Book of Persona Dolls*. Husbands Bosworth: Featherstone Education.

Provides knowledge as to how persona dolls can be used to explore a range of social issues and diversity topics with young children; contains scenarios.

Nutbrown, C. and Clough, P. (2013) *Inclusion in the Early Years*. Second edition. London: Sage.

Offers a broad examination of inclusion in the context of the early years, discussing challenges and opportunities of inclusive practice.

Robinson, K. and Jones Diaz, C. (2006) *Diversity and Difference in Early Childhood Education: Issues for Theory and Practice*. Maidenhead: Open University Press.

Provides a critical overview of contemporary social theories and how these underpin practice in early years settings.

USEFUL WEBSITES

Centre for Studies on Inclusive Education: www.csie.org.uk
Society for Advancing Philosophical Enquiry and Reflection in Education: www.sapere.org.uk

2

MASS MEDIA, SOCIAL BIAS AND THE REPRESENTATION OF MINORITY AND MARGINALISED GROUPS

CONTENTS

CHAPTER OVERVIEW

Prejudice towards minority groups is a key determinant of social exclusion and marginalisation. Therefore, challenging negative attitudes is fundamental to fostering community cohesion, as well as ensuring individuals' well-being. Although the mass media have been found to introduce and reinforce detrimental stereotypes regarding minority groups, which lead to prejudice and discriminatory action, they also have the potential to positively influence people's thoughts and feelings. It is important that early years practitioners and teachers critically reflect upon, and help to combat, the prejudice that might enter settings (including their own subconscious bias) which risks infringing upon human rights, equality and the creation of inclusive child environments.

This chapter considers:

1 Considers different forms of mass media.
2 Examines how minority groups are represented in mass media.
3 Considers the impact of mass media on children, as well as the way children are depicted in the media.
4 Fosters critical thinking and analysis skills and considers types of media bias.
5 Explores the development of social bias: stereotypes, stigma, labelling, prejudice and discrimination.
6 Considers strategies to address prejudice.

FORMS OF MASS MEDIA

Mass media are a means of disseminating information to the population. Mass media communication is used to entertain, educate, act as a political platform, advertise goods and services, and for public relations and service announcements. The general public consumes media in many different formats. 'Traditional media' is the term given to the industries that existed before the internet, such as radio, film, television and print (newspapers, magazines, books and other publications). 'New media' refers to the range of formats and platforms that have emerged since the rise of the internet (websites, blogs, vlogs, online games, podcasts, apps). The on-demand content, available through a range of digital devices (laptops, tablets and smartphones), has become a popular and viable way of accessing news sources.

Newspaper categories include 'tabloids' ('red tops' and 'middle-market' dailies) and 'broadsheets'. All major UK newspapers now have web editions. Tabloids are image-led newspapers that usually have large catchy headlines. The red tops (*The Sun, Daily Mirror, Daily Star*) have a red masthead containing the newspaper title at the top of the front page. Red tops report on politics and international news through short stories and simple language. They tend to include more pictures, celebrity talk and scandal than other newspapers. Tabloid newspapers are identified as the biggest source of 'fake news', presenting inaccurate and problematic content (Liu 2017). Dominated with sensational stories and depictions of 'otherness', they lead to many myths being founded within the general public regarding a range of social topics, including immigration, terrorism, benefit fraud and mental illness. Middle-market dailies (*Daily Mail*, *Daily Express*) refers to the target audience of these newspapers, which sits between the red tops and the broadsheets. Broadsheets (*The Times*, *Telegraph*, *Guardian*) are text led and factual. The articles presented offer more in-depth analysis. As many people tend to read only the headline or first paragraph of a news story, it is important that newspapers provide accurate headlines and do not spin a false narrative.

Historically, readership of the tabloid press has attracted the working-class and broadsheet press a more middle-class audience (Morgan and Taylor 2019). However, as online readerships and social media have changed the way that media are accessed and discussed, these distinctions have become increasingly blurred. While the tabloid press is often sensationalist and lacks credibility, its appeal for some lies in a straight-talking form of 'common sense' which is in contrast to the more politically correct and analytical reporting of the broadsheet (Morgan and Taylor 2019).

MASS MEDIA AND MINORITY GROUPS

Mass media are easily accessible, almost inescapable and highly influential. Most people do not experience a large part of the world first-hand. Instead they access media stories to keep abreast of current affairs and gain understanding of social issues. As very few people read around an occurrence or social issue in order to advance their knowledge (McQueeney 2014), it is important that the information presented within media sources is accurate and balanced. Unfortunately, misrepresentations and negative portrayals of minority groups are frequently perpetuated by the media. A report published by Ofcom (2018) suggests that a number of minority groups feel unhappy with the way that they have been represented on television: some people with disabilities feel there is too much focus on their difficulties; transgender people believe coverage to be negative and too heavily focused on medical issues; and LGB and Black African and Black African-Caribbean people feel portrayed negatively.

Furthermore, the claims and fears presented by news events and storylines, which are often grossly exaggerated, serve to introduce, reinforce or awaken prejudiced opinions. Once some individuals perceive a problem as real, they may take discriminatory action (McQueeney 2014). Thus, media producers and journalists have a responsibility with regard to how they depict minority groups, as they have the potential to create significant harm. Nazi propaganda (screened through black and white cinema footage in the late 1930s and used to ignite public hostility towards people with disabilities and the Jewish community) serves as a stark reminder of the power of the media in their ability to exacerbate prejudice and discriminatory behaviour on an unprecedented scale.

 **ACTIVITY**

Minority groups in television and film

Watch and analyse TV dramas and/or films for one week. Identify two sources and consider the following: Who are the main characters? How are they portrayed? Are any minority groups represented? If so, how are they portrayed?

The media hold a dominant position in conveying and articulating specific discourses that represent and misrepresent minority groups (Cottle 2006). 'Discourse' is a term used to define communication conveyed via speech, written text, images and other forms of expression, including propaganda. Unfortunately, discourses of deviancy frequently pervade media representations of minority groups or render minority voices almost invisible (Saeed 2007). Commentary of events or minority groups which involves emotive language or the use of imagery, and where no positive actions are presented, particularly incites prejudice (Saeed 2007; Patil and McLaren 2019). Individuals who are the primary definers of what is 'important news' and what the 'correct' perspective on what news should be (Hall 1978) have a critical role as their ideas become integrated into the concepts and content of the information presented. Politicians in particular make use of opinion polls in deciding what problems should take priority, what policies to support and what actions to take in addressing social problems (McQueeney 2014).

The information disseminated by media providers can be manipulated in order to influence the public opinions of certain individuals, groups of people and events. There is a significant body of research which asserts that the Western media's representation of minority ethnic groups is negative in its content and limited in its themes (Saeed 2007). Individuals from minority ethnic groups have consistently been depicted as 'problems': from the 'criminal mentality' of African-Caribbeans and the 'cheating Asians', to the 'Islamic fundamentalists' (Saeed 2007) and asylum seekers described as 'illegal immigrants' (see Chapter 9). Media coverage of Islam and Muslims has been identified as being particularly misleading and hostile, which has fuelled Islamophobia (Al Jazeera 2019; Patil and McLaren 2019) (see Chapter 8).

In 2018, the Muslim Council of Britain's Centre for Media Monitoring released its findings based on a study that involved the analysis of over 10,000 print articles and broadcast clips referring to Muslims and Islam. It was found that 59% of the print articles and 43% of broadcast clips associated Muslims with negative behaviour. More than a third of the articles misrepresented or made generalisations about the community; Muslim women were either 'othered' through images or silenced through a lack of prominence; and terrorism was the main theme (Al Jazeera 2019).

Positive use of media

The media may be the only contact some people have with minority groups, especially those living in homogeneous communities. Various studies suggest that increased visibility and positive representations of minority groups within the media can help to reduce the tension and prejudice that often arises, towards marginalised members. Schiappa and colleagues (2005) claim that 'parasocial contact', where viewers get to know and come to like minority group members on television (perceiving them almost as real people), may improve their attitudes towards the group in general. Where social interactions between members of the minority group and the majority group are positive, any concerns viewers may have can reduce and they may be more willing to interact with individuals from the stigmatised group (Sharples and Page-Gould 2016).

Liu (2017) compared two surveys which focused on how trans people experience the media; the first was published in 2010 and the second in 2017. Although discrimination towards the lesbian, gay, bisexual, transgender, queer or questioning, intersex and asexual/ally (LGBTQIA+) community continues, and the current negativity appears to focus on non-binary individuals and trans children and their families, the 2017 survey indicated positive change. One of the main aims of 'All About Trans 2010' was to improve the visibility as well as the portrayal of trans people in the media. In 2017, 31% of respondents saw trans people several times a week, compared with 14% in 2010. In 2010, 70% of respondents thought media coverage of trans people was negative; this had reduced to 48.5% in 2017. Asked about change in the past decade, 71% of respondents in 2017 said media coverage of trans people had become more positive, with 51% saying it had become more accurate and non-judgemental, which had helped their family and friends to better understand them. Further information regarding media portrayal of gender variant children is presented in Chapter 7.

Kallman (2017), whose work focuses on disabilities, asserts that counter-stereotypical exemplars of minority groups portrayed on television can help to reduce social biases. However, he advises that in order for messages to resonate with the audience, exemplars need to be regarded as 'realistic', with individuals with disabilities engaged in everyday situations without overt attention drawn; disability will then be viewed as natural. Kallman (2017) warns that extreme exemplars may result in individuals holding unrealistic expectations and that interactions may become negative when marginalised members do not live up to them.

CHILDREN AND MASS MEDIA

Media depictions of minority groups can have a profound impact on children's attitudes. Television programmes perceived by children as realistic are watched with more emotion and less detachment than programmes involving fantasy and animation (Hopkins 2014). Therefore, television producers have a duty to reflect diversity and think carefully about the portrayal of minority groups. However, as the case of former BBC children's presenter Cerrie Burnell shows, parents can hold significant prejudices concerning diversity which may be imparted on their children. When Cerrie started presenting on the children's channel CBeebies in 2009 she became the subject of a controversial campaign. The parents who led the campaign argued that Cerrie, who was born with part of her right arm missing, was not suitable to appear on the show as her 'limb was scaring their children', which forced them to enter into difficult conversations with their children before they were ready.

The age at which children first access digital media is becoming younger. Between the ages of 9–11, most children have regular access to a mobile phone (Howard et al. 2020). The most commonly used social media sites used by young children include Snapchat, Instagram, WhatsApp and Musical.ly (the latter is now known as TikTok) (Children's Commissioner 2018a). Although there is much concern regarding children's use of social media, it is also important to acknowledge the positives. For instance, celebrities and government departments are increasingly using social media platforms aimed at children and young people to raise awareness of and offer support towards mental health (Howard et al. 2020). Liu (2017) identifies how user-generated media (independent films, personal blogs, YouTube videos) are beginning to take over books and advocacy organisations as sources of information accessed by young people to help them understand issues relating to gender identity and sexuality. More recently, social media have been used to educate the public about the impact that bullying can have on children, as in the case of Quaden Bayles, an Australian boy who has faced relentless bullying at school because of his dwarfism (BBC 2020).

The media portrayal of children also influences decisions taken on their behalf, how adults behave towards them and how society regards them. Child Rights International Network (CRIN) (2018) asserts that the media perpetuate a collection of myths regarding children, including: sensational reporting of emotive topics that ignore broader issues confronting children; descriptive accounts which lack analysis; and children being portrayed as stereotypes – passive beings who are unable to think, speak or act for themselves girls as victims, boys as reckless or dangerous; and irresponsible teenagers. Liu (2017) alleges that trans children are at the epicentre of media backlash, with negative and sensational coverage discrediting the gender identity issues faced by some children, which could exacerbate an already challenging social environment in which 45% of trans children attempt suicide (Stonewall 2017).

CRITICAL MEDIA LITERACY AND BIAS
Media bias

Media content can be manipulated in the following ways:

- *Content commission*: Presenting false assumptions that promote a particular view (misconstruing statements made by an individual/organisation or misinterpreting statistics).
- *Omission*: Promoting a one-sided story by ignoring another side of an argument.
- *Placement*: Featuring stories that support the writer's personal stance in prominent places while hiding unaligned ones.
- *Spin*: Modifying or relocating data or a story to avert attention from negative topics or to emphasise an idealised issue.
- *Concision*: Reporting stories so concisely that it fails to provide a full account.
- *Sensationalism*: Using exciting or shocking stories, words or images to emphasise a topic to attract public interest/emotions.
- *Labelling*: Attaching extreme labels to certain groups while applying unoffensive or no labels to other groups.
- *Outliers*: Reporting unusual cases or extreme data.

(Adapted from Simon 2018)

 **ACTIVITY**

A critical review of mass media

Undertake a media search of newsprint articles relating to minority groups. It is advisable to select one group at a time to review. Using images and headlines, produce a graffiti wall (sources should be accurately acknowledged). This activity is best undertaken through group dialogue.

Once you have completed the graffiti wall, select two or three articles for critical review. For each article identify:

1   The author (individual, institution or industry) and date of publication.
2   The target audience.
3   The main messages being presented. Record the headline. Examine any images carefully. Assess the text:
     i   Identify frequent words/phrases that are stereotypical or emotive (using a coloured highlighter to categorise words is useful).
     ii   Assess the meaning of words/phrases by attaching labels according to the subject, such as hate crime; terror; financial burden; untrustworthy; abnormal.
     iii Once you have done this, consider whether the words/phrases used to represent the minority group are more positive or more negative.
4   Does the article seem to be influenced by bias, sentiment or vested interest?
5   Is the article balanced? Does it contain different viewpoints? What is left out?
6   Does the article refer to credible and current sources of literature?
7   What impact may such messages have on the marginalised group (children and families)? Consider: education, health and living standards; justice and security; community acceptance and participation.
8   How could such messages filter into child, family and educational settings?
9   Why is it important that media producers ensure that marginalised groups are portrayed accurately?

Critical media literacy is a process which can be applied to interrogate the quality of the information presented and situate print articles/media clips within the broader discourse in which they are created (McQueeney 2014). This approach, which draws upon critical and social constructionist perspectives and encourages interconnections among social problems, can help individuals unpack where subjective perceptions may have stemmed from. Critical media literacy can help individuals to become more critically informed, socially engaged and politically aware by considering multiple viewpoints and locating the evidence upon which these knowledge-claims are based (McQueeney 2014). Early years practitioners and teachers can undertake a similar exercise with young children, perhaps starting the process by sharing and discussing images of minority groups that are presented within the media. It is important that this work is carefully managed by a skilled and unbiased practitioner.

In 2013, the Equality and Human Rights Commission (EHRC 2013) (Scotland) published a resource to support the media in its reporting of issues relating to Gypsies/Travellers. The guidance presented, which aims to ensure balanced reporting, has been adapted for the purpose of this chapter as it has relevance to all minority groups.

1   Be aware of material that is likely to lead to stereotypes, hatred or discrimination.
2   Many readers or viewers have no direct contact with the minority group and so base their opinions on what they see in the media.

3   Be clear whether you are reporting fact or someone else's opinion.

4   Do not assume or suggest that the actions or beliefs of any individuals reflect a whole group, community or race.

5   Do not sensationalise or exaggerate issues involving a minority group.

6   Balance the reporting of specific 'incidents' with wider coverage and background to some of the causal factors around issues faced by the group.

7   Do not present minority groups as 'outsiders'.

8   Only describe people in a certain way if it is strictly relevant or accurate.

9   Consult people from the minority group who are directly involved.

10 Give balanced reports ensuring that the minority group's perspectives are reflected alongside those of others.

Media regulation in the UK

The media are a powerful force which can have a significant impact on people's lives, shaping attitudes and behaviours. Therefore, regulation is essential to ensure that the media operate within clear guidelines. Increasingly, interactive media allow people to share their own views and engage in debate. Media providers face the challenge of not only ensuring that their own reporting is fair and accurate but also taking a moderator's responsibility to ensure that what is published on social platforms does not involve harassment or hatred. Newspaper journalists and editors must adhere to the Editor's Code of Practice. The Independent Press Standards Organisation (IPSO) investigate complaints about any breaches (IPSO 2019). The film industry is regulated by the British Board of Film Classification, and Ofcom is the regulator of television and radio. Advertising across all media is regulated by the Advertising Standards Authority, which acts on complaints and assesses the media to ensure there are no advertisements that are misleading, harmful or offensive.

SOCIAL BIASES: STEREOTYPES, STIGMA, PREJUDICE AND DISCRIMINATION

There has been long-standing and extensive research and theorising relating to different social biases: stereotypes, stigma, prejudice and discrimination. Early psychologists focused on intra-psychic processes (attitudes held by an individual), while sociologists examined social and structural dynamics in intergroup relations. More recently, studies which draw upon social-psychology have explored the multifaceted nature of prejudice, bridging the individual-level emphasis of psychology and the group-level focus of sociology (Dovidio et al. 2013).

The chapters in this book indicate that prejudiced attitudes and actions are prevalent in the UK. These social biases, which can be limiting and detrimental, find their way into early years settings and classrooms. Therefore, critical thinking and reflective practice are paramount. Practitioners need to challenge any stereotypes, prejudice and discrimination that they encounter. They should start the process by questioning their own knowledge and value base, being aware of any possible personal unconscious bias which might influence and impact the children, families and colleagues in their setting. Practitioners should ask: How did I learn this? Is it accurate? How might this affect someone?

Unconscious biases are deep-seated beliefs (stereotypes) about different social and identity groups which all individuals form outside their conscious awareness. Unconscious biases are common and can have either positive or negative consequences.

 **ACTIVITY**

Uncovering personal bias

Complete the Implicit Association Test and challenge yourself to eliminate any personal bias/prejudiced beliefs. Available at: https://implicit.harvard.edu/implicit/

Stereotypes are a fixed set of beliefs or assumptions about the characteristics and behaviours of a group of individuals that are then applied to all individual members of that group. Stereotypes are cognitive schemas used to simplify complex social environments by categorising people into groups on the basis of social markers, such as ethnicity, religion, gender, age, disability and sexuality. Once the individual is assigned to a specific category, the stereotypes, societal assumptions and personal experiences that have framed the category then become linked to that individual. Stereotypes affect how people perceive and respond to group members.

> The human mind must think with the aid of categories. ... Once formed, categories are the basis for normal prejudgment. We cannot possibly avoid this process. Orderly living depends upon it. (Allport 1954: 20)

Stereotypes are not always negative, but they are often narrow and misleading as they ignore the variability that exists within social groups and the overlap of characteristics across social groups. It is important to realise that even positive stereotypes can be damaging, as they have the potential to place unrealistic expectations on individuals or to patronise members from specific groups. Early years practitioners and teachers should not feel guilty about having stereotypes, for it is part of human nature. However, it is imperative for them to be sociologically mindful; to recognise bias and stereotypical assumptions and take steps to eliminate them.

 **ACTIVITY**

Stereotypes

I   What characteristics are typically applied to the following people: a child in a wheelchair, a young teenager in a hoodie, a Black man, a Muslim woman in a hijab, a Gypsy/Roma/Traveller?

2   What impact could such stereotypes have on these individuals and wider society?

The stigma construct is largely attributed to Erving Goffman (1963) and Thomas Scheff's (1966) work, which focused on labelling theory and societal perceptions of individuals with mental illness. These early frameworks are criticised for locating stigma in the individual and failing to recognise its complex socio-cultural context (Mukolo et al. 2010).

Stigma is a concept of social approval based on identity and association. Goffman associated stigma with individual-level characteristics (illness, disfigurement, identity deviance) that link a person to a negative stereotype, which then taints the person's identity. Markers identified as having the power to spoil an individual's identity included 'abominations of the body (physical: genetic deformities, scars); blemishes of individual character (generalized bad character); [and] tribal (group affiliation: race, nationality, religion)' (Goffman 1963: 9). He asserted that stigma can be so powerful it has the ability to change a person's self-concept and social identity.

Stigmatisation can lead to both 'enacted stigma', where an individual is treated less favourably or excluded from society, and 'felt stigma' (imagined social reaction), which may lead to feelings of shame, guilt or depression. 'Stigma by association' is the term used to describe stigma that is extended to other individuals who are linked to the person with the spoiled identity, for example, the parents of a young person diagnosed with schizophrenia.

Labelling theory, prominent during the 1960s and 1970s, theorised that self-identity and the behaviour of individuals can be influenced or determined by the terms used to define or categorise them. It is related to the concepts of stereotyping and self-fulfilling prophecy. Scheff used labelling theory to argue that once a person is labelled 'mentally ill', they receive a set of negative responses from society, which the individual internalises to adopt the role of a mentally ill person.

Modified labelling theory later acknowledged the power relations that exist in society, which frequently sees dominant groups imposing negative labels on those deemed undesirable, whom they then devalue and discriminate. This concept draws upon a social-psychology perspective that stigmatisation is linked to human cognition through stereotyping and prejudice (Mukolo et al. 2010).

Prejudice is a multifaceted phenomenon which can manifest itself in various ways. Due to its complexity, formulating a single definition is problematic. However, it may be explained as a positive or negative orientation towards a group, or its members, based on biased and generalised prejudgements that are usually derived from inaccurate and incomplete information (Kallen 2004), which Dovidio et al. (2013) assert creates or maintains hierarchical status relations between groups.

The shift from stereotyping to prejudice or discrimination involves an emotional or behavioural response. There are usually (but not necessarily) three interlinked components: cognitive – the stereotypical thoughts and beliefs about a particular group or its members; affective – prejudice is the emotional response of stereotypes (likes, dislikes, anger, fear, disgust, hatred); and behavioural – discrimination is the biased behavioural component of stereotypes/prejudice.

Prejudice may present on a spectrum from blatant intolerance such as hate crime to subtle forms such as ignoring or excluding certain people or groups which may be subconscious and difficult to detect. Hate crimes can be defined as a range of criminal behaviour where the offender is motivated by hostility towards the victim on the grounds of their diversity. Valentine and McDonald (2004) argue that the focus given to more overt forms can obscure everyday subtle prejudice. As a result, individuals may fail to recognise their own beliefs and actions as a form of prejudice. Even those who consider themselves 'tolerant of others have implicit bias in their attitudes and behaviours which are automatically activated and often unintentional' (Scottish Government 2015: 11).

In 1954, psychologist Gordon Allport created a scale to measure the manifestation of prejudice in a society:

1   Anti-locution (verbal abuse, stereotypical jokes, hate speech)
2   Avoidance (excluding, isolating, neglecting)
3   Discrimination (denying equal access to opportunities, goods and services)
4   Physical attack (physical attacks on people or damage to their property)
5   Extermination (genocide, ethnic cleansing).

In addition to any physical harm caused, the effects of prejudice on victims can be wide ranging, including anxiety, stress, isolation, depression, low self-esteem, poor sense of identity and resentment. Prejudice frequently leads to inequality in the areas of accommodation, health, education, employment and criminal justice, and results in community discord. The impact of prejudice and discrimination is a central focus of this text, therefore detailed discussion relating to this is presented in individual chapters alongside specific marginalised groups.

In an attempt to explain the development of social biases, Dovidio et al. (2013) identify three distinct waves to reflect the different assumptions and paradigms that have been applied. The first phase (1920s and 1950s) involved theorists focusing on 'individual differences' to identify, through personality and attitude tests, prejudiced individuals so that counter-strategies could be applied. During the 1970s and 1980s, the focus was on how cognitive processes, and group processes and social identities, affect bias. Both perspectives alleged that normal psychological and social processes give rise to stereotyping and prejudice. It led to prejudice reduction strategies that aimed to change general social norms rather than targeting bigoted individuals. The third phase, from the mid-1990s and largely characterising contemporary research, focuses on non-conscious and neural processes which contribute to biases and how prejudices can become activated (Dovidio et al. 2013).

Precise explanations of prejudice are difficult to determine. Drawing upon a wide range of theories and research studies from sociology, psychology and social-psychology, basic factors have been presented by Kallen (2004) and Haslam and Dovidio (2010) as helping to explain the development and maintenance of social biases. These theories have been drawn together and presented in Table 2.1. However, it is important to view the factors and theories that follow as complementary explanations, which can combine and operate in different ways under diverse conditions (Dovidio et al. 2013).

Table 2.1 Theories and factors influencing social bias

Socialisation	Biases are learned through social interactions which occur within institutions, such as the family, education, religion, workplace, media and the government, and through personal experiences.
Authoritarian personality	After the Second World War, Adorno and colleagues drew upon 'critical theory' (a Marxist approach) to examine psychological factors which predispose individuals towards racial prejudice and fascistic propaganda. The authoritarian personality proposes that there is a personality type prone to prejudicial thought resulting in intolerance and hostility towards members of minority groups – characteristics developed during childhood as a result of hierarchical relations with punitive parents.
Frustration-aggression	Individuals who are prevented from achieving personal goals may blame marginalised groups and equality measures for their lack of success. This can lead to resentment and aggression against minority group members.
Social identity and threats to group identity	Prejudice is often biased in favour of the groups and its members to which an individual perceives they belong (in-groups) over groups they do not identify with (out-groups). Tajfel (1970) and others showed experimentally that artificially created groups, lacking any real meaning and a history of functional relations, still exhibited mild forms of prejudice. Tajfel (1969) argued that biases reflect the importance individuals place on group memberships and their attempts to understand how the actions of other groups may impinge upon their own group. Prejudice can also be the result of a social group becoming displaced from a specific role or powerful position. Members belonging to social groups perceived to be contributing towards such displacement may be regarded negatively.

Table 2.1   (Continued)

Group conflict	Competition and threat (realistic or symbolic) may generate intergroup prejudice. Prejudice often occurs between groups where there are limited economic opportunities, resulting in a need to compete for valued resources (education, housing, health services, employment, welfare support). In 1961, Sherif and colleagues carried out an experiment, 'the Robbers Cave', which encouraged conflict through a series of competitive activities between two groups of all-white, lower-middle-class 12-year-old boys at a summer camp (Sherif et al. 1961). Intergroup bias and conflict quickly developed, including aggressive acts between out-group members. However, functional relations do not have to involve explicit competition to cause biases as people often assume that members of other groups will be competitive which will prevent them from achieving their goals.
Structural power	Prejudice occurs when members of an elite group or dominant social class hold power over members of non-elite groups or lower social classes. The dominant group often views itself, its customs and beliefs as a measure of what is 'normal' and 'superior'. This is known as ethnocentrism. The expectation for minority groups to function within these values and practices invariably leads to prejudice and conflict.
Historical legacy	Although social structures and economic relationships may become more equitable within a society, the legacy of historical experiences can fuel prejudice. Many ethnic conflicts are related to recollections of past atrocities or prejudiced treatment of one group by another.
Scapegoating	When faced with social problems that involve a high level of threat (such as economic downturns), frustration and aggression are displaced onto minority groups. For instance, immigrants are often blamed for overcrowded cities and stretched resources rather than the issue being viewed as a consequence of inadequate economic and social policy. Successful minority groups are more likely to be scapegoated; for example, the Nazis blamed the Jewish community and their success in banking, business and the media for causing economic and social problems in Germany.

 ACTIVITY

Brown eyes, blue eyes

In 1968 Jane Elliott, a teacher in the United States, used a direct method to teach her class of all-white 8- to 9-year-olds the effects of racism. On the first day, she divided the class according to eye colour, 'brown eyes' and 'blue eyes', and put collars on the brown-eyed children. She told them the blue-eyed children were better and smarter than the brown-eyed children. She reinforced the division by giving the blue-eyed children privileges and removing rights from the brown-eyed children. The next day she reversed the groups. At the end of the activity the children discussed their experiences.

www.youtube.com/watch?v=oGvoXeXCoUY

Watch the YouTube clip and answer the following questions:

1   What do you think the children learned from this activity?
2   What ethical concerns are there about undertaking this activity with children today?

Discrimination can be defined as 'biased behaviour, which includes not only actions that directly harm or disadvantage another group, but those that unfairly favour one's own group, creating a relative disadvantage for other groups' (Dovidio et al. 2013: 9).

Discrimination, as is also the case for stereotypes and prejudice, can occur at the individual, institutional and cultural levels. Cultural discrimination can be entrenched in a culture's history and occurs when a dominant group has the power to impose its cultural heritage and values on other groups. Consequently, everyday activities transmit dominant group bias which impacts on individuals, socially, educationally, economically and politically, via individual actions or institutional policies and practices. People often fail to identify institutional discrimination, because the unfair and indirect methods are often so embedded in the procedures, policies, laws or objectives of organisations or governments that they have become 'normalised' (Dovidio et al. 2013).

In the UK, marginalised groups are protected by legislation and policies which are aimed at ensuring people from diverse backgrounds have a right to equal treatment before the law and the same fundamental rights as the rest of the community. However, it should not be assumed that legislation always achieves its function. The four main types of discrimination include:

- *Direct discrimination (unfair treatment)*: Happens when a person treats one person less favourably than they would another because they have a protected characteristic, someone thinks they have that protected characteristic (discrimination by perception) or they are connected to someone with that protected characteristic (discrimination by association) (EHRC 2020a).
- *Indirect discrimination (unfair exclusion)*: Occurs when a provision, policy or practice, which may appear neutral, is applied to everyone but its impact disadvantages people with a protected characteristic. For example banning all headwear would indirectly discriminate against people who wear headwear for religious reasons. If the organisation can show there is a good reason for its policy, it is not indirect discrimination. This is known as 'objective justification' (EHRC 2020a).

 **ACTIVITY**

Discrimination

Discrimination has been a feature of societies for many years. Identify examples of discrimination relating to women in developing cultures, homosexual men in the UK up to 1967, Black people in USA until the 1950s and people with disabilities.

- *Positive discrimination*: In employment, refers to actions that attempt to redress historical inequalities through a reverse principle of discrimination in favour of a disadvantaged group. However, under the Equality Act 2010, 'positive discrimination' is prohibited – it would be unlawful for an employer to recruit or promote an individual purely based on their protected characteristic, rather than experience or qualifications. The employer could, however, hire or promote an individual from an underrepresented group as long as they are as qualified and fit for the role as the other applicants.
- *Positive (affirmative) action*: Laws and policies that seek to promote equal opportunity for individuals from disadvantaged or underrepresented groups. The focus might be to redress systemic, historical or institutional discrimination or to promote diversity in public sector organisations (Jarrett 2011).

CHALLENGING PREJUDICE

Attitude formation is learned rather than innate, therefore attitudes are amenable to change. However, prejudice invariably involves a set of strong views, feelings and images that are not easily changed by providing fuller information (Kallen 2004). The Department for Communities and Local Government (DCLG) (2007) claims that prejudice reduction initiatives are more likely to be successful if the messages presented: are free of jargon and emotive language; contradict stereotypes; emphasise how groups are similar to each other; focus only on one minority group at a time; and involve repetition. The social, cultural and political context must be understood before initiatives are implemented and clear strategies for measuring the effectiveness of reducing prejudice are applied (DCLG 2007).

As there is no single explanation of the cause of social biases, a multifaceted approach to prejudice reduction is required which incorporates different perspectives and disciplines (Dovidio et al. 2013), supported by social policy and legislation, media campaigns and education. However, success rests upon whether people wish to avoid being seen as prejudiced, which is based on their personal values as well as the values held by the groups to which they belong; if their social group has bigoted views, individuals risk disapproval if they deviate by embracing tolerant views towards others.

Legislation

The Equality Act 2010 brings together a range of discrimination laws into one single Act. It places a duty on public bodies, such as schools and early years settings (including private and independent providers), to prevent direct and indirect discrimination, harassment and victimisation against individuals on the grounds of having a protected characteristic (EHRC 2020a). Those subject to the Equality Duty must reflect equality principles in the design of policies and the delivery of services in order to meet the needs of individuals listed as having 'protected characteristics' to enable them to fully participate in settings and public life (see Chapter 1).

Education – early years practitioners and teachers

In order to reduce prejudice and promote social justice and inclusion within early years settings and primary schools, there needs to be ongoing commitment from practitioners to: keep up-to-date with equality training and related initiatives; reflect on how their own gendered, social, religious and ethnic positioning may impact on children and families; raise their understanding of issues faced by marginalised groups and to use this knowledge to support and empower individuals; acknowledge the complex narrative brought about by the intersectionality of gender, race, culture, religion and social class (Hamilton and Jones 2016); and provide children with opportunities to explore the impact of power relations and the limitations of binary discourse and stereotypes, and to encourage them to become critical consumers of mass media. Chapters 1 and 2 outline two critical theory interventions that can be used with young children including Philosophy for Children (Chapter 1, pp. 22–23) and critical media literacy (Chapter 2, p. 34).

 **REFLECTION**

Addressing your own personal biases

Earlier in this chapter you were asked to identify any personal biases you may have regarding certain children and families. Now consider:

1   How this might impact the children and families you work with, currently or in the future. Think about your emotions, expectations, stereotypes and behaviour towards these individuals.
2   The steps you might take to address such bias.

KEY POINTS

- Detrimental social biases can occur at the individual, institutional and cultural levels.
- Prejudice presents on a spectrum, from hate crimes to subtle forms which may be subconscious and difficult to detect.

- Prejudice can lead to physical and mental harm and contributes to inequality in health, education, employment, accommodation and criminal justice.
- There is no single cause of social biases but contributing factors have been identified through sociological, psychological and social-psychological research; their complexity therefore requires a multifaceted approach to prejudice reduction.
- Practitioners have a crucial role to play in helping children to understand the impact of power relations, stereotypes and prejudice and to become critical consumers of media.
- Media producers have an important responsibility with regard to how they depict minority groups, as negative portrayals create significant harm. Paradoxically, the media can play a powerful role in helping to counteract social biases.
- Early years practitioners and teachers should demonstrate ongoing commitment towards equality-related training and examining their own social positioning and unconscious bias.

FURTHER READING

Dovidio, J., Hewstone, M., Glick, P. and Esses, V. (2013) *Prejudice, Stereotyping and Discrimination.* London: Sage.

Comprehensive theoretical coverage about the areas of prejudice, stereotyping and discrimination.

McQueeney, K. (2014) Disrupting Islamophobia: Teaching the social construction of terrorism in the mass media. *International Journal of Teaching and Learning in Higher Education*, 2 (26), 297–309.

Theoretical and practical advice on how to critique controversial and social news stories presented within the mass media with young people, which can be adapted for use with younger children.

USEFUL WEBSITES

Equality and Human Rights Commission: www.equalityhumanrights.com

3

CHILD POVERTY AND LOW-INCOME FAMILIES

CONTENTS

CHAPTER OVERVIEW

This chapter examines what it means to be living in poverty in the UK: the impact it has on children and families in terms of health and educational outcomes and life opportunities. Consideration is given to the scale of the problem and to individuals who are vulnerable to poverty. Theories and discourses of poverty, which underpin the legislative and policy context, are explored and attention is placed on ways in which practitioners can support children and families from low-income households in school and early years settings.

This chapter considers:

1 Definitions and statistics relating to child poverty.
2 A historical overview of legislation and policy relating to child poverty.
3 Theories and discourses of poverty.
4 Health and social disparities for children living in poverty and on low incomes.
5 Educational disparities for children living in poverty and on low incomes.
6 Strategies for supporting children and families in poverty and on low incomes.

THE PICTURE OF POVERTY: DEFINITIONS AND STATISTICS

Despite being the sixth largest economy in the world (NASDAQ 2020), the UK experiences high levels of poverty. Out of 28 EU member states, the UK had the 12th highest poverty rate in 2017 (Office for National Statistics [ONS] 2019). During the last 20 years, the UK has made significant progress at reducing poverty among individuals who had traditionally been most at risk – pensioners and children (Joseph Rowntree Foundation [JRF] 2020). However, progress has stalled, with 14.2 million people in the UK estimated to be in poverty (22% of the population), which includes over 4.2 million children (JRF 2020) – that is, 30% of children, or around 9 in a classroom of 30 (Child Poverty Action Group [CPAG] 2019).

There is evidence to suggest that poverty is rising, with more children now facing severe poverty. In 2017, over 1.5 million people were destitute in the UK, including more than a third of a million children (JRF 2020), and 7.8% of the population were in persistent poverty (ONS 2019). Rising living costs, low wages and inadequate social security benefits are resulting in increasing numbers of families living on the cusp of the poverty line (Children's Society 2020a). CPAG (2019) expect 5.2 million children to be living in poverty in the UK by 2022. The current coronavirus crisis could push disadvantaged families into poverty if parents face job losses and falls in earnings as a result of the pandemic (Children's Society 2020b).

Who is in poverty?

Poverty creates a spiral of disadvantage that often accumulates across the lifespan to trap individuals in a generational cycle of poverty (Knowles 2013a). Although individuals can move in and out of poverty over the course of their lives, households at increased risk of poverty include: families with three or more children; lone-parent families; families from certain ethnic minority groups; families with a disabled member; families who live in privately rented accommodation; families with children under the age of five; families where parents work in low-paid sectors; and families who live in certain regions of the UK.

One of the major changes in UK poverty over the last 15 years has been the fall in poverty among children living in lone-parent families. Children living in couple families now form an increasingly larger proportion of children in poverty (Social Metrics Commission [SMC] 2018). The deterioration of the terms of employment for the lowest paid 20% of workers – low wages and insecure hours and incomes – together with the high cost of childcare, have been a major cause of poverty (CPAG 2020a). Other trends regarding children and families experiencing poverty in the UK are presented below.

Poverty trends

- Wales has a higher poverty rate (24%) than England (22%), Scotland (20%) and Northern Ireland (18%) (CPAG 2020b).
- 47% of children living in lone-parent families are in poverty (CPAG 2020b).
- 70% of children in poverty live in a household where at least one person works (CPAG 2019).
- Households of Bangladeshi and Pakistani background face high rates of poverty (nearly 50%), people living in households of Indian background face poverty rates of 23% (JRF 2020); 28% of people in non-British white households are in poverty, compared with 19% of people in white British households (JRF 2020).
- Nearly half of the 14.2 million people in poverty are affected by disability. Poverty is particularly high among families where there is either a parent or a child who is disabled (JRF 2020).
- 43% of children in poverty live in families with three or more children (CPAG 2019).
- 37.9% of children in poverty live in a family where the youngest child is under the age of five (SMC 2018).
- 75% of children in poverty live in families in social or private rented accommodation (SMC 2018).

Measuring and defining poverty

There are different ways to measure poverty, but poverty is generally discussed in terms of absolute poverty and relative poverty, and is largely based on the ability to purchase items seen as essential for survival, such as food, shelter, heat and clothing.

Absolute poverty

In 1995 the United Nations defined absolute poverty as the severe deprivation of basic human needs, including food, safe drinking water, sanitation facilities, health, shelter, education and information (United Nations 1995). In 2015, in an attempt to compare poverty across countries, the United Nations set the international absolute poverty figure as being an income of $1.90 a day (United Nations 2020). Cases of absolute poverty as described in this way are unusual in the UK. However, Buttle UK (2019) reports rising numbers of homeless families in the UK falling into extreme cases of poverty. Figures published by Shelter (2019) show that 135,000 children in Britain are homeless, living in temporary accommodation. In some London boroughs, 1 in 12 children are homeless and in Manchester, in the northwest of the UK, 1 in 47 children are homeless (Shelter 2019).

 **CASE STUDY**

Prioritising household income

Jen and Alice have three children – Dai, 9 years old; Haf, 5 years old; and Rhys, 12 months old. They both work, and live in privately rented housing. They are on a low-income, living just above the poverty line.

After paying rent, food and household utilities, identify some of the other household/family costs that you would expect in order to keep them living in a similar standard to most families with young children in the UK. Think about the different needs of the children who represent different age groups. As money is tight, select and justify five key items. The section which follows might give you some ideas.

Relative poverty

When poverty is discussed in the UK, it usually refers to the notion of relative poverty. Relative poverty is where an individual's income and living standards are significantly worse than the general standard of living that is experienced or encouraged by others in their community or country. Living standards, which are based on contemporary norms and thus change over time, are not exclusively about income but also refer to the household's access to goods, services and recreational activities that allow an individual to comfortably live and participate in the societies to which they belong (Benoist 2018). There are issues with the concept of relative poverty as it does not take into account housing costs, debt repayments or changes in the cost of living. Childcare and housing are two of the costs that take the biggest toll on families' budgets (CPAG 2020b).

Each year, the UK Government publishes a survey of income poverty called Households Below Average Income (HBAI). This sets the poverty line at 60% of the median UK household income. Median income accounts for the total income, including all benefits but minus direct taxes. So, if a household's income is less than 60% of this average, HBAI considers them to be living in *relative* poverty (CPAG 2020c). In 2018–19, the median household income in the UK was approximately £29,400 per year. Therefore, households falling below 60% of this income (£17,640) in this year would be in relative poverty. *Absolute* poverty is where a household's income is less than 60% of the median as it stood in 2011 (adjusted with inflation) (CPAG 2020c). Living on an income of less than 60% of the median means that many families struggle to meet essentials such as food, housing costs, heating, transport, clothing and the extra costs of schooling (Wickham et al. 2016). Therefore, CPAG (2020c) assert that calculating poverty as an income below 60% of the median, *after* housing costs (the measure agreed by the Social Metrics Commission), gives a more accurate measure of how much families have to live on. The actual poverty line a family faces is also dependent on the size and composition of the household (JRF 2020). Thirty per cent of children live in families below the poverty line (after housing costs), which is almost double the poverty rate (16%) for pensioners (CPAG 2020c).

Being in receipt of income-related welfare benefits has also been used as a measure of poverty. In the UK, this can include being the recipient of universal credit or income support, job seeker's allowance, housing benefits, council tax benefits or working tax credit and child tax credit. Free school meal eligibility is a statutory benefit available to school-aged children from families who receive other qualifying benefits and is often used in education as a measure of childhood disadvantage related to poverty (CPAG 2020b).

Although social class is defined by more than one's profession, the UK Government utilises the National Statistics Socio-economic Classification (NS-SEC), an occupationally based classification system, for research and statistics (ONS 2016).

ONS SOCIO-ECONOMIC CLASSIFICATION 2010 (ONS 2016)

1   Higher managerial, administrative and professional occupations
     1.1 Large employers and higher managerial and administrative occupations
     1.2 Higher professional occupations
2   Lower managerial, administrative and professional occupations
3   Intermediate occupations
4   Small employers and own account workers
5   Lower supervisory and technical occupations
6   Semi-routine occupations
7   Routine occupations
8   Never worked and long-term unemployed

LEGISLATION AND POLICY

There has long been a concern for how best to provide for individuals who are living in poverty in the UK, with 'Poor Laws' first emerging in 1598 (Knowles and Lander 2011). However, histories of the welfare state usually begin after the end of the Second World War, when in 1945 the government started to rebuild Britain and address the poverty facing the country. Legislation which followed the 1942 Beveridge Report led to the establishment of the National Health Service and a system of benefits to provide social security to protect the well-being of the population (Knowles 2013a). The welfare provision introduced in the 1940s included free education, free health care, social housing, social security and other services for children. Public attitude towards supporting those experiencing poverty remained largely sympathetic until the late 1970s (Cronin 2017). In order to understand contemporary debates regarding supporting children and families in poverty, it is necessary to be aware of past measures aimed at tackling child poverty.

In 1999 the Labour government set targets to reduce child poverty by 2010 and eliminate child poverty by 2020. By doing so, the UK was the first European country to implement policies to combat child poverty. Although relative poverty fell substantially during this period, the 2010 targets to halve child poverty were missed (Wickham et al. 2016). Remaining committed to child poverty, the Coalition government passed the Child Poverty Act 2010 and a national Child Poverty Strategy. The scale of poverty during the decade that followed was not straightforward, with some decline, but also rising numbers of children from working households going into poverty. Changes to tax and benefits appear to have an explanatory role, as increased investments in families' social security led to a notable reduction in child poverty (CPAG 2020d). In 2014, the Child Poverty Strategy 2014 to 2017 was introduced, based on two core aims: (1) to support families into work and to shift away from income benefits; and (2) to raise educational attainment to prevent poor children from becoming poor adults (Wickham et al. 2016). This was followed by the controversial Welfare Reform and Work Act 2016, which abolished the Child Poverty Act 2010, the commitment to reduce child poverty and the measure of poverty based on family income. Instead, it placed a new focus on the 'root causes' of poverty such as unemployment, debt and family breakdown (Wickham et al. 2016). The 2016 Act, and its associated measures, have been heavily criticised, including concerns that the previous progress on the reduction of child poverty will be undermined. The freeze on support for children under universal credit, the two-child limit for universal credit and changes to tax credit are contentious, and critics argue that unprecedented numbers of families with young children are falling into poverty, with a serious impact on child health (Royal College of Paediatrics and Child Health [RCPCH] 2018a; CPAG 2020d).

Social mobility – the ability to move from one social class to another in an upwards direction – has featured quite heavily in social policy in the UK as this, along with the concept of meritocracy (where hardworking and talented individuals are enabled to climb the social ladder), have been popular strategies used to tackle poverty (Collett 2017). However, Collett points out how the UK has lower levels of social mobility than many other industrialised countries, and that meritocracy places the responsibility for success or failure on the individual and in so doing moves away from the wider societal structures which cause inequality and poverty. Analysis of child poverty policy suggests that, to have the greatest impact, policies should address three key areas within a framework of national economic and social policy: prioritising early childhood education and care; reducing the risk of poverty by increasing employment chances and wages of families in employment; and effective income support through the benefit and tax systems for those on very low incomes (Cheung 2018). Many commentators, including the Royal College of Paediatrics and Child Health, are urging the UK Government to prioritise child health inequalities by urgently reviewing its policies. They are calling for each government across the UK to adopt a 'child health in all policies' approach, national targets to reduce child poverty to be reinstated, the scale of cuts to public health and child services to be reconsidered and for universal credit to be reversed (Iacobucci 2017; Mayor 2017; RCPCH 2018a; Children's Society 2020a). These measures are regarded as fundamental to prevent increased numbers of children being pushed into poverty and to ultimately protect the wellbeing of future generations.

ACTIVITY

Debating discourses of poverty

Read through the statements below and discuss each with a small group of peers. Please be professional during the discussion. Once you have done this, see if you can identify which theory or discourse the statement may apply to (Social Darwinism; culture of poverty; Marxism; functionalism; cultural capital).

1   Working-class children are at a disadvantage in school because they do not share the same language and values as their teachers.
2   It is natural in society to have certain individuals who are successful and wealthy and to have others who are disadvantaged, so we should not waste time by supporting those at the bottom.
3   Working-class people have little chance to pull themselves out of poverty because the wealthy and powerful keep them positioned there.
4   Society needs people to perform different roles (doctors and retail workers), so we should encourage and reward the professionally skilled through high salaries.
5   Education is free and can open opportunities but the working class don't help themselves – they don't see the point of studying and working hard.

THEORIES AND DISCOURSES OF POVERTY

The notion that the government has a duty to provide for the poor, along with the question of why certain children and families fall into poverty, are regularly contested (Knowles 2013a; Cronin 2017). Theoretical concepts and understandings of the causes of poverty are important as these perspectives influence government welfare policy towards poverty reduction. Various studies highlight the complex interplay between social, cultural and economic factors which lead to social inequalities and poverty. However, social theories are typically centred around three causal factors: individual, cultural and structural.

Individual factors

Social Darwinism is the extension of Darwin's ideas of natural selection and biological evolution and attempts to justify an individual's success or poverty status. According to Herbert Spencer and William Sumner, social existence is a competitive experience among individuals who have different abilities and traits (Sameti et al. 2012). Spencer and Sumner asserted that individuals with better abilities are capable of being economically productive within society and that the state should not interfere with the natural course of social improvement because the social system is weakened when the poor are kept in society (Sameti et al. 2012). In line with this ideology, welfare expenditures and programmes would be kept at the minimum, provided to disadvantaged individuals only when other sources of help have been exhausted (Sameti et al. 2012).

Cultural factors and the 'underclass'

The 'culture of poverty' theory focuses on factors which exist within people's residential environment to determine either poverty or success. The theory asserts that poverty is intergenerational because working-class children are socialised into learning negative values, beliefs and psychological behaviours (not to study hard, not to plan for the future, to spend money unwisely) (Sameti et al. 2012). This ideology has been particularly used by scholars in the US (Wilson 1987, 1996; Herrnstein and Murray 1996) to study urban poverty, giving rise to the concept the 'underclass', a group that exists below the working class. Wilson argued that 'ghetto-specific culture' in inner-cities results in the 'underclass' accepting deviant behaviours, such as welfare dependence and crime, due to social isolation and the absence of economic opportunity (Sameti et al. 2012). Murray asserted that welfare systems created by the state between the 1940s and late 1970s had removed individual blame for poverty, positioning the poor as victims, which has led to the emergence of the 'underclass' who experience poverty because of a lifestyle choice that they are making (Murray cited in Cronin 2017). His work has influenced contemporary political and social attitudes, with a significant fall in empathy towards the poor since the 1990s (Cronin 2017). This ideology is criticised for focusing on the perceived character defects of individuals rather than on the wider structural and social forces associated with poverty.

 **ACTIVITY**

Media coverage

Undertake a media search to examine the news items presented about children and families living in poverty or on low incomes. Are the messages mainly positive or mainly negative? Could these messages lead to misconceptions or stereotypical thinking? What impact might such messages have for these families?

Government and media rhetoric about the 'underclass' reinforce individual explanations of poverty and are particularly seized upon when resources are stretched (Collett 2017). Negative discourses position the poor working class as a significant social problem, suggesting distinct characteristics, such as a culture of dependency, intergenerational unemployment, reckless or criminal behaviour and lone parenthood to be lifestyle choices (Collett 2017; Cronin 2017). Collett (2017: 71) asserts, 'In a climate of low-paid jobs, the distinction is no longer between non-working and working, it is between unemployed and hard-working.' The stigma often attached to low-income households frequently serves to stereotype and institutionalise the poor. Poorer families are often seen as inferior and their morals questioned (Benoist 2018). Media headlines skewed towards fraudulent claims have suggested benefit fraud is a widespread national problem leading to negativity towards claimants. For example, 'Benefit fraud in the UK hits record levels after false claims rose to £2.3 billion last year' (*Daily Mail*, 28 June 2019) and 'Disabled girl's mum from Reading in £60k benefit fraud' (BBC News, 17 January 2019). Cronin (2017) argues that the cost of benefit fraud is minimal in comparison to the money which is defrauded by tax evasion, largely committed by the wealthy, and how every year significantly more benefits remain unclaimed than are fraudulently claimed.

Structural factors

The functionalist theory is based on the belief that there are certain positions and functions in society that require special skills and knowledge, and that individuals who undergo training to hone their skills should be motivated and repaid with higher wages and privileges, otherwise society will suffer. Thus, the wage of labour is regarded as proportional to the cost of training and the individual's sacrifice, and consequently economic inequality and poverty are justified (Sameti et al. 2012).

Marx utilised the concept of capitalist exploitation to explain the cause of poverty and poor quality of life among workers during the Industrial Revolution. Social conflict perspectives argue that the privileged and powerful groups maintain their place in society through the education system. In state schools, where there is more of a social mix, this can be seen through the concentration of middle-class children in the higher academic groups, while working-class children tend to be placed in lower teaching sets (Bartlett and Burton 2007). As time progresses, any gap in ability will widen due to the impact of children being taught differently and presented with different opportunities, and teachers holding different expectations. Children come to view their positions within school as 'normal' and later replicate their order of position in society (Bartlett and Burton 2007).

Bourdieu (1984) asserted that differences in educational attainment (thus success or poverty) can be explained in relation to three forms of capital: economic, social and cultural. 'Economic capital' means wealthier parents can afford housing in catchment areas with good schools and the extra costs of education (additional tutoring, equipment) (Benoist 2018). 'Social capital' refers to relationships that individuals develop to progress in education and employment. Children living in poverty could be at a social capital disadvantage if their parents have unsociable working hours, leaving them little time to support their children with school activities (Benoist 2018). 'Cultural capital' represents the characteristics and behaviours that are associated with one's socio-cultural background. Middle-class children are often at an advantage over working-class children as education policy within the state sector is determined by politicians and civil servants, most of whom are middle class (Collett 2017). Therefore, because they are designed by individuals who hold similar beliefs and values, middle-class children have a style of language which helps them more easily access the curriculum; they know how to interact with teachers and use books; and they are aware of the importance of success at school for their future (Benoist 2018). The deficit theory often positions working-class children's cultural and linguistic differences and their work ethic and parental involvement as deficiencies in need of being 'fixed' in line with middle-class expectations.

HEALTH AND SOCIAL DISPARITIES

The importance of health and well-being in early childhood on outcomes in adult life is well established (Cheung 2018), as is the link between poor health and low income. A systematic review of the literature shows how infants, children and young people living in poverty, or on low incomes, have significantly worse physical, mental, emotional and behavioural health outcomes than children from more affluent backgrounds. Poor health in childhood has direct economic consequences for nations, due to the increased need for acute health care and greater risk of later educational failure and unemployment in adulthood (Cheung 2018).

Before the National Health Service was established in 1948, approximately 1 in 20 children died before their first birthday (Cheung 2018). Despite significant progress both in the reduction of stillbirths and neonatal, infant and child deaths, and in vaccination programmes (reducing the number of children contracting preventable illnesses such as polio, tuberculosis and measles), the poverty gap which exists in the UK means that children and young people in deprived groups experience some of the worse health outcomes in the developed world (Cheung 2018). The advance in child health has stalled; the UK now lags behind many other high-income countries when it comes to breastfeeding and reducing infant mortality, childhood obesity and rates of smoking during pregnancy (Mayor 2017; Cheung 2018). Reductions to social security have led to an increase in child poverty and cuts to welfare services (children's centres, parenting guidance, speech and language therapy, services for disabled children) have left families struggling with less support; these services are pivotal to the early identification of need and intervention (RCPCH 2018b; Save the Children 2019a).

CASE STUDY

Supporting the health and well-being of children living in low-income households

Becky lives with her boyfriend, Darnell, and two young children. Kordell, Darnell's 10-year-old son from a former relationship, also stays with them three days a week. Most days she attends the Children's Centre with Jake (2 years old) and Jaz (7 months old). Becky is struggling. She is lonely and is finding it difficult to cover the household bills. Darnell is always out working, trying to provide for the family; all he wants to do when he gets home is to unwind with a few drinks. The stress of living in poverty is causing the couple to argue on a regular basis, often in front of the children. Becky is feeling anxious as she has heard that the Children's Centre is likely to close.

1 How might the family's situation affect the children's health and well-being?
2 How can Becky and Darnell be supported?
3 What agencies do you think might be able to support the family? Alongside statutory services, identify any voluntary organisations (national and local) which may be able to assist families in poverty.
4 What might be the barriers for early years practitioners trying to support the family?

Poor health outcomes can be a consequence of cumulative exposure to deprivation or exposure during critical periods of childhood, with longer durations of poverty having more adverse effects on children's outcomes than short-term experiences (Wickham et al. 2016). As children's lives unfold, the poor physical and mental health associated with poverty often limits their development across a range of domains, leading to reduced life chances in adulthood (Wickham et al. 2016). Individuals living in poverty often have a shorter life expectancy (Mayor 2017) and experience greater illness and disability throughout life. In the most deprived areas, boys typically live 19 fewer years of their lives in good health, and girls 20 fewer years, than children in the least deprived areas (CPAG 2020e).

Since 1990, the UK has dropped several positions in the European Union rankings of child mortality (ONS 2017). In 2015, out of 28 countries, the UK ranked 20th for both neonatal deaths (2.7 deaths per 1,000 births) and under-five mortality (4.5 deaths per 1,000 births) (ONS 2017). Countries with the least amount of child deaths were Luxembourg and Finland (ONS 2017). Mortality in UK infants under age one in the lowest socio-economic group has been found to be more than twice as high as those in the highest income group, with deaths commonly associated with conditions related to preterm birth (Mayor 2017). The declining trend in infant mortality in the UK appears to have reversed, with the number of infant deaths rising since 2014. A study conducted by Taylor-Robinson et al. (2019) shows how this rise has not been experienced evenly across the population, with the gap between the most and the least deprived local authority areas in England widening by 52 deaths per 100,000 births. The rise in infant mortality has disproportionately affected the poorest areas, leaving the most affluent areas unaffected. Taylor-Robinson and colleagues assert that a third of the increases in infant mortality from 2014 to 2017 are likely to be attributed to increases in child poverty, largely due to the cuts that have been made to welfare benefits available to families.

In addition to greater mortality rates, children living in low-income families face other health inequalities, including higher rates of obesity, tooth decay, non-intentional injury, respiratory problems, mental health conditions and emergency hospital admissions for asthma or diabetes (Wickham et al. 2016; Iacobucci 2017; Mayor 2017; Cheung 2018). Physical health in infancy, such as low birth weight, whether a baby is breastfed or not, and being overweight, can have lasting effects on the risk of developing physical illness (Cheung 2018). Smoking during pregnancy is one of the most important modifiable risk factors for improving infant health. Despite reductions over the past decade, women in lower socio-economic groups are much more likely to smoke during pregnancy (Mayor 2017).

Families in poverty tend to be located in communities that have substandard housing, which is often insecure and overcrowded, with poor access to safe open play spaces (Mental Health Foundation 2018; RCPCH 2018b). Children living in overcrowded, cold and damp housing are more likely to experience respiratory difficulties and contract meningitis (CPAG 2020e). There is also evidence of escalating food poverty, with children missing out on decent meals (Children's Society 2020a) and doctors making increased foodbank referrals (RCPCH 2018b). The prices of essentials like food and fuel increasing has a significant impact on the UK's poorest families. Some parents skip meals so they can afford to feed their children, and in winter many families have to make a choice of either feeding their children or heating their homes (Children's Society 2020a). In a study conducted by the RCPCH (2018b) doctors reported a worsening of parents' and children's mental health, with the following stressors impacting on well-being: food insecurity (60%), housing problems or homelessness (60%) and financial stress (50%) (Iacobucci 2017; RCPCH 2018b). The RCPCH (2018a) also notes how poverty may prevent parents from attending appointments for sick or disabled children due a lack of transport or for fear of losing their job or money when taking time off work.

Mental health issues can lead to a series of detrimental effects on people's life chances. Even when not born into disadvantage, children who experience mental health problems are more likely to be workless and to live on benefits in adulthood (Mental Health Foundation 2018). The prevalence of mental ill-health maps closely to areas of deprivation, with children and young people living in poorer households two to four times more likely to develop a mental health problem by the age of 11 (Mental Health Foundation 2018; CPAG 2020e). The impact of poverty on mental well-being is multifaceted, with a range of environmental, social, cultural and economic factors affecting mental health.

Living in poverty can lead to feelings of shame, fear, distrust, instability, insecurity and isolation and, ultimately, a sense of powerlessness (Psychologists Against Austerity 2015). Parents may become critical of their capacity to cope financially and feel that they have failed in their ability to care for their children (Benoist 2018). Research shows how influential maternal mental health is during a child's prenatal and early years because of its impact on the child's cognitive, social, emotional and behavioural development (Save the Children 2019a). The stresses parents in poverty face in struggling to make ends meet, on low wages and in poor housing increase the probability of relationship conflict, domestic abuse, drug and alcohol misuse and mental illness within the household (Children 1st 2018). Consequently, this increases the likelihood of adverse childhood experiences (ACEs), with increased rates of depression among parents living in disadvantaged households also linked to higher rates of disorganised attachment in early childhood (Benoist 2018).

Children living in families struggling with debt are five times more likely to feel anxious, depressed, unsafe and negative about their future than children in families who do not face difficulties with debt (Children's Society 2020a). The UK's poorest children are also more likely to face repeated house moves, lack essential clothing and miss out on social events, such as school functions, holidays and family time (Mental Health Foundation 2018; CPAG 2020e; Children's Society 2020a). The cost of school life can have a significant impact on children living in deprived households. More than two-thirds of children in poverty said they had been embarrassed and felt isolated because their parents could not afford school uniform, trips and equipment. Some children go hungry at school and experience feelings of shame due to a lack of money and restricted food options for those on free school meals (Weale 2019; Children's Society 2020a). More than a quarter of children had encountered stigma and bullying at school for living in poverty (Mental Health Foundation 2018; Children's Society 2020a).

EDUCATIONAL DISPARITIES AND SUPPORT STRATEGIES

Although various factors influence children's educational achievement, there has been a long-standing relationship between wealth and education, with the attainment gap between working-class children and their more affluent peers documented through a series of reports since the 1950s and 1960s (Bartlett and Burton 2007).

Experiencing poverty for even a few years can have a significant negative impact on young children's development, particularly the under-fives, as these early stages of a child's life are a critical period for cognitive, language and social development (Benoist 2018; Save the Children 2019a). Children from poorer backgrounds lag at all stages of education, with the socio-economic gap being far more influential than the gender or ethnic gap in children's educational attainment (Collett 2017; Beniost 2018). Although socio-economic disadvantage is damaging for children of both genders, boys are more likely to fall behind (Save the Children 2016). Educational inequalities, which start in the pre-school years, typically continue to grow through primary and secondary schooling. If a child does not enter 'school ready' with basic skills this reduces their ability to make the most of learning experiences, develop social skills and establish friendships. In the longer term, falling behind in the early years disadvantages the rest of a child's school career, employment opportunities and adult life chances (Save the Children 2016).

By age five, children from the poorest homes in the UK are over a year behind their more affluent peers in terms of development, and by the end of primary school, only 75% of the poorest children reach the government's Key Stage 2 levels compared with 97% of children from the wealthiest families (Wickham et al. 2016). In 2017/18, 43% of all pupils achieved grade 5 or above in English and maths GCSEs, compared to 25% of pupils from poorer families (Department for Work and Pensions 2019). Even the performance of more able children from poorer families, who begin school on a par with more able children facing the least deprivation, falls away by the age of 16 (CPAG 2020e).

The ability to use and understand language is a significant factor in educational attainment. The range of linguistic experience and vocabulary developed among children differs greatly, largely influenced by social background. Working-class children may not be accustomed to hearing or using the elaborate code of language that is typically used at school, and so can be disadvantaged when they enter early years and educational settings (Bartlett and Burton 2007). Living in poverty can put children at significant risk of experiencing a delay in their language development (Save the Children 2016). At age five, 2 in 5 (43%) children in poverty in England were struggling with basic skills (unable to speak in full sentences, follow simple instructions and express themselves) compared to 1 in 4 (26%) wealthier children (Save the Children 2018). This can have major consequences for the development of early reading skills. Being able to read well is vital for a child's prospects at school and in life in general. Yet every year, one-third of children growing up in poverty leave primary school unable to read well, preventing thousands of the UK's poorest children from fulfilling their potential (Save the Children 2015). Research suggests that in order to engage children in the reading process at school, they need to be presented with texts they are familiar with, which may include digital texts and comics, neither of which are routinely used by schools (Knowles and Lander 2011).

Language skills develop best when children experience stimulating, language-rich environments. Simple activities such as talking, playing and reading have the potential to transform a child's life (Save the Children 2015). However, many low-income families have complex, challenging and stressful lives juggling work, managing the household budget and facilitating childcare. Some families have little choice but to prioritise work and income above their child's learning at home in order to meet the family's basic needs (Save the Children 2019b). Financial constraints can result in lower exposure to resources and activities which support learning; toys, books, computers and laptops may be second hand and there may be limited opportunity for extra-curricular activities (Save the Children 2019b). Furthermore, living a transient lifestyle or in temporary accommodation may mean toys and learning resources can be difficult to look after and may get mislaid (Argent 2017).

Promoting and supporting positive parental engagement in children's early learning is critical in mitigating the impact of poverty on children's life chances. However, parents who have grown up in poverty may not necessarily have experienced a nurturing parenting style themselves, or had positive experiences of school, which can leave them less ready to support their child's learning (Save the Children 2019a). It is therefore important to consider the impact of the increased closure of child and family centres, as these have been evidenced as playing a pivotal role in promoting parents' confidence in supporting children's learning in the early years (Save the Children 2019a). Supportive intervention in the early years and throughout primary education is paramount, as raising attainment among children from low-income households can help to prevent them from becoming the next generation of disadvantaged parents (Knowles 2013a).

Key to reducing child poverty are government measures which relate to the provision of appropriate welfare benefits for families with young children, narrowing the education gap at all stages, and the provision of high-quality, universal early childhood and family services. On a micro level, practitioners working with families experiencing poverty need to have a sensitive approach, be familiar with the importance of multiagency working, signposting and providing emergency advice, and be aware of the setting's policies regarding supporting families who are unable to fund the extra costs of schooling. As practitioners it is essential to avoid making assumptions based on socioeconomic status about differences in parenting, pre-school education and resources available to families (Collett 2017), and to remember that the effects of poverty are multiple and personal circumstances are different for everyone (Argent 2017). While the many ways in which low-income families can be excluded from early years settings and schools should be fully considered, inclusion policies must guard against singling out individual children and families, to prevent stigma (Collett 2017).

 **REFLECTION**

Thinking critically about the potential impact of poverty

Now that you have reached the end of this chapter, consider the following:

1   What factors can impact a child's ability to reach their academic potential when living in poverty or within a low-income family?
2   What key factors are important in establishing an effective relationship with families facing severe deprivation?
3   What support could a school/early years setting be able to offer?

KEY POINTS

- Rising living costs, low wages and inadequate social security benefits are resulting in increasing numbers of families living on the cusp of the poverty line, with rising numbers of children living in poverty where at least one adult works.
- Poverty often accumulates across the lifespan to trap individuals in a generational cycle of poverty.
- To understand debates regarding supporting children and families, it is necessary to be aware of past measures aimed at tackling child poverty and the theoretical discourses that exist to explain why certain families fall into poverty.
- Government and media discourse frequently portrays the poor working class as 'deviants' who are making (damaging) lifestyle choices, which moves the focus away from wider societal structures that lead to social inequalities and poverty.
- The link between child poverty and poor health, well-being and educational outcomes are long established.
- Early years and primary school practitioners have an important role to play in supporting children and families from low socio-economic households, creating enabling environments which do not single out individuals, and also through multiagency working, signposting and providing emergency advice, where required.

FURTHER READING

Benoist, F. (2018) Supporting and including children from low-income families. In Knowles, G. (ed.) *Supporting Inclusive Practice and Ensuring Opportunity is Equal for All*. Third edition. pp. 153–68. Abingdon: Routledge.

Offers a sound theoretical overview of issues associated with poverty with an emphasis on an educational context, and some useful scenarios.

Cronin, M., Argent, K. and Collett, C. (2017) *Poverty and Inclusion in Early Years Education.* Abingdon: Routledge.

Presents a good theoretical overview of poverty as well as addressing practicalities of working with low-income children and families.

Wickham, S., Anwar, E., Barr, B., Law, C. and Taylor-Robinson, D. (2016) Poverty and child health in the UK: Using evidence for action. *Archives of Disease in Childhood*, 101 (8), 1–7.

Provides a critical overview of historical legislative and policy context for tackling poverty.

USEFUL WEBSITES

Child Poverty Action Group: www.cpag.org.uk

Children's Society: www.childrenssociety.org.uk

Joseph Rowntree Foundation: www.jrf.org.uk

Poverty and Social Exclusion: www.poverty.ac.uk

Save the Children: www.savethechildren.org.uk

4

STIGMA OF MENTAL ILL-HEALTH IN CHILDHOOD

CONTENTS

CHAPTER OVERVIEW

Despite sustained efforts by the government and various charities, which have led to increased awareness of mental health, children and young people in the UK are still being subjected to prejudicial attitudes and behaviours on the grounds of mental health conditions (YMCA 2017; Bowman and West 2018). This chapter explores concepts of mental health and mental ill-health, examines risk and resilience factors and considers how schools and early years settings can both support children's mental well-being and promote understanding of the impact of stigma and prejudice.

This chapter considers:

1   Terms and concepts of mental health and mental ill-health.
2   Potential indicators of mental ill-health in children.
3   Statistics relating to mental health conditions in childhood.
4   Risk and resilience factors, including intersectionality.
5   The process and impact of stigma associated with mental illness.
6   Ways of addressing mental health in early years and primary school settings.

DEFINITIONS, CONCEPTS AND INDICATORS OF MENTAL ILLNESS

Mental health is a broad concept which is difficult to define, as it is culturally determined and thus subject to change.

ACTIVITY

Defining mental health and mental illness:

1   Identify terms and phrases used by the general public to describe 'mental health' and 'mental illness'. What observations can you make?
2   Look at the list of terms and phrases generated and identify those you think are most likely to be used with young children when discussing mental health. Why do you think these terms are chosen?

Various definitions are presented but the most commonly cited is that offered by the World Health Organization (WHO) (2014), which defines mental health as:

a state of well-being in which every individual realises his or her own potential, can cope with the normal stresses of life, can work productively and
fruitfully, and is able to make a contribution to her or his community.

It is suggested that mental health be perceived 'as a continuum, ranging from having
good mental health to poor mental health and from having no diagnosis of mental illness to a diagnosis of severe mental illness' (Mental Health First Aid [MHFA] 2016: 32).
Individuals will change their position along this continuum at different stages in
their life course.

With regard to poor mental health, numerous terms are utilised including mental
illness, mental health disorders, mental health problems, mental health conditions
and mental health issues. These terms are often used interchangeably. Poor mental
health also refers to emotional and behavioural issues. It is not the intent of this
chapter to examine different mental health disorders; definitions and characteristics
of individual disorders can be found in the *International Classification of Diseases 11*
(WHO 2018a) and the *Diagnostic and Statistical Manual of Mental Disorders 5* (American Psychiatric Association 2013).

An individual may be identified as having a 'mental health disorder' if they have
severe symptoms and persistent problems which interfere with their ability to function and impact upon their everyday life and relationships. Mental health disorders are considered a disability and are protected against discrimination under the
Equality Act 2010, when there is significant impact upon a person that lasts longer
than 12 months. Only a minority of individuals have serious ongoing mental health
disorders (MHFA 2016). A 'mental health issue' is a broader term including mental
disorders and symptoms of mental illness that may not be acute enough to necessi-
tate a clinical diagnosis. Some people have only one episode of mental illness in their
lifetime, while others have frequent episodes with periods of wellness in between
(MHFA 2016).

Children and mental health

In children, symptoms and behaviours may indicate a mental health disorder when
they occur regularly, last a long time, present at an unusual age and cause considerable disruption to the child's ability to: develop and maintain mutually fulfilling
relationships; develop a sense of right and wrong; and play and learn to reach age-
and context-appropriate psychological and behavioural benchmarks (Burton 2014).
The most common mental health problems for children and young people are emotional disorders (depression and anxiety in particular), conduct disorders, eating disorders and neurodevelopmental conditions, such as attention deficit hyperactivity

disorder and autism. Post-traumatic stress disorder – a consequence of persistent neglect, physical or sexual abuse, violence, severe bullying or witnessing a disturbing event – are also recognised (Howard et al. 2020).

Somatising and behavioural indicators in children include headaches, faecal soiling, sleep disturbance, stomach ache, changed eating patterns, changes in behaviour, an inability to focus, low self-esteem, social withdrawal and attachment and relationship difficulties (Howard et al. 2020). A deterioration in nursery/school attendance or the child's learning and development profile might also signify that a child has a mental health problem (Glazzard et al. 2019). However, the child should be monitored over a period of time, in a range of contexts, to determine if the problem is persistent, as these signs may not be the result of a mental health issue. The symptoms observed might be associated with physical illnesses, other behaviours or life events. Furthermore, it is important that 'normal' development for children and young people is seen on a continuum of change, as mood changes, emotional outbursts and risk-taking behaviours might be typical to a particular life stage (Burton 2014; Howard et al. 2020).

It is crucial that children are encouraged to talk about their feelings at a young age using the correct terminology. However, Danby and Hamilton (2016) found that mental health often remains the 'elephant in the room', with many early years and primary school practitioners reluctant to expose young children to the terms 'mental health' and 'mental illness'. Instead, there has been a tendency to approach the topic with children by cushioning any coverage with the term 'emotional and social well-being'. It is fundamental that practitioners avoid seeing words that are associated with mental illness as taboo, or it may cause children to perceive mental health issues as being abnormal and something to fear and be kept hidden. By talking about it, it becomes normalised.

Statistics

Much work has been done in recent years to improve mental health outcomes. However, mental health issues among children and young people appear to be on the increase and prevalent at an increasingly younger age. Research suggests that 50% of all mental health problems are established by the time an individual is 14 (Mental Health Foundation 2018), with 12.8% of children, aged 5–19 years, having been diagnosed with a mental health condition (Sadler et al. 2018). In 2018, the Health and Social Care Information Centre (HSCIC) published its survey *Mental Health of Children and Young People in England*, including 'under-fives' for the first time. The statistics indicated emotional disorders (depression and anxiety) were the most prevalent across all age groups, with rates higher in girls (10.0%) than in boys (6.2%); 9.5% of 5- to 10-year-olds, and 5.5% of children aged 2–4 years, had at least one mental health disorder.

Behavioural issues, more prevalent among boys than among girls, were the most common conditions experienced by children aged 2–10 years.

It is reported that 70% of children and young people who experience a mental health problem do not receive interventions at a sufficiently early age (Mental Health Foundation 2016). With timely and appropriate specialist support, these problems can be managed and perhaps prevented. There is current concern about the number of children, particularly those diagnosed with autism, who have been admitted for lengthy periods to a hospital or facility that is located a significant distance away from their home (Children's Commissioner 2019). Some of these institutes have been found to be using restrictive practices, which can be traumatising for young children (Children's Commissioner 2019).

 ACTIVITY

Thinking critically about statistics

1   Why do you think conduct disorders are more prevalent in boys than girls?
2   Why do you think there is a higher incidence of emotional disorders in girls across the age range?
3   What are the concerns relating to diagnosing and labelling young children with mental health conditions?
4   Are statistics reliable? Could there be an alternative explanation for the increase in mental health issues among children and young people?

Questioning the epidemic

Claims that mental health issues among children and young people are rising is rarely challenged and the suggestion to do so is perhaps contentious. However, it is important that early years practitioners and teachers strive to consider alternative perspectives beyond the contemporary discourse of early childhood adversity, protection and vulnerability, in order to understand the sharp increase in mental health issues in childhood. There may be other explanations: (1) The growth of mental health campaigns has led to better recognition of symptoms and diagnosis, increased awareness of support agencies and reduced stigma, resulting in individuals opening up about their problems. (2) The publication of the *Diagnostic Statistical Manual* and the *International Classification of Diseases* may see emotional and behavioural changes that have traditionally been regarded as 'normal' stages of development being categorised as new disorders (Burton 2014; Ecclestone 2014). (3) Society's preoccupation with safeguarding children has resulted in a culture of protecting them, sometimes from 'stressful situations' and 'uncomfortable feelings' arising from daily occurrences; by so doing this reduces opportunities for children to develop resilience (Ecclestone 2014, 2015).

RISK, RESILIENCE AND INTERSECTIONALITY

Many mental health issues can be traced back to childhood. Different theoretical models used to understand mental ill-health can be situated within one, or across, the following domains: (1) medical or biological (an individual's genetics); (2) psychological (cognitive and emotional factors); (3) systemic, social and environmental impact of context (family stressors, traumatic events) (Burton 2014).

Mental health and mental ill-health are the result of biological factors (such as genetics and brain development), and psychological determinants (including coping strategies), and how these interact with either positive or adverse environmental circumstances (Howard et al. 2020). Experiences in early childhood impact on brain development and it is the effect of these encounters on a child's characteristics and temperament that shapes their psychological development (Howard et al. 2020). Risk factors (stressors) which make individuals vulnerable to poor mental health are wide ranging. Some of the potential risk factors or 'stressors' are outlined in Table 4.1.

Table 4.1 Risk factors (many factors overlap and this is not a complete list)

The child	The family and school	Community and environmental
Genetic factors	Child has experienced abuse	Socio-economic disadvantage
Low self-esteem	(physical, sexual, emotional,	Prejudice/discrimination
Gender identity conflict	neglect)	Poor accommodation/homelessness
Neurological disorder	Family conflict/breakdown	Disadvantaged neighbourhood
Learning differences;	Parental illness (physical or	(antisocial behaviour/crime, lack of
developmental delay	mental)	social facilities, environmental decline)
Chronic physical	Domestic abuse	High level of unemployment and
disability/disfigurement	Parental criminality	inadequate financial support
Sexuality	Bereavement	Impact of social media
Communication/	Change in family structure	Consumerism
language difficulties and	(divorce, birth of a sibling)	Traumatic event (war, terrorism,
differences	Parental alcohol/substance	natural disaster)
Body image issues	misuse	
	Main carer for a relative	
	Poor attachments with	
	parents; hostile and rejecting	
	relationships	
	Children moving into care,	
	fostering, adoption	
	Moving countries/schools	
	School attainment – testing,	
	exam pressures	
	Bullying/discrimination	

(Prever 2006; Burton 2014)

CASE STUDY

Supporting Abbie

Abbie has had a challenging start to life. Her mum, a single parent, had Abbie when she was 16 years old. Mum struggled to bond with her daughter, but Abbie's Granddad, who they lived with, formed a strong attachment with Abbie – the two were inseparable. Unfortunately, six months ago, the day before Abbie's fourth birthday, Granddad passed away suddenly in the family home. Abbie witnessed the paramedic team trying to resuscitate him. Mum's mental health has deteriorated so much that it is affecting her parenting capacity. Abbie has been placed in temporary foster care. She has started to present difficult behaviours, including sleep disturbance and an unwillingness to leave the foster home, refusing to go to school.

Questions

1   Identify the stressors that might lead to Abbie having a mental health problem.
2   What other signs and symptoms might Abbie present, which could indicate a mental health problem?
3   How can the early years team at Abbie's school support her?

Intersectionality

A causal factor of mental ill-health is social bias (prejudice, stigma, discrimination). Thus, poor mental health is something which individuals from all minority groups may be susceptible to because perceived social differences (sexuality, disability, race, ethnicity, religion, socio-economic status) frequently make people a target of prejudice. Individuals who present signs of mental illness may be at risk of double or multiple prejudice from members within their own minority group if they deviate from accepted norms, as well as being discriminated against by the wider population. Consideration will now be given to the marginalised groups featured within this textbook to highlight the intersectionality and interconnectedness between mental health and other aspects of social diversity.

Socio-economic status and family context

Social inequalities in society are closely linked to mental health inequalities, with disorder rates higher in children living in households with the lowest income (Mental Health Foundation 2018; Glazzard et al. 2019). Various studies have highlighted the stigma faced by children living in poverty (Inglis 2016; Children's Society 2020a), which, in addition to poor health, low educational attainment and social exclusion, puts children at increased risk of developing a mental health issue. The stressors associated with living in poverty, or on a very low income, frequently take their toll on family functioning, impacting on parental health, mental well-being and potentially parenting capacity. A high percentage of children who enter the care system are from disadvantaged backgrounds (Bywaters and Brady 2019); these children often have low levels of social and emotional health.

Traumatic events occurring during childhood are known as adverse childhood experiences (ACEs); these are most common among lowest-income families (Children 1st 2018). The first ACEs study was undertaken in the USA (Felitti et al. 1998). The study found that individuals who face four or more ACEs during childhood are more likely to develop poor health, commit violence and be incarcerated later in life (NHS Health Scotland 2019). Ten ACEs used to predict negative health and social outcomes include: five 'personal factors' (physical abuse, verbal abuse, sexual abuse, physical neglect and emotional neglect) and five 'family-related factors' (domestic abuse in the household, a family member diagnosed with mental illness, a member of the household in prison, parental separation or loss – bereavement, divorce, abandonment – and adults in the household experiencing alcohol or substance misuse). There is increased awareness of the frequency with which domestic and sexual abuse, alcohol and substance misuse and mental health problems coexist, to have a detrimental impact on young children's development, well-being and safety (Hardy 2018).

It is essential that poverty in itself is not regarded as an ACE. ACEs occur within all racial/ethnic groups and across the socio-economic spectrum but more affluent families often have the material resources and social support necessary to counter the negative effects of adversity (Children 1st 2018). Although not all children experiencing ACEs will have a poor outcome, children with four or more ACEs are four times more likely to have low levels of mental well-being (Young Minds 2018).

 **ACTIVITY**

The impact of ACEs (supporting children 7–11 years)

Watch the video clip. Think about the impact that substance/alcohol abuse and domestic violence can have on the lives of young children aged 7–11 years.

www.youtube.com/watch?v=XHgLYI9KZ-A

1   How might a practitioner notice that some of these issues are happening in children's lives?
2   How could children be supported to deal with emotions resulting from witnessing such incidents?

3   Identify some local and national support agencies which could support a child/ family experiencing some of these difficulties.

4   Reflect upon your own childhood. How many ACEs were you exposed to? Although you do not have to disclose your experiences, you could record the number of ACEs you encountered on a piece of paper. This would allow your tutor to count the average number of ACEs faced within the group.

Sexuality

Many children and young people struggling to understand their gender identity, and those who have disclosed their sexuality or are living in same-sex parent or trans families, are at risk of prejudice which may contribute to mental ill-health. A range of challenges can exacerbate mental ill-health among LGBTQIA + children and young people; family conflict and rejection are common, as is bullying and isolation from their peer group (MHFA 2016). Revealing one's sexuality can be particularly difficult for individuals of a religious faith. LGBTQIA + children have been found to be reluctant to seek professional help (Stonewall 2018).

Special educational needs and disability (SEND)

Mental and physical health and impairment are closely interrelated. Physical illness often triggers depression; equally individuals with a mental health condition are at risk of developing physical health problems. Of children diagnosed with a mental health disorder aged 2–19 years old, 71.7% also had a physical health or developmental problem (HSCIC 2018). SEND children often encounter multiple forms of disadvantage and prejudice. These children are more likely to be isolated at school, excluded from mainstream settings and to leave school with poor educational outcomes, which increases the chance of living in poverty and poor mental health (Shaw et al. 2016). It is important to note that high-functioning children, who typically set high expectations for themselves, and who may appear different to their peers, are also vulnerable to mental ill-health arising from prejudice and peer isolation (Potential Plus UK 2020a).

Culture, ethnicity and religion

Racism and language, cultural and religious differences may present children from Black, Asian and minority ethnic (BAME) communities with various challenges. Having a religious faith has been found to act as a protective factor against mental illness, including aiding recovery. Individuals with a religious identity are reported as being less likely to die by suicide, experience depression and misuse substances (MHFA 2016). Many refugee and asylum seeker children will have experienced traumatic events, such as witnessing the death of loved ones, torture and political oppression. These children are at risk of numerous stressors, including prejudice and challenges within the community where they have migrated, which may lead to complex mental health issues (MHFA 2016). Interestingly, rates of mental health disorders are lower among Black British and Asian and/or Asian British children, compared to white British children, who are reported to have significantly higher levels of mental illness (HSCIC 2018). However, these statistics should be reviewed with caution as institutional racism and language and cultural differences, together with a mistrust of health services by some families, may prevent children (or their parents) from seeking help and specialist support (MHFA 2016; UK Parliament 2019). Therefore, there may be children from minority ethnic groups who remain unknown to public health services who are not represented in the statistical data available.

Resilience

Resilience is a complex and dynamic construct, largely dependent on how risk (life stressors) and protective factors interact. Some children will succumb to stress, whereas others remain relatively unscathed. Even siblings living within the same household, subjected to the same adverse situations, may react differently to the stressors encountered. Children and young people have been found to have greater resilience to mental ill-health when faced with an acute, unexpected, short-term risk than those exposed to ongoing stressors (Roffey 2016). However, resilience should not be regarded as a static characteristic, as an individual who reacts adversely to a particular stressor might be able to cope with that same stressor at another stage in their life (Rutter 1987).

Children who are resilient 'bounce back' from adversity but the ability to bounce back is only one aspect of resilience (Glazzard et al. 2019). Resilience should be viewed as a resource that is shaped across developmental pathways. Protective factors, which help individuals to become resilient to life stressors, include secure attachments, self-esteem, social skills, familial compassion and warmth, stable family environment, social support systems and a skill or talent (Burton 2014). Many of these protectors are absent from children with ACEs.

Resilient children tend to have a positive sense of self-worth, are able to acknowledge and communicate how they feel, will seek support and are able to learn from and adapt to negative and stressful experiences (Glazzard et al. 2019). These are all attributes and skills which early years and primary school practitioners can help children to foster. But as resilience can only be nurtured through exposure to risk or stress (Burton 2014), children need safe environments in which they can experience a certain amount of risk.

STIGMA OF MENTAL ILLNESS
History of stigma

In order to understand the stigma associated with mental illness in contemporary society, it is necessary to examine the past. During the late nineteenth century, a clinical approach based on observation and classification emerged to categorise the sick or impaired. This 'medical model of disability' helped to support influential members of the Eugenics Society for managing the 'problem classes', including those with impairments (Boronski and Hassan 2015). Individuals with mental health problems and physical disabilities came to be perceived as a burden and a threat to the well-being of society, and asylums were founded. By the early 1900s, Victorian institutions had become the norm in the UK for segregating the 'impaired' and the 'defective' (Boronski and Hassan 2015).

Psychiatry became a recognised field of medicine, with medics using asylum patients to master their field. Treatments were of their time, in that they were rudimentary and today considered controversial, such as electroconvulsive therapy, lobotomy and aversion therapy (used until the late 1950s to 'treat' homosexuality) (Gould 2008). Asylums were feared by the general public and patients stigmatised. The term 'mental health' was introduced in the early 1900s to reduce the stigma surrounding mental illness and prejudice against individuals in asylums. Medical terms at this time, such as 'lunacy' and 'insanity', were used until they were gradually replaced by 'mental illness' (Science Museum 2020).

The growing involvement of the state in public education led to psychologists and educationalists classifying children into groups based on their perceived educability. In the early twentieth century Mary Dendy, a member of the Eugenics Education Society, argued for the permanent detainment of children classified as 'feeble-minded' in 'colonies', asserting that this would prevent 'weakness' being passed on to future generations. The Mental Deficiency Act 1913 and the Elementary Education Act 1914 enabled this to happen by removing 'defective' children into special schools (Boronski and Hassan 2015). Under the 1913 Act, a 'Board of Control' was established to manage four categories of people: idiots, imbeciles, feeble-minded persons and moral imbeciles. It specified that children and adults identified as 'idiots' or 'imbeciles' should either be placed in a colony or closely supervised in the community (Historic England 2020a). Cyril Burt's (a leading psychologist and advocate of eugenics) method of intelligence testing was adopted to identify 'backward children' and support the segregation process (Boronski and Hassan 2015). The 1913 Act was repealed by the Mental Health Act 1959.

Towards the end of the Second World War, the 1944 Education Act came in to effect, based on the philosophy that all children should benefit from education. Disabled children were to be taught in mainstream schools, with special provisions made to support them. Only 'ineducable' children would remain the responsibility of health professionals (Borsay 2012). Despite the promise of integration the number of pupils in special schools doubled under the Act, a consequence of the medical classification system at the time, which placed children in one of 10 categories ranging from 'physically handicapped' to 'educationally subnormal'.

Criticism of the detention and care of asylum patients led to the Conservative government establishing the Percy Commission in 1954. The report which followed, in 1957, recommended that people with mental illness should be treated in the community and given the same level of care and liberty as that afforded to people with physical disabilities, and that psychiatric hospitals should operate on the lines of 'normal' hospitals (Percy Commission 1957). These principles, enshrined by the 1959 Mental Health Act, were extended by the National Health Service and Community Care Act 1990, which made it a legal requirement for local authorities, where possible, to care for physically and mentally disabled people in the community rather than admitting them to institutions.

Theory of mental health stigma

For over a decade, various bodies and campaigns have been launched to combat the stigma faced by individuals who experience mental health difficulties. Although there is evidence to suggest a positive shift, in that public knowledge about mental health issues has increased and social acceptance of people with mental illness has accelerated (Time to Change 2017), there continues to be much room for improvement. There remains a powerful stigma attached to mental ill-health, and individuals with difficulties face significant prejudice and discrimination in many aspects of their lives.

The stigmatisation of individuals with mental illness is typically a sequential process which involves the negative association of behavioural characteristics that appear to deviate from a 'normalised' state of being. The process starts with stereotyping, leading to status loss and separation of the labelled person, which may generate prejudicial attitudes among those who support the negative stereotypes, and subsequently can result in discriminatory behavioural actions. Mukolo et al. (2010) present three interrelated constructs for understanding the relationship between stigma and child mental health disorders: (1) the dimensions of stigma (negative stereotypes, devaluation, discrimination); (2) the context of stigma, where the stigmatising event is occurring (self, institutional, general public); and (3) the targets or victims of stigma (the child, family members, services).

 **ACTIVITY** ————————————————————————

Reflecting on labels

Watch the video clip 'How to talk to a child about their autism'.
www.bbc.co.uk/news/av/education-51877434/autism-how-to-talk-to-a-child-about-their-autism

Questions

1   Identify arguments for and against the use of labels to describe children who have mental health conditions.
2   Draw upon the concepts presented within this section to identify the type of stigma/prejudice Isaac may encounter.

According to Mukolo et al. (2010), children are less likely than adults to be assumed responsible for their condition and so the disorder rather than the child tends to be stigmatised. However, they assert that as the child progresses to adolescence, the distinction of the 'individual' from the 'condition' becomes blurred and public stigma towards the condition becomes synonymous with the stigma towards the young person. Additionally, parents who have a child with a mental health disorder may be 'stigmatised by association': blamed for something that they did or did not do during a developmental stage of the child.

'Self-stigma theory' explains how individuals with mental health conditions may internalise public stigma by devaluing themselves and modifying their attitudes and behaviour. Although young children can form negative perceptions of mental illness, it is not clear at which stage of the developmental trajectory a child may start to interpret prejudicial environmental cues and self-stigmatise (Mukolo et al. 2010).

Media and stigma

Various studies have indicated the detrimental impact mass media can have in influencing public stigma towards mental illness (Barber 2012; Bowman and West 2018). Historically, media have presented a negative depiction of mental ill-health, individuals with conditions being presented as dangerous, violent, immoral or unpredictable, or as suffering victims who are unable to live normal lives (Bowman and West 2018). Individuals characterised by externalising problems are more likely to be stigmatised. For instance, people with attention deficit hyperactivity disorder, depression and schizophrenia are often portrayed to be violent and likely to engage in antisocial behaviour (Mukolo et al. 2010; Bowman and West 2018). The fear generated, a consequence of harmful stereotypes, may partly explain the reluctance of some parents and practitioners to engage in related discussions with children, thus making it difficult for young people to 'open up' about mental health issues (Danby and Hamilton 2016).

Media have a powerful role to play in de-stigmatising mental illness and influencing constructive public policy (Mukolo et al. 2010). Consequently, there has been increased focus on the positive use of media to combat the prejudice surrounding mental health issues. Celebrities, such as Adele, Miley Cyrus and Stormzy, have begun to utilise the media to share their own struggles with mental ill-health. Younger members of the Royal Family have also been proactive, launching in 2017 'Heads Together', an initiative aimed at tackling stigma and encouraging conversation on mental health issues. Increased visibility of positive representations of people with mental health conditions, including the portrayal of celebrities who young people can relate to, may help to reduce stigma and encourage children and young people to talk about any difficulties they might be experiencing.

 **ACTIVITY**

Media and mental health

Undertake a media search to examine news stories about individuals with mental health conditions. Are the messages mainly positive or mainly negative? Could these messages lead to misconceptions or stereotypical thinking? What impact might stigmatising and prejudicial messages have on children (or their parents) who have mental health issues?

Mental illness stigma, children and families

Stigma and discrimination exacerbate the challenges associated with mental health problems and can trap children and families in a cycle of illness and disadvantage. Stigma experienced by children and young people can lead to poor self-esteem, social withdrawal, school absence, low educational attainment, poverty, risky behaviour and reduced life expectancy and be a barrier to recovery (YMCA 2017; Bowman and West 2018). Negative public attitudes towards mental disorders in children include the avoidance of the child and their family, blaming parents for the child's problems, and a preference for the institutionalisation of the child (Mukolo et al. 2010).

In 2012, Time to Change reported that 9 out of 10 young people had experienced negative treatment from others (often people known to them) because of their mental health difficulties: friends (70%), parents (57%), medical professionals (47%) and teachers (40%). Fear of encountering stigma (or self-stigma) is the main factor preventing young people from speaking out about mental health issues (55%) and seeking help (40%) (YMCA 2017). When young people had disclosed or shown symptoms of mental health difficulties, 67% were accused of 'attention seeking', 51% 'faking it', 50% told to 'snap out of it' or to 'cheer up', and 48% 'it's all in your head' (YMCA 2017). Fear of stigma may also cause some parents to delay or avoid accessing specialist support for their children.

YMCA (2017) claims that stigma is mainly manifested through harmful language and negative stereotypes; 81% of young people have heard derogatory language and stereotypes used about people experiencing mental health difficulties. Social media (60%), followed by school/college (56%) and public areas (47%), are the places where these terms are being used, with the words 'retard' (79%) and 'mental' (71%) used by peers in everyday language (YMCA 2017). This lack of understanding is fuelling harmful stereotypes and consequently having a damaging impact on young people's lives. Although 88% of young people recognised the need to confront stigmatising words and stereotypes, only 48% had taken action to challenge them (YMCA 2017). Education has a critical role to play in de-stigmatising mental illness, by creating environments in which prejudice is addressed and children and young people are not afraid or ashamed to speak out about mental health difficulties.

SUPPORTING MENTAL HEALTH

Mental health has become a central focus of government policy in the UK. In 2017, the English government demonstrated its commitment through *Transforming Children and Young People's Mental Health Provision: A Green Paper* (Department of Health [DoH] and Department for Education [DfE] 2017), followed by *Government Response to the Consultation on Transforming Children and Young People's Mental Health Provision: A Green Paper and Next Steps* (Department of Health and Social Care [DHSC] and DfE 2018) and *Relationships Education, Relationships and Sex Education (RSE) and Health Education* (DfE 2019a). Wales and Scotland have developed their own policies and strategies.

Fundamental to creating a system which supports the mental health of children and young people is a partnership approach that meets needs across universal, targeted and specialist services (DoH 2015). Schools are regarded as the driving force of a universal services-led approach in promoting mental well-being, resilience and the early identification of mental health problems (DoH 2015). An effective universal approach is dependent on a 'whole school approach', which should pervade all aspects of school life (DHSC & DfE 2018) (see Table 4.2 for an overview). Settings

Table 4.2 Key components essential to a whole school approach to mental health

Leadership, management and an inclusive school culture	Senior leaders need to demonstrate clear commitment to school change and implement a well-developed whole school policy for mental health and well-being. To be successful, the policy must reflect the changing needs of the setting and be reviewed regularly, developed in conjunction with other school policies and based upon an agreed definition of mental health, social and emotional well-being (Howard et al. 2020).

School cultural changes must be based on genuine commitment and resourcing by school leaders. An inclusive school ethos is pivotal, where individuals can disclose their difficulties and concerns in a supportive, tolerant, respectful and non-threatening environment. Priority should be placed on developing children's self-esteem and resilience, and providing targeted support, such as quiet areas and nurture groups, where children who are struggling can talk through their emotions with skilled practitioners without feeling stigmatised. |
| *Curriculum* | The curriculum has the potential to empower young people with the knowledge and skills required to deal with stressful situations, and to facilitate positive change without eroding their mental well-being. In 2020, 'RSE and Health Education' (DfE 2019a) became a compulsory part of the curriculum in England, which includes mental health and mental ill-health. Going beyond the 'wellness model' that schools have traditionally adopted, by introducing children to the concept of mental ill-health, will help to counter the stigma associated with mental illness. It is important that children understand the concept of mental health and mental illness as being a continuum which individuals typically move along throughout life and where they may sometimes require additional support (Prever 2006). Furthermore, Ecclestone (2014, 2015) asserts that in order to foster resilience, the discourse of children as 'psychologically and emotionally vulnerable' needs to be challenged, as the language of vulnerability and protection leads to a self-fulfilling prophecy of need and dependency. This will require early years practitioners and teachers to strike an appropriate balance between safeguarding children and young people and the provision of experiences that involve 'measured risk'; it is the latter that will help to foster the resilience required to ensure positive psychological well-being.

The development of social and emotional skills (emotional intelligence, resilience, problem solving, conflict management, tackling stigma) can be built through the wider curriculum and not just through 'RSE and Health Education' and 'Spiritual, Moral, Social and Cultural Development' (DfE 2014b). Emotional literacy (which is where these skills are essentially situated) is a regular feature in early years settings, addressed through the use of persona dolls, puppets, circle time, role play, worry boxes and 'life issues' books. These methods allow children to discuss their feelings and develop strategies to deal with difficult topics through fictional scenarios. Certain topics will need to be addressed sensitively and skilfully, as there may be children in the setting who are experiencing similar personal challenges. |

Continuing professional development	Studies suggest that teachers have previously lacked the knowledge and skills required to support children, particularly those with complex needs who are waiting for specialist support (Danby and Hamilton 2016; YMCA 2017). Ongoing mental health-related training is essential for child practitioners. In recognition of this, since 2017, the government has offered mental health first-aid training for all secondary school teachers, with the intention to roll this out to primary school teachers by 2022 (Howard et al. 2020).

It is important that practitioners reflect upon their own attitudes and behaviours, as well as the policies and procedures within their work setting. This will help to identify any personal bias and institutional prejudice that may impact on supporting and promoting children's mental well-being. |
| Voice of children | Mental health rests on an individual's ability to have a sense of control and self-efficacy. It is therefore vital that children feel empowered. This can be achieved by keeping children informed of matters which affect them and by providing children with opportunities to voice their needs, concerns and ideas. It is important to recognise that those most marginalised within settings are individuals more likely to struggle to be heard and need to be listened to (Howard et al. 2020). |
| Effective partnerships | Government policy reflects the need for schools and early years settings to work in partnership with parents/carers and specialist agencies to support children's development and well-being. A multidisciplinary model is encouraged, where specialist agencies assist schools with the delivery of interventions and children who exhibit mental health needs (DHSC and DfE 2018). |

most likely to be effective in supporting children's mental well-being are those which have: the genuine support of senior leaders, effective and closely monitored policies, an ethos of open dialogue and respectful relationships, ongoing opportunities for staff development, readily available specialist support for children and teachers, a safe environment to share mental health, and social and emotional difficulties without the fear of prejudice and stigma.

Certain barriers may render government policy and a whole school approach to mental health idealistic, as the level of effectiveness will be determined by sufficient funding to support training and safeguard practitioners' workload and their own mental well-being (Danby and Hamilton 2016; O'Reilly et al. 2018). It also relies on an assumption that all practitioners will endorse the responsibility; some individuals may feel there is a limit to their professional role and expertise in the amount of support they can or should provide to the mental health of children and families (Ekornes et al. 2012).

 REFLECTION

Promoting mental wellbeing and reducing stigma in practice

Now that you have reached the end of this chapter, consider the following:

1   How can early years practitioners and teachers promote understanding of mental health and mental illness among children and reduce the associated stigma?
2   Can you think of any factors that might help a child to be resilient when faced with adversity? How can early years practitioners help to foster resilience in young children so that they are better equipped to deal with difficult life events?

KEY POINTS

- Although there has been a positive shift in public attitudes towards mental illness, the stigma associated to it has been difficult to shake, largely a consequence of nineteenth-century discourse and practice of classification and segregation.
- 50% of all mental health problems are established by the time a person is age 14.
- Stigma may prevent young people from talking about their difficulties and seeking support, trapping children and families in a cycle of illness and disadvantage.
- Stressors which make people vulnerable to poor mental health are wide ranging; however individuals in marginalised groups are at higher risk of mental ill-health due to social bias.

- Since 2017, the government (in England) has demonstrated commitment towards mental health through a series of policies and initiatives, including the compulsory requirement of the teaching of 'RSE and Health Education' (DfE 2019a), in which mental health is a prominent feature.
- Schools are regarded as the driving force of a universal services-led approach in promoting mental well-being and the early identification of mental health problems. However, if children are to build resilience, they need experiences which involve 'measured' risk.

FURTHER READING

Glazzard, J., Potter, M. and Stones, S. (2019) *Meeting the Mental Health Needs of Young Children 0–5 Years*. St Albans: Critical Publishing.
Examines risk factors which can result in mental health needs in very young children and provides guidance regarding policy, transitions and working with parents/carers.

Health and Social Care Information Centre (2018) *Mental Health of Children and Young People in England: A Summary*. Available at: https://files.digital.nhs.uk
Provides a useful overview of the prevalence and trends of mental health conditions affecting children and young people aged 2–19 years.

Howard, C., Burton, M. and Levermore, D. (2020) *Children's Mental Health and Emotional Wellbeing in Primary Schools: A Whole School Approach*. London: Sage.
Comprehensive coverage regarding the mental health of primary school children and how settings can support children's social, emotional and mental well-being.

USEFUL WEBSITES

Mental Health Foundation: www.mentalhealth.org.uk
Mind: www.mind.org.uk
Time to Change: www.time-to-change.org.uk
Young Minds: https://youngminds.org.uk

5

CHILDREN WITH SPECIAL EDUCATIONAL NEEDS AND DISABILITIES

CONTENTS

CHAPTER OVERVIEW

The key focus of this chapter is to explore how children with special educational needs and disabilities (SEND) have been historically stigmatised and marginalised within education settings and wider society. It examines concepts and theoretical models of disability and impairment, which help to explain reasons for prejudicial and reductionist thinking. Critical consideration of intersectionality is given – the way in which disability frequently overlaps with other aspects of identity. Legislation and policy relating to the education of children with SEND are also included.

This chapter considers:

1   Definitions, statistics and areas of special educational needs (SEN) and disability.
2   Models of disability: historical and cultural perspectives and influences.
3   Social and educational outcomes and support strategies for children with special educational needs, including intersectionality.
4   Stigma, prejudice, bullying and the impact of the media.
5   Educational policy and complexities regarding the education of children with special educational needs (SEN) and disability.

The term SEND will be used throughout this chapter to represent all children and young people who have special educational needs and/or disabilities, other than where primary source documents have undertaken research or produced statistics relating to specific sub-groups of this community (i.e. special educational needs [SEN]).

DEFINITIONS AND STATISTICS

Fifteen per cent of the world's population are believed to experience some form of disability (World Bank 2020); it is one of the few minority groups that anyone can unexpectedly join at any time. Disability prevalence is higher for developing countries, as individuals in these countries are more likely to be affected by disability caused by communicable, maternal and perinatal diseases, and conflict and war (UK AID 2010). In 2017, 13.3 million of the population in the UK were identified as having a disability (1 in 5 people) (Disabled Living Foundation [DLF] 2017). Of these individuals, 17% were born with their disabilities, meaning that most people acquire their disability later in life (DLF 2017). It is estimated that 1 in 20 children under the age of 16 have a disability in the UK, and of these children, 99.1% are supported by their families at home (Contact 2020).

The concept of disability is a complex and multidimensional phenomenon, and its interpretation varies in different countries (Devarakonda 2013). According to the World Health Organization (WHO) (2020), 'disability' is a term which covers impairments (a problem in body function or structure), activity limitations (a difficulty encountered by an individual in undertaking a task or action) and participation restrictions (a problem experienced by an individual in involvement in life situations). The WHO (2020) explains that disability reflects the interaction between the features of a person's body and the features of the society in which they live, and that overcoming the difficulties that individuals with disabilities face is reliant on the removal of social and environmental barriers.

In the UK, under the Equality Act 2010, an individual is considered to have a disability if they have a 'physical or mental impairment and the impairment has a substantial and long-term adverse effect on his or her ability to carry out normal day-to-day activities' (HM Government 2011, p.7). 'Substantial' means it is likely to take longer than it usually would to complete a daily task, whereas 'long-term' is clarified as meaning that the disabling condition affects the person for 12 months or more. Some conditions which deem a person to be disabled are present from birth (autistic spectrum conditions, foetal alcohol syndrome); others can occur at certain stages in life and a person may recover (cancer, asthma), while some may be progressive, slowly having a disabling effect (motor neurone disease).

With regard to education, the term 'special educational needs and disability' (SEND) is used in England to describe a range of disabilities, disorders and learning difficulties that children and young people may have (See Table 5.1 for the broad areas of need). In Scotland, 'additional support needs' (ASN) is used, while in Wales 'additional learning needs' (ALN) has been adopted. The *SEND Code of Practice: 0 to 25 Years* for England makes an important distinction between disability and Special Educational Needs (SEN), recognising that children with disabilities may not have a SEN; but it acknowledges the significant overlap between disabled children and young people and those with SEN (Department for Education [DfE] and Department of Health [DoH] 2015). It offers the following definition (p. 86):

Table 5.1 Broad areas of need (DfE and DoH 2015)

Communication and interaction	Children with speech, language and communication needs, including those with autistic spectrum disorder, Asperger's syndrome and autism, have difficulty in communicating with others.
Cognition and learning	This includes moderate and severe learning difficulties (where children may require support in all areas of the curriculum) and problems with mobility and communication, through to profound and multiple learning difficulties, as well as a physical or sensory impairment. It also includes specific learning difficulties such as dyslexia, dyscalculia and dyspraxia.
Social, emotional and mental health	These difficulties manifest themselves in many ways, including disruptive behaviour or the child becoming withdrawn or isolated. These behaviours may reflect underlying mental health issues such as anxiety, depression, self-harming or eating disorders. Other children may have conditions such as attention deficit hyperactivity disorder or attachment disorder.
Sensory and/or physical	Children with a physical disability, vision or hearing impairment or a multi-sensory impairment (combination of vision and hearing difficulties) are likely to require ongoing specialist support and/or equipment. These difficulties can be age related.

A child or young person has a learning difficulty or disability (which calls for special educational provision to be made for him or her) if he or she has a significantly greater difficulty in learning than the majority of others of the same age, or has a disability which prevents or hinders him or her from making use of facilities … provided for others of the same age in mainstream schools. (DfE and DoH 2015: 16)

As 97% of children in the UK attend state-funded early years education or care provision between the ages of three and four (Frederickson and Cline 2015), many difficulties can be identified early on in a child's life. Some conditions, such as physical impairments, may be relatively straightforward to identify, unlike some forms of SEN which can be less obvious and their diagnosis problematic and contested (Joseph Rowntree Foundation [JRF] 2016). Early identification is complex, particularly when children are young, so it is inevitable that mistakes will be made. Children may be identified as having serious difficulties when this is not the case ('false positives'); or they may not be identified as having difficulties when they do ('false negatives') (Frederickson and Cline 2015). Early years practitioners are not expected to be experts in special needs, but they should have a good understanding of child development and an awareness of the common types of SEN that they may encounter when working with young children (Rodgers and Wilmot 2011).

 **ACTIVITY**

Supporting children with different types of SEND

For each category of SEND select one condition/difficulty and identify: (1) some of the signs which the child may present; (2) some of the difficulties the child could encounter in schools and early years settings and ways they could be supported; (3) sources of further information and support agencies.

According to the DfE (2019b), the number of children in England with SEN across all school types has increased for a third consecutive year to 1,318,300 in 2019, representing 14.9% of the pupil population. Of the total pupil population, 11.9% are on SEN support (with no Education, Health and Care [EHC] plan) and 3.1% have an EHC plan. The most common primary type of need across pupils aged 4–17 on SEN support is speech, language and communications needs, and for those on an EHC plan, autistic spectrum disorder is the primary need. Of 4-year-olds on SEN support 59% have a primary type of need of speech, language and communication.

Moderate learning difficulty and social, emotional and mental well-being are the more prevalent needs in older pupils (DfE 2019b).

MODELS OF DISABILITY

Models of disability provide an understanding of the needs of individuals with disabilities, guide policy development and help to explain the prejudice encountered by people with disabilities. Historically and across cultures, various beliefs have shaped perceptions and attitudes towards people with disabilities. This section considers six of the most dominant models.

Traditional or religious

This is the oldest model of disability and underpinning it is the belief in religion or the supernatural. Within this model, disability may be regarded as a punishment from God for a sin that has been committed, a test of faith or an opportunity presented by God for character development (Retief and Letšosa 2018). People with disabilities may be perceived to have supernatural qualities; or to be possessed by demons, bring bad luck or be linked to witchcraft; or their impairment is believed to be contagious (Bond 2017; Rieser 2018). During the 'Great Witch Hunts' (1480–1680), it is estimated that over 60,000 people, mainly women, were put to death as 'witches' across German speaking regions of Europe, as a result of their impairment or giving birth to disabled children (BBC News 2009; Rieser 2018). Although this model is not as prevalent as it once was, there are certain cultures which still hold a mysticism perspective to explain illness or disability. In societies which adhere to this model, individuals with disabilities can be severely marginalised. Children born with disabilities may lead to an entire family (often especially the mother and child) being ostracised by the community, with assumptions that this is punishment for a family member having sinned (Anderson 2013). The stigma of having a child with disabilities means that mothers can be put under pressure to abandon or kill infants born with impairments (Bond 2017).

Medical

From the mid-1800s, due to advances in scientific understanding, the medical model of disability began to replace the traditional or religious model. Under this model, disability is regarded as a tragedy, something to be prevented and if possible cured. The focus is on the limitations associated with the individual's impairment, and wider aspects of their life and conditions which might contribute to their disability are disregarded (Retief and Letšosa 2018). Due to the growth in industrialisation, people (including children) with physical and mental impairments were increasingly regarded as a social and educational problem and incarcerated in workhouses, asylums, colonies and special schools where many became institutionalised (Rieser 2018). Features common to life in these institutions included abuse and neglect, social stigma, depersonalisation and loss of liberty and autonomy (Boronski and Hassan 2015). However, they may have offered refuge for individuals who had nowhere else to go. In 1981 the 'Care in the Community' Green Paper, which promoted a programme for people with learning disabilities and mental health needs, marked the end of the asylum. Over the following two decades, tens of thousands of people returned to the community from hospitals and institutions. A new era of supporting people with disabilities in mainstream communities began (Historic England 2020b).

In the last part of the nineteenth century there was a growth in 'eugenics' ideology, at a time when industrialised countries were competing to create empires, and it was used to argue that people with impairments weakened the nation (Rieser 2018). This philosophy contributed to controversial measures such as the involuntary sterilisation and euthanasia of people with disabilities (Boronski and Hassan 2015; Retief and Letšosa 2018). Laws sanctioning the sterilisation of women with physical and mental impairments remained in place in some countries until the 1990s (Rieser 2018); Rieser asserts that genetic research, such as the former Human Genome Project, is controversial as it could lead to the eradication of many forms of impairment. It also causes significant debate about the religious and moral ethics of 'designer babies', how to measure the quality of someone's life, and that there is agreement about the boundaries between normal variation and disability.

Today, the medical model of disability remains strongly criticised. Under this model, power is assigned to professionals who diagnose children against developmental stages. Failure to meet physical and cognitive milestones by a certain age may result in the child being seen as 'deficient' and in need of fixing; the impairment is the focus rather than the holistic needs of the child. Discourses of 'diagnosis', 'cures' and 'normalisation' lead to a cycle of labelling, low expectations and dependency which is difficult to break and which empowers professionals to make decisions about where children with disabilities go to school, where they live, what support interventions are put into place and what benefits they are entitled to.

Social

The social model asserts that disability is a situation caused by the way the able-bodied community has organised society, rather than by a person's impairment or difference. The model, which emerged as a result of the disability movement in the 1960s and 1970s, is concerned with addressing societal change through the elimination of social, environmental and economic factors, institutional practices and government policy that impose restrictions and barriers to participation (Wearmouth 2017). An important distinction is drawn between impairment and disability. 'Impairment' is defined as the loss or limitation of physical, mental or sensory function on a long-term or permanent basis, whereas 'disability' is defined as the loss or limitation of opportunities in participation in mainstream activities (Retief and Letšosa 2018). Within the social model of 'disability' the child is included and their diversity welcomed, relationships are nurtured, barriers are removed and the child's strengths and needs are identified by the child in consultation with others (Anti-Bullying Alliance 2014), with an emphasis on empowering the child to take more control over their own life (Knowles 2018a).

Human rights

This model offers a theoretical framework for policy development that emphasises the civil, political, economic, social and cultural rights of people with disabilities (Retief and Letšosa 2018). It acknowledges that some people with disabilities are confronted by challenging situations, and offers proposals for improving the life of individuals with disabilities (Retief and Letšosa 2018), including an emphasis on the right to take control of one's life through personal assistance rather than care.

Charity

Under this model people with disabilities tend to be viewed as victims of their impairment. In attempts to fund-raise, the media and campaigns often portray people with disabilities suffering in tragic circumstances. Although the charity model may seek to benefit people with disabilities, it can contribute to harmful misconceptions by depicting individuals as helpless, depressed and dependent on others for care and protection (Retief and Letšosa 2018).

Identity

The identity model acknowledges that disability is socially constructed but claims disability as a positive characteristic. Under this model, disability is a marker of collective identity and membership in a recognisable minority group. The identity model has inspired many individuals in the disability community to adopt a positive self-image that celebrates 'disability pride' and fights for societal change through equal opportunities and civil rights (Retief and Letšosa 2018).

SOCIAL AND EDUCATIONAL OUTCOMES

Children with SEND are more likely to experience poorer health and education outcomes, and lower levels of employment in adulthood. Having a child with disabilities can have a significant impact on family life. Parents and carers often encounter a challenging combination of emotional, social, physical and financial pressures that may impact on family life and well-being (Anti-Bullying Alliance 2011). Stress, depression and lack of sleep are issues commonly experienced among parents; and 53% of parents say that caring for a child with disabilities has caused major difficulties or the breakdown of their relationship (9%) (Contact 2020). Fifty-six per cent of parents report there to be a lack of appropriate childcare to accommodate their children and only 1 in 13 children with disabilities receives a regular support service from their local authority (Contact 2020). Furthermore, as the annual cost of raising a child with disabilities is estimated to be three times greater than that of bringing up a child who does not have disabilities (Disabled Living Foundation [DLF] 2017), 52% of families with a child with disabilities are thought to be at risk of poverty (Contact 2020).

Most children with SEN in the UK go to mainstream schools, with fewer than 10% attending special schools (Mencap 2020). In 2018, 228,315 children in mainstream education in England had a primary SEN associated with a learning disability (Public Health England 2019). However, the proportion of children with a learning disability who have Education, Health and Care (EHC) plans/statements of SEN being educated in mainstream schools has decreased over the last decade from 36% to 26% (Public Health England 2019). Pinney (2017) claims that rather than this being a drift away from inclusion, it reflects rising numbers of children with extremely complex needs in the education system in general.

Children with SEND tend to have low attendance at school and a high exclusion rate from school, and are less likely to leave with qualifications that will give them access to well-paid and secure employment opportunities (JRF 2016; Contact 2020). In 2019, 43% of pupils with SEN met the phonics standard in Year 1 compared to 88% of pupils with no recorded SEN (DfE 2019c), and 22% of pupils with SEN reached the expected standard at the end of Key Stage 2 in reading, writing and maths, compared with 74% of pupils with no identified SEN (DfE 2019d). It is crucial to close the attainment gap, as many children with SEND end up in poverty in adulthood (JRF 2020); a disproportionate number of children in youth custody have speech, communication and language difficulties (The Communication Trust 2014); and prison populations have a high prevalence of people with learning difficulties (JRF 2016).

Intersectionality

SEND provision reflects a wide range of learners and there are many overlaps with other dimensions of diversity. In Chapter 4 (p. 71), the interconnectedness between mental health and physical health was explored and how impairment to one dimension can have a detrimental impact on the other. Of children diagnosed with a mental health disorder aged 2–19 years old, 71.7% also had a physical health or developmental problem (Health and Social Care Information Centre [HSCIC] 2018). There is a strong link between poverty and SEND and also evidence that ethnicity and gender play a part in increasing the likelihood of children being identified as having SEND (Frederickson and Cline 2015; JRF 2016). Important questions to be asked in relation to the prevalence and diagnosis of SEND include: (1) To what extent is intersectionality considered? (2) What part do arrangements for identification and assessment play? (3) Do differences in SEND categories reflect broader structural inequities in society (Frederickson and Cline 2015)?

Boys tend to outnumber girls by a large margin for SEN support (Frederickson and Cline 2015). Figures published by the DfE (2019b) show boys were almost twice as likely to be on SEN support than girls, and 4.4% of boys compared to 1.7% of girls had an EHC plan. Speech, language and communication needs was the most prevalent primary type of need among boys with SEN support (25%), compared with 20% of girls (DfE 2019b). Behavioural issues are also more common among boys (HSCIC 2018). The most prevalent primary type of need among girls with SEN support was moderate learning difficulty (26%), compared with 21% of boys (DfE 2019b). Statistics also show emotional disorders (depression and anxiety) to be higher in girls (10.0%) than in boys (HSCIC 2018).

Since the 1970s there have been disproportionate numbers of children from some minority ethnic groups in certain categories of SEND (Frederickson and Cline 2015). Black Caribbean boys continue to be more likely to be identified as having behavioural, emotional and social difficulties (JRF 2016), and to be excluded from school (Frederickson and Cline 2015). There is an increased risk of Bangladeshi and Pakistani pupils being categorised with learning difficulties, visual impairment, hearing impairment and multi-sensory impairment, as well as profound and multiple learning difficulties (Frederickson and Cline 2015). Children from Gypsy, Roma and Traveller (Irish heritage) communities continue to be more likely than any other group to be identified as having SEN and to live in poverty, experience poorer education outcomes, drop out of school early and encounter negative teacher attitudes, racism and bullying (JRF 2016). In contrast, pupils from all

Asian groups (in particular Chinese ethnic groups) are underrepresented in SEND categories such as moderate learning difficulties, specific learning difficulties and autistic spectrum disorder (JRF 2016). Of pupils with EHC plans, Travellers of Irish heritage (4.5%) and Black Caribbean (4.4%) pupils had the highest percentages and Indian pupils the lowest percentage (1.9%), compared with 3.1% of all pupils (DfE 2019b). Pupils whose first language is English are more likely to have SEN (15%) than those whose first language is other than English (12%) (DfE 2019b). Over-representation of pupils in SEN categories might result from differential attitudes among practitioners held about certain groups of children. More subjective forms of SEN categories (emotional and behavioural difficulties) can involve unconscious bias and be due to a lack of understanding regarding cultural, ethnic and linguistic diversity. Additionally, when pupils are learning English as an additional language, it can be difficult to determine whether any academic problems children encounter are caused solely by language differences or by underlying specific learning difficulties (Hamilton 2013b).

There is considerable overlap between children who have SEND and those who are living in poverty – a situation that is common to all four nations of the UK (JRF 2016; Mencap 2020). Children with SEND from low-income families face multiple disadvantages and increased vulnerability in early childhood that have negative impact on well-being, education and social outcomes (JRF 2016). These children are often less likely to receive effective interventions that can help to address their SEND, partly because their parents are less successful in seeking support (JRF 2016). Factors associated with poverty, such as smoking and consuming alcohol during pregnancy, low birth weight, low levels of parental education, parental stress and family breakdown, contribute to the likelihood of a child being born with an inherited SEND and developing SEND in childhood, and make it difficult for children to move out of SEND categories while at school (JRF 2016). Further-more, the hereditary nature of some disabilities and learning difficulties (such as dyslexia and autism) which has caused parental poverty is also likely to lead to the same future for children with disabilities from these families (JRF 2016). Children with SEND from low-income families have poorer educational outcomes across all stages. More than half of children with behavioural difficulties or physical difficulties were living in poverty at the age of nine months (JRF 2016). Pupils eligible for free school meals are more likely to have SEN support (28%) and have an EHC plan (33%) compared to their more affluent peers (13% SEN support and 27% EHC plan) (DfE 2019b). Children from poorer backgrounds are overrepresented in being assessed with both moderate learning difficulties and social, emotional and mental health problems as their primary type of need (Frederickson and Cline 2015; DfE 2019b).

CASE STUDY

Disability and intersectionality (Ayra and Harry, age 4)

Ayra and Harry are pupils at Mountain Primary School. Both children are struggling with 'communication and interaction' (language development, inability to communicate in simple sentences and follow instructions). Ayra's parents, who are police officers, are in contact with an external speech and language team and are engaging daily in activities to stimulate her language development. The family are well supported by Ayra's grandparents. However, Harry's parents are both juggling part-time jobs and have no extended family to offer support as they were both children in care. They are a happy family but not having had a positive school or parenting experience themselves, they are struggling to support Harry's early development, and money for toys and learning resources is limited.

1   How could the early years teacher support these children?
2   Can you think of other services that might be supporting Ayra and Harry?
3   What factors might exist to widen the gap between Ayra and Harry as they progress through school?
4   What additional advice/support could the early years teacher give to Harry's parents to help promote his development?

STIGMA, PREJUDICE AND BULLYING

There has been a long history of prejudice, oppression and marginalisation experienced by people with disabilities. For readers interested in learning more about the history of disablement, Richard Rieser (2018) (listed under Further Reading) provides a comprehensive overview of the injustice and atrocities encountered by the disabled community. In many countries people with disabilities are stigmatised and remain a target for stereotyping (Bond 2017; Kallman 2017). The media have reported a 150% rise, over a two-year period, in hate crime against disabled children in the UK (BBC News 2017; *The Independent* 2017). Detrimental attitudes and practices can lead to serious personal, social and economic consequences. Some of the families represented in the media discuss how they feel unable to take their children out into public spaces or to post images onto social media for fear of being verbally abused or targeted online (BBC News 2017; *The Independent* 2017). Many people with disabilities live in poverty and on the margins of society, excluded from education and employment opportunities and health and public services, which increases vulnerability to physical and psychological abuse, neglect and exploitation (Bond 2017).

Media and disability

Many of the prejudicial attitudes that exist today regarding people with disabilities have their roots in historical influences. Implicit social biases as to what is considered 'normal' are persistently reinforced by mass media. One of the most powerful examples to illustrate the damage that can be caused by mass media is the way in which Germany, under Hitler's Third Reich, used film as propaganda to justify the concept of compulsory sterilisation and 'mercy killing'. Silent black and white film was used to dehumanise and criminalise people with mental and physical impairments, portraying them as a burden to the state, with captions included to show the cost of keeping them alive. In 2003, the German government acknowledged that 240,000 people with disabilities (including children) were murdered between 1939 and 1940 (Rieser 2018).

Stereotypes used by the media to represent people with disabilities may include individuals being portrayed as: pitiable or pathetic, an object of curiosity or violence, sinister or evil, the 'super cripple', as creating a negative atmosphere, laughable, their own worst enemy, a burden, non-sexual and being unable to participate in daily life (Hunt 1991 cited in Wood 2012). Nearly three decades later and both older and newer digital forms of media are still portraying people with disabilities as 'intimidating, lazy, incapable, isolated and emotionally unstable' (Kallman 2017: 644). In today's digital entertainment culture which reinforces the tendency to judge people by their appearance, disabled children are often stigmatised because their bodies do not function or look in line with 'social norms'. It is important that the media present disabled characters and individuals with disabilities as 'real people' in a positive and non-stereotypical way, while also providing a realistic account of issues they may encounter (Rieser 2018).

 **ACTIVITY**

Media and disability

Undertake a media search to examine how individuals with special educational needs (SEN) and disabilities are portrayed in children's television, films and books.

Are the messages mainly positive or mainly negative? Could these messages lead to misconceptions or stereotypical thinking? What impact might prejudicial messages have on children who have disabilities?

School bullying

At age seven a child with SEND is two to three times more likely to be bullied than a child with no SEND (Chatzitheochari et al. 2016). Children with SEND who are eligible for free school meals face 'double disadvantage', composed of both limiting contexts and greater risk of frequent bullying due to their perceived impairment and socio-economic status (Anti-Bullying Alliance 2017). The most common form of bullying that children with disabilities experience is verbal (including cyberbullying) (Anti-Bullying Alliance 2011). Other forms of abuse encountered include physical, emotional and manipulative bullying, sexual abuse, conditional friendship, exclusion from friendship groups and damage to personal property.

Bullying is often used to attain social status in the school network hierarchy, with vulnerable populations such as children with disabilities making 'easy targets' (Chatzitheochari et al. 2016). Furthermore, the SEN label typically used in mainstream schools has been found to draw attention to 'normality' and 'differences', creating boundaries between children with and without disabilities (Chatzitheochari et al. 2016). Children with SEND are less likely to report themselves as happy than children without SEND (JRF 2016). This may be due to the fact that they tend to have fewer friends (59%) compared with 92% of children without SEND, and participate less in social and recreational activities (JRF 2016; Mencap 2020).

The derogatory language often used in the UK to describe physical and mental differences (such as 'invalid', 'cripple', 'spastic', 'handicapped' and 'retarded') draws on many outdated notions of impairment derived from the medical model (Retief and Letšosa 2018). The original meaning is often no longer understood, but the negative messages conveyed can be detrimental to the self-esteem of those targeted and can serve to 'other' and isolate children with SEND (Anti-Bullying Alliance 2014). Studies suggest that the disability bullying encountered in childhood can have a lasting impact across psycho-social dimensions in adulthood (Chatzitheochari et al. 2016).

'Special educational needs' (SEN), a label initially introduced to move away from negative categorisation in the past, now raises many issues. Teacher expectations can differ in relation to labels allocated to children (Richards 2016). Children with disabilities may internalise the labels and negative views assigned to them to adopt lower expectations for themselves by focusing on their deficits rather than their abilities (Kallman 2017). These children may develop feelings of low self-esteem, worthlessness and underachievement, which reinforce non-disabled people's views of their capabilities (Anti-Bullying Alliance 2014; Bond 2017).

 **ACTIVITY**

Bullying of children with disabilities

Watch the video clip and consider the following questions.

https://youtu.be/38mZLDWMNe4

1   What are the different ways in which children with special educational needs (SEN) and disabilities might be bullied or discriminated against?
2   What is the possible impact of such bullying?
3   How can early years practitioners and primary school teachers promote understanding of special educational needs (SEN) and disabilities among children to reduce stigma?

It is important to find ways to communicate with and empower children who are being bullied because of their disabilities. Contact (2019) advises that parents and practitioners find creative ways to encourage children to open up about their experiences. For example, by asking them questions about the games they played and who they interacted with, and to help children build resiliency and skills to deal with conflict and bullying through the use of toys, persona dolls, puppets, drawings, social literacy stories, a worry box, scales to rate how the child is feeling (traffic light system, facial expressions), communication boards (visual symbols organised by topic), cue cards (messages presented in pictorial or written format) and maps of the setting which children can colour to indicate how safe they feel in different areas. Equally, it is crucial to promote understanding and positive attitudes among staff and other children of physical and mental differences.

EDUCATION POLICY AND COMPLEXITIES

The education of children with SEND has revolved around three broad concepts: segregation, integration and inclusion. Traditionally medical ideas have played a significant part in the identification and placement of children within the school system, and special schools have their origins in the charitable institutions founded for children with learning disabilities and visual and hearing impairments, from the 1760s (see Table 5.2 for a historical overview).

Table 5.2 Special education timeline, England 1870–2010

1870 Elementary Education Act	Universal primary education introduced. Attendance between ages of five and ten made compulsory in 1880. Children with significant learning difficulties were deemed 'ineducable' and those with milder learning difficulty went to 'educationally sub-normal schools'.
1944 Education Act	Introduced medical system of classification. Children assessed against one of 11 categories of 'handicap' (severely subnormal, educationally subnormal, blind, partially sighted, deaf/partially deaf, epileptic, maladjusted, physically handicapped, speech defect, delicate, diabetic) to identify if they required special treatment.
1978 Warnock Report	Baroness Mary Warnock advocated greater inclusion of pupils with impairments in mainstream schools. Identified two groups of children with impairments: those who experienced difficulty but who could have their needs met within mainstream schools and those with more complex learning difficulties who required specialised provision.
1981 Education Act	Enacted many recommendations of the Warnock Report, including statementing. Defined special educational needs (SEN) and outlined the responsibilities of mainstream schools in assessing and supporting children, and rights of parents to appeal against decisions. More children with SEN were integrated into mainstream education but children were expected to adapt to meet the requirements of their school.
1988 Education Reform Act	Introduction of a national curriculum which all children, whether in mainstream or special education, should follow. Aim is a balanced and broadly based curriculum relevant to children's individual needs.
1993 Education Act	Introduced a Code of Practice on the Identification and Assessment of Special Educational Needs. Schools and parents given more involvement in the statementing process.
1994 Salamanca Statement (UNESCO)	Framework for Action – a commitment to providing mainstream education for all children. Advocated schools assist children with SEND to become economically active and to provide these children with the skills needed in everyday life.
2001 Special Educational Needs and Disability Act (SEN Code of Practice)	Outlawed discrimination against SEND students in schools, colleges and higher education. Settings must adapt to meet the needs of individual children. Parents can go to tribunals to ensure this right.
2004 Strategy: 'Removing Barriers to Achievement'	Focused on raising expectations for SEN pupils in mainstream schools; aimed to reduce the number of children attending special schools and reliance on statements.
2005 Warnock: 'Special Educational Needs: A New Look'	Baroness Warnock backtracked on her 1978 report, condemning the closure of special schools, statementing and forcing some children into mainstream education. Emphasised the impact of poverty on SEND.
2010 Equality Act	Children with SEND have the right to have (1) discrimination eliminated, equality of opportunity promoted and good relations fostered and (2) reasonable adjustments made so they are not at a disadvantage.

(tes 2005; Boronski and Hassan 2015; Wearmouth 2017)

Note: This is not a complete list and the language used is reflective of the time era.

Current policy

Children and Families Act 2014 / SEND Code of Practice 2015 (England) (DfE and DoH 2015)

Section 19 (Part 3) sets out the general principles that local authorities must have regard to when supporting children and young people with SEND (from birth to 25 years).

- The Code of Practice provides guidance for schools and local authorities on how to meet the duties placed on them.
- A local authority must help families find an appropriate early years option for their child, which may include a specialised nursery for children with complex needs.
- Specialist settings are normally only available to learners who have an EHC plan.
- A single category of 'SEN Support' has replaced School Action/School Action Plus.
- Provision for SEND is based on an integrated approach. Children referred to a local authority for assessment are considered under the EHC plan assessment process. An EHC plan, drawn up by the local authority in consultation with partner agencies, details the support that is to be provided to a child identified as having SEND.
- Children and parents have been given more power to direct government funding towards provision that best meets their needs.

SEND and the Early Years Foundation Stage framework (EYFS) (England) (Contact 2020)

All early years providers must follow the EYFS framework for children aged 0–5 years. This includes having arrangements to identify and support children who have SEND. Settings cannot refuse to take a child because they have SEND. Early years settings will use the EYFS framework to observe and review how a child is learning, and parents' insights are an integral part of this. The framework includes two formal reviews: (1) one at age two, looking at language and communication and physical, personal, social and emotional development; (2) one at age five, looking at literacy, mathematics, understanding the world and expressive arts and design.

Early years settings that receive government funding must have a Special Educational Needs Coordinator (SENCO). This is a teacher who is responsible for making sure children with SEND have the support they require. Children should also have a named key worker who is responsible for them on a daily basis. If it is decided necessary to provide 'SEN support', detailed records must be kept in consultation with the child and their family.

The approach to support children with SEND includes a graduated approach:

- *Assess*: The setting, SENCO and parents should work together to explore the cause of any learning delay or difficulty.
- *Plan*: Practitioners should talk to parents about any additional support the child requires and signpost them to other sources of information. The support recommended should be written in the form of a plan.
- *Support*: The child may need additional specialist support.
- *Review*: The setting should agree with the family when the child's progress will be reviewed and whether the child requires additional or a different type of support.

Additional Learning Needs and Education Tribunal (Wales) Act 2018 (Welsh Government 2019)

The new statutory support system for children and young people, aged 0–25, with additional learning needs (ALN) will come into force in September 2020.

- The terms 'special educational needs' and 'learning difficulties and/or disabilities' are replaced with the term 'additional learning needs'.
- All children and young people with ALN regardless of the severity or complexity of their learning difficulty or disability will be entitled to a statutory support plan called an Individual Development Plan (IDP).
- Children and young people with ALN will receive support called additional learning provision which will be set out in their IDP.

 **CASE STUDY**

Mainstream or special school?

Neo is a 7-year-old boy who has Down's syndrome. His parents desperately want him to remain in mainstream education, but he is struggling, academically and socially. Lately he has been coming home with unexplained bruises and has begun to refer to himself as 'stupid' and 'idiot'. His parents are worried about him as he has started to become very withdrawn. Discussions are being held to determine whether Neo should enrol in a special school.

1   What do you think might be happening to Neo? How can the staff and his parents help him to deal with any bullying he might be facing?
2   Where do you think he is best educated? Identify advantages and disadvantages to both mainstream education and special provision.

 **REFLECTION**

The education of children with SEND remains a significant topic of debate; even within the disabled community there is disagreement (Rieser 2018). Rieser asserts that as long as models of inclusion for children with SEND are based on mapping into a national curriculum that has been designed for mainstream pupils, some children will remain disadvantaged.

Thinking critically about the education of children with SEND

Now that you have reached the end of this chapter, consider some of the arguments and complexities that exist around the education of children with SEND:

- Educating children together, irrespective of any disability, helps integration into wider society and can remove detrimental stereotypes and ignorance towards individuals with impairments.
- If children remain segregated in special schools, they will be prevented from achieving their potential.
- Whose needs should be adhered to when there are differences of opinion regarding the child's provision? The child, parent, school or local authority?
- The closure of specialist schools would prevent parents and children from having freedom of choice, and the needs of some children with severe and complex conditions may be more effectively addressed in a special setting.
- It is economically more sustainable for the government to locate specialist facilities, staff and resources in one educational setting for children who have complex learning and medical differences.
- Children with SEND attending mainstream settings will be the target of bullying. However, in all social contexts, there will be individuals who wish to be at the top of the social hierarchy, so bullying may also happen in special schools.
- Some children with SEND may be more confident in segregated classrooms when they are in the company of children with similar difficulties.
- Including children with SEND in mainstream education can be at the expense of other children. For example, a child with SEND in a mainstream class might need extra attention from the teacher or be disruptive, impacting on other pupils.

KEY POINTS

- Overcoming the difficulties that individuals with disabilities face (inaccessible physical environments, inappropriate educational contexts, gaps in service delivery, prejudice) is reliant on the removal of social and environmental barriers (World Bank 2020; WHO 2020).
- Children with SEND are more likely to live in poverty, experience poorer education and social outcomes, and be bullied at school.

- Prejudicial attitudes regarding disability have their roots in historical influences, shaped by the traditional/religious model and medical model of disability.
- The education of children with SEND has revolved around concepts of segregation, integration and inclusion.
- The education of children with SEND continues to be debated; complexities and tensions exist even within the disabled community.
- Early identification of SEND requires practitioners to be confident in understanding 'typical' patterns of child development and when a child's behaviour or learning falls outside the expected age (Stobbs et al. 2014).
- SEND training should incorporate intersectionality to promote awareness of the overlaps with other dimensions of diversity and subconscious bias (JRF 2016).

FURTHER READING

Frederickson, N. and Cline, T. (2015) *Special Educational Needs, Inclusion and Diversity*. Third edition. Maidenhead: Open University Press.
Comprehensive text which consists of three broad sections: principles and contexts, assessment in context and areas of need.

Rieser, R. (2018) 'Achieving disability equality: The continuing struggle'. In Cole, M. (ed.) *Education, Equality and Human Rights*. Fourth edition. pp. 192–229. Abingdon: Routledge.
Provides a detailed overview of the history of disablement and prejudice, putting into context the disabled rights movement and quest for equality and human rights.

Wearmouth, J. (2017) *Special Educational Needs and Disabilities in Schools: A Critical Introduction*. London: Bloomsbury.
Critical consideration is given to various issues relating to SEND, including a historical perspective and the current legal position.

USEFUL WEBSITES

Anti-Bullying Alliance: www.anti-bullyingalliance.org.uk
Contact (for families with disabled children): https://contact.org.uk
Council for Disabled Children: https://councilfordisabledchildren.org.uk
Mencap (learning disability): www.mencap.org.uk

6

CHILDREN IN CARE, FOSTERING AND ADOPTION

CONTENTS

CHAPTER OVERVIEW ━━━━━━━━━

This chapter will consider the incidence of children in care and adopted children in the United Kingdom and reasons why children enter the care system. Children in care and adopted children often experience many challenges and disparities relating to their learning, health and social well-being. Inequalities relating to these aspects of development will be considered, and ways children and their families can be supported in early years and school settings discussed.

This chapter considers:

1   The incidence of children in care and adopted children, reasons why they enter the care system, where they live and the stability they experience.
2   Differences between fostering and adoption.
3   The impact of early adversity on children's health, developmental and behavioural outcomes.
4   Children's experiences within education and their educational outcomes.
5   Ways to support children and their families in early years and school settings.

CHILDREN IN CARE
Facts and figures

Under the Children Act 1989 (HM Government 1989), if a child is deemed to be suffering or at significant harm, a local authority has a legal obligation to attain a care order to protect them. Where a court makes a care order, the local authority must undertake parental responsibility for that child. It is then the responsibility of social workers to find a place for the child to live. A child who has been in the care of their local authority for more than 24 hours is known as a 'child in care'. A child will stop being in care if they return home, are adopted or when they turn 18. Young people in care are entitled to support from the local authority until they are 21, receiving assistance with accommodation, finances and employment. Each UK nation follows its own legislation, policy and guidance regarding children in care.

The number of children in care has increased every year since 2010, although trends vary across the UK (National Society for the Prevention of Cruelty to Children [NSPCC] 2019). As of 31 March 2019, the number of children in care under 18 years, by local authorities in England, was 78,150. This is equivalent to a rate of 65 children per 10,000 – up from 60 per 10,000 in 2015 (Department for Education [DfE] 2019e).

ACTIVITY

Analysing statistics – trends and characteristics

The DfE publishes statistics relating to children in care on an annual basis.

Using the link below, access the most current document available to identify:

www.gov.uk/government/collections/statistics-looked-after-children

1 The total number of children in care and the number of children adopted.
2 Characteristics of children in care (age, gender, ethnicity).
3 Reasons why children in care have entered care.
4 Where children in care have been placed.

Where do children in care live?

As noted above, on 31 March 2019, 78,150 children in England were in the care of local authorities:

- 72% lived with foster carers (including kinship care).
- 12% lived in secure units, children's homes or semi-independent living.
- 7% were placed with their parents.
- 4% lived independently or in residential employment.
- 3% were placed for adoption.

(DfE 2019e)

Most children in care are accommodated in foster placements, with an increasing number placed with a relative or friends. A minority of children live with their birth families, where either the local authority or another family member will take parental responsibility regarding the child's education and welfare. Residential children's homes, which usually accommodate no more than 10 children, allow siblings to remain together. Children who have committed a criminal offence, or who are thought to be of risk to themselves or others, may be placed in secure accommodation, where they receive 25–30 hours on-site education per week.

Reasons for being in care

When a child is assessed by children's services their primary need is recorded. The main reason for children entering into care is due to abuse or neglect (DfE 2019e).

This figure may be an underestimate because very young children and some children with disabilities may not be able to understand or articulate what has happened to them. Children may also be in care due to: family dysfunction (where parenting capacity is critically inadequate); the family facing a short-term crisis that diminishes the parental capacity to meet children's needs; there being no parents to provide for the child (including unaccompanied asylum-seeking children); the child's or parent's disability or illness; and low income or socially unacceptable behaviour.

ACTIVITY

Children in care – Sam's story

Watch the following video clip, which has been written by children in care.

www.youtube.com/watch?v=F8_A_01U0ng

What are the main messages that Sam is delivering? Would this be a suitable resource to use within an early years setting to promote understanding of children in care? Justify your reasons.

Stability in care

Many children in care will have experienced significant adversity before arriving into care. A stable home environment that nurtures children provides the foundation for them to form positive relationships that enable them to flourish. Additionally, a supportive early years or school environment, together with consistent and timely support from professionals, can help these children to readjust and thrive.

The Stability Index, launched by the Children's Commissioner in 2017, provides data that allow stability to be monitored and guide improvements for children in care. The Stability Index gives an annual measure of three domains of stability regarding the welfare of children: stability at home, stability at school and stability in professional support. The Children's Commissioner (2018b) reported that: (1) most children in care experience some kind of instability throughout the course of a year; (2) only 1 in 4 children experienced no placement move, no school move and no social worker change within a year; and (3) only 1 in 10 children experienced none of these changes over two years.

FOSTER CARE

Foster carers may look after children from a couple of nights to a number of years but legally children remain part of their biological family and have contact with their birth parents, if it is safe for them to do so. Often children return home once the issues that caused them to go into care have been resolved and their parents are able to look after them safely. However, some children may stay in long-term foster care and will move on to live independently, while others may be adopted.

Fostering is normally arranged through the local authority but there are also private fostering agencies. Foster carers receive remuneration to cover their caring costs. Applicants will have been through a Disclosure and Barring Service process, have undergone training about the needs of children entering into care, and they are reviewed on an annual basis to confirm they are suitable to continue fostering (Holmstrom 2013a). They will receive regular visits from a social worker before they are matched with a child. Priority is given to placing children with carers who share a child's ethnic origin, culture and language. This is deemed important as Black, Asian and minority ethnic foster carers are often better placed to empathise with birth parents' difficulties and help to promote and support children's ethnic, cultural, religious and linguistic heritage, as well as helping them to deal with any racism or stereotypes that they may encounter (Coram 2017). However, a report published by Ofsted suggests that 68% of the local authorities in England have a shortage of Black, Asian and minority ethnic foster carers, with 83% of all foster carers being white (Ofsted 2019; BBC News 2020).

When a child is taken into care their initial foster placement is usually a brief one while social workers identify an appropriate placement. Ideally, placements should be in the same area as where the child lived before entering into care. Unlike with adoption, the parental responsibility for the child is held by the local authority and the child's birth parents although some decisions will be shared by the local authority with the foster carers.

 TYPES OF FOSTER CARE

Short-term: Children stay for a couple of nights with foster carers while plans are made.
Long-term: Children live with long-term foster carers until they have reached 18 years of age (sometimes longer).
Respite: Children with special needs, disabilities or behavioural difficulties stay with a family to give their own family or foster carers a break.
Specialist: Young people are placed with specialist foster carers as an alternative to custody or where experienced carers look after children with complex needs.
Parent and child: A parent is placed into a foster home with their child.
Kinship: Children are cared for by relatives or other adults associated to the child.

(British Association for Adoption and Fostering 2020)

For some children the placement may be long-term foster care, not adoption. For example, carers of children with disabilities may feel they will receive more financial support if the children are fostered, older children may not want to sever the legal ties to their birth family, and some birth parents may wish to maintain parental responsibility despite being unable to care for their child. There are also individuals from some minority ethnic groups who opt for long-term fostering, as adoption may be at odds with their cultural beliefs.

ADOPTION

Most children enter the adoption system after spending time in foster care. Adoption is a legal procedure in which all parental responsibility is transferred to the adopter as though the child had been born into that family. Those wishing to adopt have to be over 21, although there is no upper age limit. Potential adopters must undergo a Disclosure and Barring Service check and a medical examination, and undertake training to prepare them for being parents. They are assigned a social worker and after various checks and references they will be matched with a child. They will be introduced to the child over a series of meetings, which normally includes the foster carers. After 10 weeks, adopters can apply for an adoption order and when it is approved the child becomes a legal member of their family; the child's surname changes and the adopters are listed as the child's parents on the adoption certificate. Once an adoption order has been granted it cannot be reversed except in rare circumstances. When children are 18 years of age, they are entitled to a copy of their original birth certificate (Holmstrom 2013b).

 **CASE STUDY**

Types of adopters – Ebony

Ebony is 4 years old. Her birth parents are Black British – her family originally came from the Caribbean. She has physical, cognitive and emotional delays because of her early home life experiences. She is in the process of being adopted. Social workers are considering a match. Families include:

1 A single woman in her twenties.
2 A same-sex female married couple.
3 A heterosexual couple with two birth children under the age of seven years.
4 A heterosexual couple who are living on benefits.
5 A hearing-impaired couple.
6 An older couple in their late fifties.
7 A same-sex Black British male couple.
8 A single mum who has a 14-year-old daughter.
9 An Indian family, who are practising Hindus.

Questions for group discussion

Which family you think would be the best match for Ebony? Rank the families in diamond order – 1 'most suitable', to 9 'least suitable'. Justify the adopter/s you feel would be the best match. Are there any adopters you feel Ebony should not be placed with? If so, explain your reasons.

The number of children placed for adoption has continued to fall. In 2019, 3,570 of children in care were adopted compared to 2015 when 5,360 children were adopted (DfE 2019e). According to the DfE (2019e) 88% of children were adopted by couples and 12% by single adopters; 14% of children were adopted by same-sex couples. The average time between entry into care and adoption was 1 year and 11 months, with older children waiting longer.

Since the Adoption Act 2002 (HM Government 2002), there have been increasing numbers of lesbian, gay, bisexual and transgender adopters, many of whom choose 'harder to place' children. Many lesbian, gay, bisexual and transgender adopters/carers will have learned resilience in the face of marginalisation and prejudice. This can make them better equipped to empathise with and support children who might be encountering discrimination or who are questioning their own identity, gender or sexuality (Sharples 2017). However, there is still work to be done with regard to challenging stereotypes as to who can foster and adopt, including younger people, single people and those who have never parented.

 **CASE STUDY**

The needs of 'harder to place' children – Freddie

Freddie is 9 years old. He was physically abused by his parents when he was a toddler and walks with a limp as a result. Freddie has unpredictable responses to events and behaves inappropriately, often lashing out by hitting, kicking and swearing at key adults who are trying to support him. He has been in the care system for six years. He has experienced multiple foster placements, which break down quickly. There is no sign of him being adopted.

Questions

1   What factors might be preventing Freddie from finding a home with long-term foster carers or adoptive parents? Identify other groups of children who might be 'harder to place'.
2   What perceptions and concerns might be held about children in care like Freddie who have complex needs and behaviours?
3   Identify the different practitioners likely to be involved in supporting Freddie.
4   What knowledge, qualities and skills do potential foster carers need to have to effectively support Freddie?

Within the UK there are twice as many children waiting to be adopted as there are families willing to adopt. Children waiting for 18 months or above for a permanent family are referred to as 'harder to place' children. They include: sibling groups; older children (over the age of four); children with special educational needs, disabilities or challenging behavioural difficulties; and Black and minority ethnic children (*The Guardian* 2015; Coram 2020).

Many adopters are reluctant to adopt older children due to a fear that the children will be too traumatised and that attachment difficulties will result in adoption break-down. Instead, there is a preference to adopt babies or very young children. It is important that adopters are made aware of the difficulty in detecting long-term developmental issues in babies. For example, the full impact of drugs and/or alcohol on the foetus will often not show until later on in childhood (Family Futures 2020). The number of adoption breakdowns is low – approximately 3% (Meakings et al. 2018). However, this figure should be considered in the context that many children will have experienced multiple placement moves and changes in social workers prior to adoption (Children's Commissioner 2018b) which can make positive attachments difficult, placing strain on family relationships and well-being.

Children who enjoy a positive relationship with their adoptive parents may feel guilty for missing or wanting to establish contact with their birth parents. These feelings may intensify as the child gets older. Research relating to identity development shows how important it is for children to have an understanding of and, if appropriate to do so, contact with their birth family and culture. Very young children should be made aware as early as possible that they have been adopted. This is to avoid children learning that they have been adopted from anyone else or perceiving adoption negatively as it was kept hidden. Face-to-face contact between a child and their birth parents is rare and would have to be undertaken with the consent of the child's adoptive parents (First4Adoption 2020). However, contact between siblings who have been placed separately is encouraged. Where there is contact with birth parents or grandparents it is most likely to be 'letterbox' contact, where an exchange of written information is managed through a central point (usually the adoption service). In this way, contact details are kept confidential, and inappropriate content can be extracted.

HEALTH, DEVELOPMENTAL AND BEHAVIOURAL OUTCOMES

Many children in care and adopted children will have experienced significant childhood trauma, loss and turmoil and are thus at risk of a range of negative outcomes. Nearly half of these children exhibit emotional, social or behavioural problems and many experience poor mental health (Jones 2018). Complex externalising behaviours include aggressive, disruptive, hyperactive and impulsive conduct, and internalising issues involve anxiety, depression and somatic (physical) conditions (Solomon et al. 2017). Many families, particularly adoptive parents, report there to be inadequate professional assistance to support children's complex needs (Meakings et al. 2018).

Poor health among children in care and adopted children is the result of a complex interaction of pre-existing mental health conditions, length of exposure to maltreatment, and biological risk and resilience (NSPCC 2015). Children in care are over five times more likely to have a diagnosed mental disorder than non-disadvantaged children (NSPCC 2015; DfE 2019e). In 2019, for children aged 5–16 years who had been in care for at least 12 months, 78% had an average Strengths and Difficulties Questionnaire (SDQ) score of 14.2. A score of 0 to 13 is considered normal, 14 to 16 borderline, and 17 to 40 a cause for concern. Of the 78%, 39% had scores which were a 'cause for concern' (DfE 2019e). The high rate of behavioural disorders is also concerning, with 2 out of every 5 children in care having a diagnosed disorder (DfE 2019e). Numerous placement disruptions, together with changes in social workers, can have further negative impact on children's mental well-being (Fisher 2015; Children's Commissioner 2018b), determining how they settle into a new family, early years setting and school.

 **CASE STUDY**

The impact of early adversity on health, developmental and behavioural outcomes – Kisha

Kisha is 3 years old. She was severely neglected by her parents, lacking clothes, food and social interaction. She spent most of her time in her bedroom, rarely attending pre-school or appointments with the health visitor. She is a very anxious and socially withdrawn child. She is developmentally behind the majority of her peers. An adoption order has been granted and she will soon be moving into her new home. However, she is showing signs of distress about leaving her foster mother with whom she has built a close attachment.

Questions

1   Identify the impact that early adversity may have had on Kisha's health and behavioural development.
2   What challenges might Kisha face in settling into her adoptive family?
3   How can Kisha's social worker and foster mother prepare her for the transition?

There can be additional impacts on the health, developmental and behavioural outcomes of children in care:

- They are more likely to be the subject of case reviews.
- They are more likely to struggle with relationships and coping with change.
- Two-thirds have at least one physical health condition (speech and language problems, bedwetting, coordination difficulties and eye or sight problems).
- They are more likely to engage in risky behaviour (alcohol and drug misuse, early and unprotected sex) and to become teenage parents.
- They are four to five times more likely to self-harm in adulthood.
- They are twice as likely to be cautioned or convicted for a criminal offence.
- An increasing number of young people are being placed in unregulated homes which lack adult supervision, putting them at risk of sexual exploitation and crime.
- Care leavers who have poor mental health are at risk of becoming homeless.

(NSPCC 2015, 2019; Local Government Association 2016; BBC News 2019).

There has, however, been progress in some areas. The DfE (2019e) report that most children in care are up to date with immunisations (87%), have had an annual health assessment (90%) and have visited a dentist (85%), and that most under-fives are up to date with development assessments (88%).

Attachment difficulties

Attachment theory will help parents and practitioners to understand the impact of early trauma, loss and separation on the socio-emotional development of children. The relationship between the extent of early childhood trauma and the degree of attachment issues is complex. However, the older the child with a chaotic life is, where they are placed and the number of moves they have experienced will increase the risk and level of attachment difficulties. If a child is in an institution where there are a number of children requiring attention, secure attachments might be difficult. Research has shown that children placed in foster care, adopted or cared for by biological family members before the age of seven are more likely to make a more successful recovery from early adversity than children who have remained in residential care (Knowles 2011a; Fisher 2015). Nonetheless, it is important that children in care and adopted children are not seen homogeneously or as victims. Despite challenges, some children develop resilience or remain relatively unscathed as a result of early trauma (Fisher 2015). Even siblings who have faced the same adversity will not necessarily have similar needs or difficulties, and they may have different levels of resilience.

ACTIVITY

Attachment difficulties

Think of a child in care or adopted child who you know or have worked with in a setting. Identify behaviours they might present which could indicate an issue linked to attachment.

Children who have attachment difficulties can be overly anxious to please; some withdraw, while others express challenging behaviour. There are several signs that a child might have an attachment disorder: they do not turn to their main caregiver when upset; they avoid being touched or comforted and lack appropriate eye contact; they are unusually withdrawn, anxious or depressed; they have extreme control issues (clingy and demanding behaviour); they show aggressive behaviour towards others; they are inappropriately friendly to people they don't know; or they do not appear upset in situations where you would expect them to be upset.

Stigma

Homogeneous assumptions, negative labelling and stigma exist around children in care and adopted children, which may diminish their mental health and impact other outcomes. Many children in care: (1) think the public see them as damaged, uncontrollable and problematic, with the assumption that they are troublemakers or criminals; (2) report being faced by reactions of curiosity or sympathy when people find out they are in care; (3) believe the longer they spend in care the worse they will be treated by teachers, employers and potential landlords (Ofsted 2009; Coram Voice 2015).

ACTIVITY

Media coverage

Undertake a media search to examine the news items presented about children in care and adopted children. Are the messages mainly positive or mainly negative? Could these messages lead to misconceptions or stereotypical thinking? What impact might such messages have for these children?

EDUCATIONAL EXPERIENCES AND OUTCOMES

Although there has been progress, lower educational outcomes of children in care and adopted children remain an issue in the UK. Because of their disrupted childhood, complex situations and fractured relationships, these children often find it difficult to attend and focus in school. Even children who appear to be settled can have periods of distress and difficulty at different stages of their school career.

The link between social and emotional well-being and educational attainment is widely documented. Children who have a higher incidence of emotional and behavioural difficulties are more likely to truant, be excluded from school, leave without qualifications and have poorer employment outcomes (NSPCC 2015; Adoption UK 2017). Over two-thirds of children in care and adopted children have a special educational need/disability, most commonly related to social, emotional or mental health (DfE 2017; Adoption UK 2017). Many children struggle with executive functioning, sensory processing, managing feelings, social skills, forming relationships and coping with change (DfE 2018). It may take a number of years before they make the expected academic progress for their age, with a lack of achievement in the primary phase often having a cumulative effect. For example, only 25% of children in care and 30% of adopted children in England achieved the expected standard at Key Stage 2 in 2016, compared to 54% of children from the general population (Adoption UK 2018). Although these children have poorer educational outcomes, children who are continuously in care have been found to have better educational attainment than children in need (NSPCC 2019).

Schools can help children to build resilience as they provide a structured routine and opportunities to form friendships. However, the histories of many children in care and adopted children often make it difficult for them to regulate their emotions, leading to insecure attachments and poor peer relationships. So, where children struggle with this, school can present a significant challenge. Peer relationships which lead to isolation, intimidation or rejection are predictive of social, emotional and behavioural problems, including school drop-out. Thus, it is important that practitioners remain vigilant of children who are struggling with positive peer relationships. They can assist by supporting children to develop social skills and manage difficult feelings, particularly during non-structured events such as playtime, and by warding off any invasive questions asked by other children.

In 2009, the Department for Children, Schools and Families announced that schools in the UK do not do enough to support children in care (DCSF 2009b). Despite developments, these children continue to struggle at school. Many adopters/foster carers are concerned that their children's educational needs will not be adequately addressed and that teachers do not have enough understanding of how trauma and attachment issues affect their children. Parents are particularly anxious about the transition to secondary school. Their fears may be justified as these children have been found to struggle with the larger, more impersonal nature of secondary school (Selwyn and Meakings 2018). In 2018, Adoption UK reported how adopted children's well-being was supported in school. The survey revealed that:

- 70% of parents feel their child's progress is affected by their well-being.
- 60% of parents do not feel that their child has an equal chance at school.
- Over a third of parents stated how their child had refused to go to school, ran away from school or played truant.
- 79% of adopted children agreed to feeling 'confused and worried at school'.
- 47% of adopted children said they had been bullied or teased at school (children are often targeted because of their birth parents, low self-esteem, behavioural differences, health and speech issues or academic delays).

Young people in care have highlighted various issues linked to negative labelling, assumptions and stigma which exist within schools. They report how they: dislike being treated as a homogeneous group; are afraid of prejudice and being treated differently (many do not want to 'stand out'); believe teachers hold low expectations about what they can achieve; and want teachers to have more training so they understand their needs and the issues they face, and can help to reduce the stigma of being in care (Coram Voice 2015; Become 2019).

Supporting children and families

The needs of children in care and adopted children, and the relationships that exist within their families, are often so complex that it is important that early years and school practitioners have access to high-quality training, continuing professional development and specialised support. However, the provision of training relating to the needs of these children is said to be patchy across the UK (Adoption UK 2018). There are calls for, among practitioners, an increased awareness of attachment and resilience theories and the impact of early adversity on children's development and learning, and also for content on foster care and adoption to be addressed through the curriculum. Adoption UK (2018) asserts that attention also needs to be given to bridging gaps in empathy, resources and attainment, as only then will adopted, looked after and other traumatised children have an equal chance in school. Schools which invest in the social and emotional welfare of pupils, prioritising this above academic achievement, will enable these children to achieve greater personal well-being and, in turn, academic outcomes.

ACTIVITY

Thinking about Freddie

Reflect back to the case study of Freddie (p. 109) and the knowledge, qualities and skills you identified as being important for foster carers to have to be able to support him. As you read the next section, are any additional features outlined as being essential when working with children in care and adopted children? Do you think early years practitioners and teachers should have an appreciation of the challenges often faced by foster carers and adoptive parents? Please justify your answer.

The NSPCC (2014) stress it is essential that adults (parents, carers, practitioners) should be prepared to take on a challenge, have good communicative openness and recognise success in small steps forward in these children. A patient and responsive approach where adults pay close attention to the child's verbal and non-verbal cues, in an attempt to understand their needs, temperaments and actions, is important. By depersonalising challenging behaviours, where emphasis is put on assisting the child to self-regulate rather than on the adult containing the behaviour, can reduce confrontation (NSPCC 2014). Adults who acknowledge children's agency and encourage them to partake in the decision-making process can also promote socio-emotional growth and positive bonds with children (Zeleke et al. 2018).

Far more understanding and skills are typically required by foster carers and adoptive parents than biological parents, as they are likely to be supporting children with extreme needs and behaviours, as well as managing complex relationships. During the early stages, families are often in a state of turmoil, with parents assisting children to cope with numerous losses and unfamiliar surroundings, people, rules and routines. Hamilton and Forgacs-Pritchard (2020) identified various challenges encountered by adoptive parents, including: rushed and difficult adoption transitions where there had been tensions with foster carers; children arriving into families with little background knowledge of each other; parents feeling unsupported and disheartened a few months into receiving the child; and strained family relationships where siblings with diverse needs and personalities had been placed together. The need for continued access to timely and appropriate support from a range of agencies as the child grows cannot be underestimated. Awareness of what families may be experiencing can help practitioners to understand changes in a child or parent's behaviour or why information about a child might be missing, and to allow them to take an informed approach to assist a child in building a positive sense of self.

Early years practitioners and teachers play a fundamental part in promoting the acceptance of diverse family structures. It is therefore essential that they remain mindful of the messages that children in care and adopted children receive at school about their family background and living arrangements. However, Hamilton and Forgacs-Pritchard (2020) suggest that some teachers are not always as considerate about the children in their care as they should be. Parents in this study identified examples of insensitive classroom practices, including tasks that were difficult for their children to complete and which risked them 'standing out' from their peers, making them a potential target of teasing or bullying.

 **CASE STUDY**

Insensitive classroom practices – Filip

Filip is 10 years old. His teacher set the class a writing task 'The best day in your life'. Filip wrote about the day that he and his siblings went into care. The teacher displayed the work on the wall. Following this task, the children were asked to take photographs into school from when they were a baby. As Filip did not have any baby photographs, he took one in of himself with his foster mum.

These activities alerted Filip's peers to his family background, which resulted in awkward questions and regular teasing. Filip, who had previously been thriving in school, started to become distressed about having to attend. It was only when Filip's foster mum went into the classroom for parents' evening that she noticed his writing task (which contained his birth siblings' details) and the photograph on the wall. She felt angry and dismayed.

Questions

1 Discuss the impact these experiences may have on Filip, his foster family and possibly his birth siblings.
2 How could the teacher work more effectively with Filip and his foster parents to ensure that he is better supported?
3 Make a list of things you would want to know to help you support a child in care in your care.

Personal writing tasks (for example, 'The best day of your life' and 'What did you do over summer?') can result in children revisiting difficult past events or revealing limited family interaction. Alternatively, such tasks may offer a medium through which children can voice, and make sense of, a negative experience. Whatever the view, it is important that such activities are carefully considered, discussed with parents prior to taking place, undertaken with sensitivity and include work around tasks for children who might find the exercise too challenging to complete.

Adopted children and children in care normally require support in understanding their past, where they belong and who they might become (NSPCC 2014; Zeleke et al. 2018). Their disrupted backgrounds often lead to a poor or confused sense of self. This may be compounded where lifestyle factors (socio-economic, sexuality, cultural, religious) have been particularly diverse within the birth family, across foster placements and the adoptive home. Early years practitioners can play an essential part in raising awareness and normalising the family background of children in care and adopted children. Information regarding children's birth families should be dealt with sensitively and their current family structure represented positively through classroom materials and content, and the choice of language and activities must not make children feel devalued or uncomfortable because their family does not fit the 'norm'. Teachers who have awareness of self-identity, attachment and loss theories can support parents with this important aspect of a child's readjustment.

Removing barriers

The Children and Families Act 2014 requires local authorities in England to appoint a Virtual School Head (VSH) to act as the lead officer for improving the educational experiences and outcomes of the authority's children in care. Although the main focus is on supporting children from the foundation stage to the end of Year 11, the VSH will support the transition of children into the foundation stage, and from Year 11 to post-16 education, employment or training. The VSH has responsibilities relating to Personal Education Planning (PEP) and for managing the funding schools receive for children in care – the Early Years Looked After Pupil Premium (EYPP) or Looked After Pupil Premium (PP+) (National Association of Virtual School Heads 2018).

Since 2009 it has been statutory in England for a designated teacher (DT) to champion the educational needs of children in care in their school. The DT works alongside the VSH in partnership with carers/parents, other teachers and specialist agencies. The DT should take the lead in devising and monitoring the progress of the child's PEP and implementing actions to provide equality of access to learning. The child and their parents/carers should be involved in creating the PEP, which must encompass extra-curricular activities in addition to academic targets.

It is important to note that it has taken some years for adopted children to gain parity with the provision that is available for children in care. In 2013, legislation was amended to give adopted children the same rights as children in care by giving schools access to Pupil Premium Plus funding (DfE 2013). Then in 2017, under the Children and Social Work Act (HM Government 2017), the roles of the VSH and DT were expanded to also act as advocates for adopted children.

The following are important for supporting these children in education: (1) admissions procedures which ensure these children have access to early years settings and schools that best support their needs; (2) continuity between the different adults supporting these children (teachers, support staff, social workers) and open communication with parents/carers; (3) sensitive sharing of information, with key/ appropriate adults, regarding the child's needs, difficulties and support strategies.

Early years settings and schools have a vital role to play in supporting children in care and adopted children (DfE 2018). This will require practitioners to have enhanced theoretical knowledge and skills relating to attachment difficulties, trauma and loss, and how such issues affect children's ability to learn, together with an understanding of how this can be translated in practice. Although issues of inclusion, diversity and adverse childhood experiences have gained prominence in early years and initial teacher education programmes and in-service training, various studies suggest that gaps in awareness remain. With so many diverse social groups to consider, it is argued that adoption/fostering is one of the more marginalised topics, receiving insufficient attention.

While the number of children in care and adopted children in a classroom may be small, the issues faced by these children are so complex, and have the potential to significantly hinder educational and well-being outcomes, that it is essential that practitioners gain an in-depth understanding regarding their needs and those of their families. Such knowledge will help these children to feel a sense of security, belonging and positive sense of self, thus optimising the conditions required for enhancing social, emotional, behavioural and academic outcomes.

 **REFLECTION**

Supporting children in care in practice

Now that you have come to the end of the chapter, imagine that you are advising a colleague on how best to support the needs of a 5-year-old foster child who has just started in your setting. What key points of advice would you give?

KEY POINTS

- Certain groups of children are identified as being 'harder to place'.
- Children in care and adopted children have poorer outcomes across a range of measures.
- Homogeneous assumptions should be broken down, and misconceptions and stereotypes regarding adopted and children in care should be dispelled.
- Awareness should be raised of the challenges faced by these children, and when addressing family diversity, foster and adopted families should be normalised.
- Better guidance is needed to enable these children to have equality of learning and social opportunities, without making them 'stand out'.

- Increased awareness is needed of the complex relationships that often surround foster and adopted families, which might influence child and family engagement.
- A patient and responsive approach is required by practitioners, who recognise small steps in children's success and help them to build positive relationships.

FURTHER READING

Adoption UK (2018) *Bridging the Gap: Giving Adopted Children an Equal Chance in School.* Available at: www.basw.co.uk/system/files/resources/bridging-the-gap.pdf Detailed report outlining the challenging reality of school life for adoptive families and their children; considers various aspects of children's social and emotional well-being and their educational progress.

Department for Education (2019) *National Statistics: Children Looked After in England (including Adoption), year ending 31 March 2019.* Available at: https://assets. publishing.service.gov.uk/government/uploads/system/uploads/attachment_ data/file/850306/Children_looked_after_in_England_2019_Text.pdf Statistics publication which provides comprehensive coverage on various characteristics of children in care, including placement type, health and behavioural outcomes.

Hamilton, P. and Forgacs-Pritchard, K. (2020) The complex tapestry of relationships which surround adoptive families: A case study. *Education 3–13: International Journal of Primary, Elementary and Early Years Education.* Published online 17 March 2020.
Provides understanding of the complexities which may exist within adoptive families, to help practitioners to identify strategies that can be used to promote children's well-being and their capacity to function and learn inside classrooms.

Jones, A. (2018) Looked after children, fostering and adoption. In Knowles, G. (ed.) *Supporting Inclusive Practice and Ensuring Opportunity is Equal for All.* Third edition. pp. 140–52. Abingdon: Routledge.
Detailed overview of who children in care are, the barriers they face and how these children can be supported in an educational context.

USEFUL WEBSITES

British Association for Adoption and Fostering: https://corambaaf.org.uk
Family Futures: www.familyfutures.co.uk
Fostering Network: www.thefosteringnetwork.org.uk
National Society for the Prevention of Cruelty to Children: www.nspcc.org.uk

7

GENDER DEVELOPMENT AND IDENTITIES: INTERSEX AND TRANSGENDER CHILDREN

CONTENTS

 **CHAPTER OVERVIEW**

This chapter explores the development of gender identity and problematises gender binaries and stereotypes, which restrict and oppress individuals within societies. It discusses the issues faced and experiences encountered by gender variant, intersex and transsexual children. Consideration is given to how children from these groups can be supported in early years settings and schools, and the role child practitioners can play in counteracting dominant gender discourses and prejudice.

This chapter considers:

1 The development of gender identity, stereotypes and binaries.
2 Terms and concepts.
3 Issues faced by intersex children.
4 Issues encountered by gender variant and transgender children.
5 How intersex, gender variant and transgender children can be supported in early years settings and schools, including strategies for challenging dominant gender discourses, stigma and prejudice.

GENDER DEVELOPMENT, IDENTITY, STEREOTYPES AND BINARIES

When the child emerges into the world, every physical movement and spoken word, every toy touched and game imagined, are coloured by the power of gender role expectations. (Burke 1996: 3)

Many cultures and societies are systematised by gender. Gender binaries, stereotypes and power relations are at the core of most societal structures, with binary gender norms so embedded in Western cultures that they are internalised as 'natural' (Sweeting et al. 2017). Cultural binaries pervade modern life, defining 'masculinity' and 'femininity' (also 'heterosexuality' and 'homosexuality') in opposition through everyday language, policies and practices, restricting and marginalising the lives of some individuals, while empowering others. However, in some cultures and different historical periods, more than two sex categories are, or have been, recognised. Infants born intersex demonstrates that there is a natural area between complete 'maleness' and complete 'femaleness' (Sweeting et al. 2017).

Forming a positive sense of self is a fundamental aspect of a child's development. Unfortunately, despite increased legal protection in the UK for people who identify as lesbian, gay, bisexual, transsexual, queer or questioning, intersex and asexual/ally (henceforth LGBTQIA+), social acceptance often lags behind. Individuals who challenge gendered expectations of their birth (natal) sex, as well as those who fail to conform to heterosexual norms, frequently face stigma and prejudice. Early years settings and schools are not gender-neutral places, as children and practitioners bring with them firmly established gender roles and behaviours: gender atypical behaviour is often noticed and strictly regulated (Smith and Chambers 2016). An important responsibility of a child practitioner is to promote social equity: a central aspect of this is to problematise restrictive binaries. However, it is not uncommon for practitioners to fall short of this task by introducing gender binaries and stereotypes through the language and resources they use, the activities and subjects they encourage pupils to partake in, and how staff interact with, and have different expectations of, boys and girls (Hamilton and Roberts 2017).

Terms and concepts

Gender identity is complex and multifaceted. Gender can be best understood as a spectrum rather than being restrictive binary categories of masculine and feminine (Brighton and Hove City Council Education Team [BHCCET] 2018). Confusion often exists around the concepts of sex, gender and sexual orientation. There are numerous terms connected to these (see 'Trans Inclusion Schools Toolkit', BHCCET 2018); as names, pronouns and terminology vary widely, it is important that children and young people are given opportunities to voice how they identify or describe themselves rather than labels being ascribed to them.

TERMINOLOGY

Sex represents physiological characteristics (hormones, chromosomes and the appearance of external genitalia) used to categorise humans as either female or male. For many people their sex will also be the gender they assign themselves to. However, this is not always straightforward as some individuals are born intersex.

Gender refers to the social construction of masculinity and femininity. Gender is about how individuals are positioned in society and the relationships they have that result from their birth or chosen gender. These are not only the relationships they decide to have, but also how other people view and treat them because of the gender they portray (Knowles 2018b). Gender concerns the internal sense of self; there is much diversity in how people feel about and express their gender identity.

People whose gender identity corresponds with their natal sex are known as *cisgender*. *Gender variant* individuals consider their gender identity to be fluid and may describe themselves as non-binary, gender diverse or agender. Aligning one's self to a binary category of either female or male carries certain behaviours which society expects from that gender: how one should look, attitudes that should be held and social roles which should be undertaken. However, gender is not fixed, so what is expected of females and males varies geographically and across time.

Sexual orientation is concerned with whom someone is romantically or sexually attracted to (BHCCET 2018). Sexual orientation is complex and may change over time. Although some young people with gender identity issues will later identify as LGBTQIA+, this is not always the case (Grossman and D'Augelli 2007). Just like cisgender people, transgender people can have any sexual orientation as it is independent from gender identity.

LGBT, an acronym for lesbian, gay, bisexual and transgender, emerged in the 1980s when it replaced the term 'gay' to create a blanket term for referring to individuals who did not identify as heterosexual (Lesbian & Gay Community Services Center 2020). With increased awareness about the spectrum of sexuality and gender identities, additional letters have since been added, for example, LGBTQIA+ (lesbian, gay, bisexual, transgender, queer or questioning, intersex and asexual/ally) or LGTBQ+ (the '+' represents all other subgroups) (Lesbian & Gay Community Services Center 2020). Throughout this chapter the term LGBTQIA+ is used, other than where primary source documents have undertaken research or produced statistics relating to specific sub-groups of this community.

Theoretical explanations of gender identity

There are numerous theoretical accounts and long-contested debate as to how children develop gender-related identities, attitudes and behaviours. The dichotomy as to what extent a child's genetic heritage is the major influence, compared to the impact of the social environment in which they have been raised, is referred to as 'nature or nurture' (Knowles 2018b).

 **ACTIVITY**

Gender fortunes

In a recent poll, 1,000 members of the general public were asked to name:

1   Two of the most popular toys bought for 'girls' and 'boys'
2   Two personality traits associated with 'girls' and 'boys'
3   Two professions undertaken by 'women' and 'men'

Record what first comes to mind. Then, share your ideas with a group of peers. Are answers stereotypical? What might the impact be if gender-typing is left unchecked? Can you identify any connections between the categories?

Biological determinist explanations, used heavily until the mid-twentieth century in the UK, have dominated understandings of gender identity, leaving an imprint which is difficult to shift. Biological theories assert that physiological sex characteristics determine an individual's interests, personality traits, roles, skills and abilities. This dominant discourse is used in many societies to normalise power relations between men and women, and because of this, there persist many disparities in aspects of daily life (family, social, economic, political).

Feminist writers such as Oakley (1975) argue that biological accounts, which perpetuate a myth of male superiority, are part of male social control (Bartlett and Burton 2016). Harber (2014) explains how some dominant traits of male identity maintain patriarchal power and privilege, reinforcing male dominance and female subordination and oppression. This can be seen globally, with females in some societies and cultural groups facing significant barriers in accessing equality in education and employment, and with issues regarding their safety and welfare.

Neuroscience examines how hormones and chromosomes explain differences in brain development and function, resulting in oppositional patterns of behaviour, skills and cognitive abilities in women and men. It is argued that the female brain and male brain are wired differently; girls and boys have preferred learning styles (Gurian 2011) and their hormonal make-up causes them to behave differently (Featherstone and Bayley 2010). Females are said to be genetically positioned to be nurturing and caring, while physicality and competitiveness are traits typically assigned to males. Neuroscience has served as the basis for the implementation of many contemporary 'brain-based learning' and educational initiatives (Griffin 2018).

Biological theories are strongly contested, with critics arguing that they fail to acknowledge the diversity among women and men across history and societies (Marchbank and Letherby 2014) and the intersectionality of ethnicity, class, religion and sexuality. Essentialist ideology, based on inconclusive facts (Fine 2010, 2017), needs to be problematised as it adds strength to the polarised dualism of masculinity and femininity, reinforcing cultural sexist beliefs about gender and restrictive ways of 'doing' gender (Hamilton and Roberts 2017). Fine (2010, 2017) asserts that there are studies which indicate that neurological differences in gender can be shaped by environmental factors, thus challenging the concept of 'hard wiring'. She presents examples of how biological differences between male and female animals have no impact on parenting roles, such as male rats who will 'mother' their offspring if left without a female, and where male macaque monkeys in different parts of a continent engage in different levels of paternal care (Griffin 2018).

 **ACTIVITY**

The influence of adults on children's play in the early years

Watch the BBC clip 'Girl toys vs boy toys: The experiment', and consider why adults make gender stereotypical assumptions and the impact that this might have on children.

www.youtube.com/watch?v=nWu44AqF0il

Social constructivist theories maintain that men and women, and notions of mas-culinity and femininity, are essentiality products of culture and society. Cognitive social learning theorists (Bussey and Bandura 1999, 2004) propose that social agents deliver and encourage models of gender-normative behaviour for children to observe and imitate, thereby shaping and reinforcing gender role attitudes and behaviour (Spinner et al. 2018). According to gender schema theory (Bem 1981, 1983), deeply embedded gender binaries in cultural discourse and social structures promote the growth of gender-based schemas in young children, where children evaluate, organ-ise and filter information in terms of what it means to be masculine or feminine (Spinner et al. 2018). Cultivation theory argues that media represent a powerful socialising agent as they constantly convey cultural definitions of gender normativ-ity in numerous contexts (Spinner et al. 2018).

Although gender identity is initiated at 24 months (Kohlberg 1966), it is from app-roximately the age of five years that children begin to enforce gender conformity with zeal (Devarakonda 2013). Children look to significant others (parents, teachers, siblings, peers) and the media for guidance, picking up on explicit rules and implicit cues as to what it means to be a 'proper' girl or boy (Soylemez 2010). Fearful of straying from gen-der outlines, some children strictly regulate each other about what they can and cannot do (Bloom 2014). This 'policing' process is a regular feature in pre-school. Children new to early years and school settings quickly establish how to become accepted members in a community of masculinity or femininity by observing the behaviour of other chil-dren, particularly during free play when children typically segregate into groups of boys and girls (Martin 2011). Martin claims that established children patrol play borders by telling other children when they are doing something unacceptable for their gender, with only the more confident child able to cross enforced gender boundaries.

Critics of early socialisation theories warn against accepting a simplistic view of social learning and assert that a more dynamic conceptualisation is required of the way gender identity is learned and (re)produced (Robinson and Jones Diaz 2006; Francis et al. 2008).

Poststructuralist theory perspectives propose that increased attention needs to be given to power relations, the fluidity of identity, children's agency and intersectionality, as gender cannot be experienced or performed separately from other social contexts and aspects of individual identity. Children are known to be active agents in the con-struction of their own gendered identities. Although many children adopt behaviour that reinforces traditional gender norms, some ignore or reject certain discourses of masculinities or femininities. Not all children identify with, and choose to model, a same-sex parent or friend (Ryle 2015). Griffin (2018: 34) claims that children 'don't just soak up their identity from people and institutions'; instead they form and reshape their gendered identities as they interact within different social settings, where they may hear diverse and contradictory messages.

Traditionally, early years practitioners and teachers have focused on challenging gender binaries by expanding children's views about non-traditional gender roles, play and occupations. However, simplistic sex-role-theory approaches have had limited success (Skelton 2002). Instead, a more critical style of thinking is required, where children are introduced to the concept of power relations (Robinson and Jones Diaz 2006) and are encouraged to dismantle stereotypes, polarised concepts and oversimplified explanations (Norwich 2013) associated to gender. Practitioners should also appreciate the influence of 'stereotype threat' and subtle messages in the environment which promote a negative stereotype about one's group (Griffin 2018). For example, the absence of one's own gender in a subject or occupation, such as nurses or engineers within story books or television programmes, has been shown to affect both self-belief and the ability to do or achieve something.

Gender, colour and toys

Children's play is a critical site for learning their birth sex, gender and sexual construction, with colours and toys having a significant impact on brain development, how children see themselves and what skills they learn – later influencing subject choices and career pathways. Gender-related knowledge is acquired early in childhood, highly embedded and difficult to change (Banse et al. 2010).

Developmental research indicates that by the age of two most children know whether they are a girl or a boy (Grossman and D'Augelli 2007). It is from this age that children start to build gender stereotypes typical of their culture, using this knowledge in an increasingly rigid manner until they are 6 years old (Spinner et al. 2018). After that, the use of gender stereotypes becomes increasingly flexible and children may adopt a more open-minded attitude around gender roles (Spinner et al. 2018). However, although there is increasing effort to counteract gender stereotypes in early settings, many children continue to express stereotypical ideas about what each sex should feel, wear and do.

 **ACTIVITY**

Gender and play

1   Do adults engage differently in their play with girls and boys?
2   How influential are gendered toys on children's lives?
3   Do children 'police' each other on the grounds of gender? If so, in what way?
4   What are your own memories of playing? Who did you play with and what games did you play? How gendered was your playing? Have expectations changed?

Children as young as 2 years old can have gender stereotypical preferences for objects, colour and people (Banse et al. 2010; Fast and Olson 2018). Between three and five years of age, children draw upon higher levels of gender stereotypical knowledge to guide their own toy choices (Wong and Hines 2015), outfit choices (Halim et al. 2014), colour preferences (Wong and Hines 2015) and expectations of others' appearances and activities (Grossman and D'Augelli 2007). By the age of six, many children will have developed a strong preference for playing with children of the same gender, further promoting gender-typed behaviour (Spinner et al. 2018).

Children tend to play with gender-typed toys and generally avoid toys associated with the 'other' gender; by the ages four and five, children know that girls usually play with dolls and boys with contact sports (Grossman and D'Augelli 2007). Gendered marketing of toys drives gender stereotypes. From 18 months, toys are increasingly presented as 'for boys' or 'for girls', directly through words used on labelling or indirectly through the sex of the child shown playing with the toy, or the colour of the product or packaging (Fine and Rush 2018). Colour is the main factor influencing children's classification of ambiguous toys as being more appropriate for one gender than the other (Karniol 2011); boys' toys are often manufactured coloured blue and girls' toys are typically coloured pink (Wong and Hines 2015).

Critics argue that the toys and activities provided to young children contribute to social and economic inequalities between men and women later in life. 'Boy toys' (action, transportation, construction, technology) elicit physicality, dominance and spatial and problem skills, while 'girl toys' (dolls, arts and crafts, domestic-themed, beauty) facilitate nurturance, domesticity, verbal and social skills, fine motor skills and concern with appearance (Fine and Rush 2018). Toys, co-varied with colour, can lead to children gender-typing traits and occupations, with children aged 3 to 6 years old associating different adjectives ('gentle'/'strong') and professions ('nurse'/'firefighter') to dolls on the basis of the colour of clothing (Karniol 2011). The development of different sets of knowledge and skills may partly explain men's reluctance to seek support with mental ill-health and their dominance in highly paid science, technology, engineering and mathematics (STEM) occupations. Children need the chance to foster growth in all aspects of development. However, although there is generally more acceptance for girls to engage in 'typical boy' activities, boys are frequently stigmatised for crossing gender binaries (Spinner et al. 2018).

Enforced heterosexuality has also traditionally been manifested in the socialisation of children's play, through the messages delivered to young children via books, toys and the media (Kilvington and Wood 2016). One way to understand the impact of heteronormativity is to consider the relationships which are commonly represented in children's play (mummies and daddies in the home corner, rehearsing weddings, princess stories, kiss-catch), where girls and boys are expected to fall in love with someone of the opposite sex; by contrast, queer instances of sexuality emerge as off-limits (Morgan and Taylor 2019). Children who do not readily identify with heterosexual norms may view their alternative sexualities and genders as socially unacceptable, which can lead to confusion, anxiety and isolation.

INTERSEX/DSD CHILDREN

Gender is important; the first question typically asked of expectant parents is 'Is it a boy or a girl?' This cannot always be easily answered, as some individuals are born with ambiguous external and/or internal genitalia. The term 'intersex' refers to people whose biological attributes cannot be clearly classified as one or the other sex. Intersex results from congenital conditions in which the development of chromosomal, hormonal or anatomic sex is atypical. The term is not applicable to individuals who have deliberately changed their own anatomical characteristics (Organisation Intersex International United Kingdom 2012). Intersex characteristics may appear as genitalia that are not exclusively male or female; internal sex organs that do not match the external sex characteristics; varied chromosomes (XXY, XYY); hormone levels that are unusual for the assigned sex at birth; or having both testicular and ovarian tissues (OutLife 2018). Tests are normally undertaken shortly after birth to determine which condition a baby has (Griffiths 2015). However, some individuals do not discover their condition until adolescence. For example, a child born with complete androgen insensitivity syndrome (CAIS) is genetically male but the external appearance of their genitals looks entirely female; CAIS is usually only discovered when a female's menstrual cycle does not commence.

The language used to describe intersex individuals is contested. The term 'intersex', introduced in the early twentieth century, is supported by many intersex people as it highlights the ability of the body to cross rigid social boundaries (Danon and Kramer 2017). In contrast, individuals with a preference for Disorders of Sexual Development (DSD) believe it to be less stigmatising as it emphasises biological factors (Sweeting et al. 2017). Those who reject the pathologising 'disorder' label suggest 'Differences' or 'Divergences' (of Sex Development) be used instead (Sweeting et al. 2017).

Statistics published for the number of intersex/DSD babies born globally differ but it is considered to be about 1 in 1,500 or 2,000 births (Intersex Human Rights Australia 2013). Reasons for a lack of reliable data include variations in what counts as intersex/DSD; subtle forms of sex anatomy variations not becoming apparent until later in life; and underreporting due to the stigma of having an intersex infant. It is thought that around 130–150 intersex/DSD babies are born in the UK each year (Griffiths 2015; Dsdfamilies 2020).

Before the twentieth century there was no medical management of intersex/DSD. In the 1950s, psychologist John Money and colleagues introduced the biomedical system 'optimal gender policy' (OGP) to 'correct' intersex bodies (Danon and Kramer 2017). The OGP was based on the belief that infants are born psychosexually neutral and can be directed to a binary gender if guided before the age of two (Sweeting et al. 2017). Under the OGP, babies born with intersex bodies were considered a medical and social emergency, to be assessed by a clinical team who would determine the child's sex based on genital examinations (presumed future fertility, endocrine function and pubertal development) (Sweeting et al. 2017). Intersex infants younger than 18 months underwent, and in many countries still undergo, surgery to external and internal sexual organs to normalise their bodies to either one or the other binaries, 'female' or 'male' (Danon and Kramer 2017).

The case of David Reimer (1965–2004) demonstrates the limitations of, and potential damage caused by, the OGP. In 1966 at the age of seven months, John, one of a set of twin boys, suffered serious burning to his penis during surgery. After consulting with John Money, the child's parents consented to their son's reassignment. At 20 months the infant had his penis removed, was renamed Joan and socialised as a female. 'Joan' experienced significant psychological difficulties being raised as a female. At age 14, after discovering the truth of his birth gender, he assumed a male identity, calling himself David, and underwent reversal surgery. There is much interest in this case because having had surgery at such a young age, Reimer had little/no recollection of gender differentiation prior to reassignment, thus potentially promoting understanding as to whether gender is largely the result of biological factors or social learning.

In the 1990s there was growing activism of intersex/DSD people who challenged the need for surgery on infants, highlighting the psycho-social-physical damage caused by medical interventions (Danon and Kramer 2017). These (often irreversible) procedures performed during infancy without the informed consent of the individual can cause infertility, incontinence, loss of sexual sensation, painful scarring and long-term mental health issues (United Nations Free and Equal [UNFE] 2017). Many intersex/DSD adults exposed to such surgery as children discuss the stigma associated with attempts to 'fix' their intersex traits, with some feeling forced into sex and gender categories they do not associate with (UNFE 2017).

According to Danon and Kramer (2017: 1563), parents of intersex/DSD children remain 'problematically positioned between their children's need for care and wellbeing and the social-medical forces that aim to "normalize" them'. Due to fear of stigma, many parents of intersex/DSD infants isolate themselves from family and friends. Often unfamiliar with the complex concept of intersexuality, parents rely on medical professionals to guide them to make the 'best choice' for their child's future physical, psychological and social welfare (Danon and Kramer 2017). However, information provided from a medical perspective typically pathologises intersex/DSD conditions, leading to parents agreeing to early surgical interventions to 'fix' their children's bodies. Without conclusive research for or against early surgery, there is a risk of submitting children to multiple surgeries, genital examinations and treatment, resulting in irreversible damage (Danon and Kramer 2017).

In 2013, Germany was the first country in Europe to pass legislation to allow intersex/DSD infants to be registered as 'intermediate sex', and in 2015 Malta passed a law to prohibit surgery and treatment on the sex characteristics of children without informed consent. In the absence of legislation, the UK Intersex Association (2011) recommends a staged approach to diagnosis, treatment and long-term support, of both the child and their family. There continues to be much controversy regarding the diagnosis and surgical intervention of intersex/DSD infants.

TRANSGENDER CHILDREN

Gender dysphoria describes the discomfort or distress caused by the mismatch between an individual's birth sex/anatomical body and their gender identity. Transsexualism is an extreme form of gender dysphoria and may be so intense that an individual undergoes a transition from male to female (trans woman/girl) or female to male (trans man/boy) in order to be accepted as a member of a sex other than that assigned at birth. Some individuals regard themselves as non-gender or elsewhere on the gender spectrum. Although listed within the *International Classification of Diseases (ICD-10)*, a document published by the WHO containing morbidity and mortality statistics, gender dysphoria and transsexualism are not considered to be forms of mental illness (Ahmad et al. 2013). However, issues stemming from unmanaged dysphoria and the stigma attached to transition may result in psychological problems (Ahmad et al. 2013).

Transition describes the steps (social and/or medical) that an individual takes to live in the gender they associate with. It is reported that approximately 40% of young trans people realised that they were trans when they were aged 11 or under (Metro Youth Chances 2014 cited in BHCCET 2018). With increased social understanding, more children are now socially transitioning while at primary school (Women and Equalities Committee [WEC] 2016). Of the few studies involving trans children in the early years, gender development is identified as being similar to that of gender-typical children. Fast and Olson (2018) note the key difference among transgender children, aged 3–5 years, to be that these children were less likely to believe that their birth gender matched their current gender or that their birth gender was stable across time. The social transition that children make is reversible and usually involves changing names, pronouns, dressing differently and using toilets and changing rooms appropriate to their gender identity. Not all children who wear clothes associated with a gender different to that they were assigned at birth will be questioning their gender identity. For example, a young boy who likes wearing dresses will not necessarily be experiencing gender dysphoria or transsexualism (BHCCET 2018). For many children their gender dysphoria will not continue into adulthood; however, as some young people approach puberty, they may proceed with medical transition to physically alter their body. This is often contentious.

There is no accurate record of numbers of trans children in the UK. However, the Tavistock Centre (Gender Identity Development Service [GIDS] 2020), a specialist service for young people presenting with gender identity difficulties, reported 2,470 referrals for children aged between 3 and 17 in 2018–19. While most referrals involve young people aged between 12 and 16, the number of pre-pubertal children accessing the service is increasing; 128 children aged 3–8 years were referred in 2018–19 (GIDS 2020). Each child has an individual plan, and treatment is only provided after a long period of assessment. Although GIDS does not provide any form of surgical intervention, hormone-blocking medication is available from the onset of puberty (regardless of chronological age) (WEC 2016). This delays puberty, allowing the young person the chance to consider their gender identity issues. Cross-sex hormone therapy is available from the age of 16, but only after 12 months of hormone-blocking treatment. Some of the changes brought about by cross-sex hormone treatment and surgery are difficult to reverse (WEC 2016). Media report high rates of regret among young people who have had irreversible treatments or reconstructive surgeries. However, the World Professional Association for Transgender Health (WPATH) assert that strict protocols are followed, and that only 1–3% of individuals who undergo gender transition which involves irreversible procedures regret doing so (WPATH 2020). They claim that regrets are usually due to the individual's lack of support or acceptance from their family, social groups or work (WPATH 2020). The Gender Recognition Act 2004 (GRA) enables individuals who can evidence a diagnosis of persistent gender dysphoria and who have taken steps to live in the new gender role for the rest of their lives to be formally recognised as their chosen gender. The GRA 2004 does not require that sex change surgery has taken place for a Gender Recognition Certificate to be issued (Knowles 2018b).

 **CASE STUDY**

Transgender children – Henry

Henry is 10. At an early age, he had strong male gender preferences in toys, clothing, sports and books. He refused to wear dresses, would not play with girls and rejected stereotypical 'girl toys'. Initially his parents thought he was a tomboy but, after talking to the early years team at his school, and noticing increasing signs of distress, they realised it was something more. He used to tell them that he felt he was 'born in the wrong body'. After getting some advice, at the age of five, his parents made the decision to have him socially transition and live as a boy. Since then Henry has legally changed his name and his birth certificate and is in the process of getting a hormone-blocker.

Questions

1   Why do you think the number of young children with gender dysphoria who are socially transitioning is increasing?
2   Should pre-pubertal children be prescribed hormone-blockers?
3   What are some of the challenges faced by gender variant and trans children?
4   What concerns might cis children and their parents have about gender variant and transgender children in early years settings and primary schools?
5   How can gender variant and trans children be supported in early years settings and primary schools?

Although many gender variant and trans children face different challenges in their lives, problems are often exacerbated because of the prejudice (transphobia) they encounter. Transphobia is the fear, abuse or dislike of trans people and of those who do not conform to traditional gender norms, and is often linked to sexist and stereotypical ideas (BHCCET 2018). Transgender children may experience negative reactions from family members and peers. Stonewall (2017) identified that 51% of young trans people are bullied at school for being trans, 58% are not allowed to access the toilets they feel comfortable using and 33% are not able to be known by their preferred name at school. Forms of discrimination encountered at school include verbal bullying (61%), physical bullying (13%), death threats (9%) and sexual assault (6%) (Stonewall 2017). The report claims that despite an increasing number of schools supporting trans pupils, there are many that fail to do so. Due to victimisation and rejection, young transgender people are at increased risk of disrupted education, homelessness, high risk behaviours and mental health disorders, including depression, self-harm and suicide (Grossman and D'Augelli 2007; Stonewall 2017; Mangin 2018). According to Stonewall (2017), 45% of young trans people and 35% of young non-binary people have attempted to take their own life.

In 2010, the Trans Media Watch's survey 'How Transgender People Experience the Media' revealed that 70% of transgender respondents thought representation of trans people in the media was negative (Liu 2017). The 2017 survey (Liu 2017) reported an encouraging change, as over 70% of transgender respondents claimed that media representation of trans people in the UK has become more positive. However, Liu warned that prejudice has shifted onto non-binary individuals and the negative media coverage of trans children and their families. Of the 48.5% of transgender respondents considering media portrayal of trans people to be negative, 78% felt angry, 69% felt unhappy, 69% felt bad about society, 49% felt excluded and 41% felt frightened (Liu 2017). The report highlighted the negative impact of the media on trans people's well-being. Mermaids (2019) also asserts that articles based on anecdotal claims made by a minority – using emotive and sensational language such as 'Hundreds of transgender youths who had gender reassignment surgery wish they hadn't ...' (*Daily Mail* 5th October 2019) and 'Girls skipping school to avoid sharing gender neutral toilets with boys as they feel unsafe and ashamed ...' (*The Sun* 6th October 2019) – are misleading and serve to undermine, frighten and demonise transgender children and their families.

 **ACTIVITY**

Media portrayal of gender variant and trans children

Undertake a media search to examine news stories about gender variant and trans children.

Questions

1   What are the main messages being delivered? Are the messages mainly positive or mainly negative?
2   What impact might prejudicial messages have on gender variant and trans children and their families?
3   How can early years practitioners and teachers support these children through policy and the curriculum?

PROMOTING GENDER EQUITY IN SCHOOLS

Schools have a duty to raise awareness of and support children and young people with issues relating to gender and sexuality, and to prevent sexist, transphobic and homophobic bullying, under both the Equality Act 2010 and the national curriculum. The Relationships Education, Relationships and Sex Education (RSE) and Health Education (England) Regulations 2019 (DfE 2019a) make Relationships Education compulsory for all primary school pupils, and RSE compulsory for all pupils receiving secondary education. They also make Health Education compulsory in all schools except independent schools. All schools must have in place a written policy for Relationships Education/RSE which is shared with parents. Parents/carers can request their child to be withdrawn from sex education delivered in primary schools but not Relationships Education or Health Education. With regard to reference to gender, gender identity and sexual orientation the following general guidance, for primary and secondary education, is given (DfE 2019a: 14–15):

31. Schools should be alive to issues such as everyday sexism, misogyny, homophobia and gender stereotypes and take positive action to build a culture

where these are not tolerated, and any occurrences are identified and tackled. Staff have an important role to play in modelling positive behaviours …

36. In teaching Relationships Education and RSE, all pupils should understand the importance of equality and respect. Schools must ensure that they comply with the relevant provisions of the Equality Act 2010, under which sexual orientation and gender reassignment are amongst the protected characteristics.

37. Schools should ensure that all of teaching is sensitive and age appropriate in approach and content. At the point at which schools consider it appropriate to teach pupils about LGBT, they should ensure that this content is fully integrated into their programmes of study for this area of the curriculum rather than delivered as a stand-alone unit or lesson. … Schools are free to determine how they do this, and we expect all pupils to have been taught LGBT content at a timely point as part of this area of the curriculum.

Under the theme 'respectful relationships', primary and secondary pupils learn about the impact of bullying and the consequence of detrimental stereotypes. Additionally, secondary pupils should examine how 'stereotypes based on sex, gender, race, religion, sexual orientation or disability can cause damage (e.g. how they might normalise non-consensual behaviour or encourage prejudice)' (DfE 2019a: 28). Although there is no direct mention of these concepts within the themes listed for primary education, the guidelines suggest that LGBT parents could be one of the diverse family forms that children are introduced to. Schools are asked to pay careful consideration to the religious background of pupils when planning teaching, to ensure that topics are appropriately handled (DfE 2019a). However, the looseness of terminology within the guidelines should be noted, as the phrases 'Schools are free to determine how they do this' and 'we expect all pupils to have been taught LGBT content at a timely point' create a gloss that can have multiple interpretations (Morgan and Taylor 2019), which might mean that LGBTQIA+ issues go unaddressed.

Tackling gender identity and sexuality with children are controversial topics and, because of potential conflict, there is often a reluctance to approach them (Leadley-Meade 2018). Morgan and Taylor (2019) discuss how attempts to cover LGBTQIA+ issues within primary schools have resulted in a backlash of criticism. In 2016, the press presented negative coverage of a transgender equalities initiative that was to take place in a primary school in East Sussex. Sensationalist headlines from the period include 'Parents pull children out of primary school in outrage at planned "transgender day" for children as young as FOUR' (*Daily Mail* 16th March 2016). Then in 2019, school gate protests were heavily televised, with parent activists objecting to the delivery of the 'No Outsiders' programme, concerned that it conflicted with their religious beliefs (Haynes 2019). The programme, created by Andrew Moffat, aims to teach young children about all characteristics protected by the Equality Act 2010, including issues around gender stereotyping and LGBTQIA + families, using age-appropriate resources.

ACTIVITY

Evaluating resources

1   Undertake a web search on books available for young children involving LGBTQIA+ characters and same-sex parent families.
2   Access resources available for young children from Stonewall, Mermaids or the 'No Outsiders' programme.

What messages are contained within these resources? What is the value of using these resources with young children? What concerns might there be about using them?

The resistance to exposing children to gender variant and transgender education is framed by conceptions of childhood 'innocence' and the protection of a 'natural' state of cisgenderedness (Morgan and Taylor 2019). In the case of sex education, there is a discourse around the need to 'protect' children from adult information. Morgan and Taylor (2019) explain that while transgender is not linked to any sexual orientation, it creates ideas of the sexed body and is often associated with queer sexual perversions. Coverage of transgender issues for children may be viewed as 'ridiculous' owing to the presumption that pre-pubertal children are too young to identify as trans and 'dangerous' because it has the potential to corrupt children's minds or wrongly pigeon-hole them as trans (Morgan and Taylor 2019).

Many gender variant and transgender children do not feel included in the typical 'male'/'female' and heterosexual normativity of their classrooms and frequently encounter prejudice (Mangin 2018). Addressing gender equality, gender variance and trans issues via a whole school approach, in line with the Equality Act 2010 and Relationships Education, will help children (or their family members) whose gender expression and sexual orientation are diverse to feel acknowledged and safe in their social and learning spaces. Furthermore, laying the foundations of positive, age-appropriate understanding in the early years will ensure that gender variant children have the vocabulary to voice their needs, feelings and identities. Table 7.1 presents an overview of a whole school approach to these issues.

Table 7.1 A whole setting approach to gender equity and trans inclusion

Policy	A clear gender equity and transgender policy should sit within the general equality and inclusion framework. Reference should be made to intersectional issues, for example, the needs of Black and ethnic minority children and young people or those with SEND who are also transgender. Effective anti-bullying and equality policies are required which record and challenge all forms of prejudicial incidents.
Senior staff	Supportive head teachers/managers are central to creating an inclusive culture. Head teachers can establish links with specialist organisations which will facilitate opportunities for staff, pupils and parents to learn about gender variant and transgender children. Difficult decisions may have to be made to ensure that the rights of gender variant children are met without compromising the rights of other children.
Training	Practitioners need to be provided with equality training which will develop confidence in understanding gender and trans presentation and terminology. Practitioners can create gender-inclusive cultures by changing their language, using non-gendered terms and non-gendered ways to manage the classroom, for example forming groups in accord with children's favourite foods.
Curriculum	Resources, and teaching and learning approaches, should be closely monitored to ensure inclusive practice that challenges gender stereotypes, sexism and transphobia. As well as providing age-appropriate resources through continuous provision, practitioners should design specific activities which go beyond cisgender identities and binary categories, and which expand children's critical thinking. Parents/carers should be kept informed of the work that children will be covering.
Collaboration	Schools and early years settings are encouraged to support gender variant and trans children and their families. Positive relationships include listening and responding to individual needs and preferences and sign-posting children and families to specialist agencies for guidance. Confidential information must not be shared with parents/carers without the child's permission unless there are safeguarding reasons for doing so.

(Adapted from BHCCET 2018; Mangin 2018)

 **REFLECTION**

Too much, too soon?

Now that you have come to the end of the chapter, do you think young children should learn about gender stereotypes, gender identity and age-appropriate messages regarding sexuality? Please justify your answers.

KEY POINTS

- Gender-related binaries, stereotypes and power relations are at the core of societal structures, marginalising some individuals, while empowering others.
- Early years settings and schools are not gender-neutral places; gender atypical behaviour is often strictly regulated and non-conforming individuals risk prejudice.

- There is a long-contested debate as to how children develop gender and sexual identities, attitudes and behaviours, based on biological determinist, social constructivist and poststructuralist explanations.
- Children's play is a critical site for learning natal gender and sexual construction.
- Intersex, gender variant and trans children show the complexity and fluidity of gender identity.
- Early years settings and schools have a legal duty under equality legislation and the national curriculum to promote awareness of gender and sexuality and to prevent sexist, transphobic and homophobic bullying. However, addressing these topics with children is often contentious.

FURTHER READING

Brighton and Hove City Council Education Team (2018) *Trans Inclusion Schools Toolkit.* Available at: https://mermaidsuk.org.uk

Provides information and guidance to schools on how to effectively support trans and gender-questioning pupils and prevent transphobia.

Griffin, H. (2018) *Gender Equality in Primary Schools: A Guide for Teachers.* London: Jessica Kingsley.

Comprehensive text for primary school teachers providing guidance on how to challenge gender stereotypes and implement gender equality in all areas of school life.

Knowles, G. (2018) Gender and inclusion. In Knowles, G. (ed.) *Supporting Inclusive Practice and Ensuring Opportunity is Equal for All.* Third edition. pp. 22–36. Abingdon: Routledge.

Provides a detailed account of the development of gender roles, identity and transgender children, and children's experiences of gender in educational settings.

USEFUL WEBSITES

Gender Identity Development Service: http://gids.nhs.uk
Gendered Intelligence: www.genderedintelligence.co.uk
Mermaids: https://mermaidsuk.org.uk
Stonewall: www.stonewall.org.uk

8

RELIGION, ANTISEMITISM AND ISLAMOPHOBIA

CONTENTS

CHAPTER OVERVIEW

It is not the intention of this chapter to outline characteristics of individual world faiths; rather it will explore the role of religion along with the complexities, tensions and prejudice that may arise within early settings, schools and society as a result of religious faith, with specific consideration given to Antisemitism and Islamophobia.

This chapter considers:

1   Reasons why practitioners should understand the importance of religion in some people's lives and why they should be aware of their own values and beliefs.
2   Single-faith schools.
3   The impact of Antisemitism on children, families and communities.
4   The impact of Islamophobia on children, families and communities.
5   How religion may clash with aspects of social justice for children, women and LGBTQIA+ people.
6   Legislation, policy and statutory duties of schools and early years settings regarding religious extremism and religious prejudice.

UNDERSTANDING THE IMPORTANCE OF RELIGIOUS FAITH
Examining values and beliefs

All individuals bring cultural (and for some religious) norms and practices to early years settings and classrooms, which affect their social interactions. Sometimes the prejudices people carry are so deep they are subconscious (unconscious bias). It is important that practitioners reflect on their own value and knowledge base before attempting to promote understanding of, or deal with conflict associated with, religious beliefs and differences. In order to uncover any biases, practitioners should consider:

- What value judgements do I bring to the discussion?
- How do I know what I know? Is this fair/balanced?
- What impact might my values have on the children and families in my care?

ACTIVITY

The role and function of religious faith

1   Why should early years practitioners and teachers have an understanding of the religious backgrounds of the children and families in their settings?
2   What does following a religious faith mean to, or provide, some individuals?

Role of religion

Most societies contain elements of religious faith. Predominant religion/s, past or present, are often central to the way in which a society is structured and operates. Religious faith remains of significant importance to many individuals worldwide. According to Ipsos MORI (2011), which conducted research across 24 countries, 73% of people (aged 35 or under) said religion was important to their lives. However, the survey revealed marked differences across the world, with 94% of those with a religion in primarily Muslim countries saying it was important in their lives compared to 66% in Christian majority countries. While having a religion is core to some people's identity and everyday life, holding a secular or atheistic approach can be equally as important to others.

Having a religious faith may fulfil various functions: helping to explain the meaning of and purpose for daily life, providing guidance and rules relating to personal choices and daily living (diet, dress, family life, parenting), bringing communities together and fostering a positive self-identity. Appreciating the role that religion may play in some people's lives can help practitioners to meet the needs of children and families, support children to develop a positive identity, understand reasons behind attitudes and behaviours, avoid offending children and families, meet government and institutional obligations, and promote inclusive school and early years settings and community cohesion.

ACTIVITY

Whose religion? Examining similarities

Read the following statements and decide which of the three Abrahamic religions (Judaism, Christianity and Islam) the statement is applicable to. It may be applicable to one, two or all three religions. The answers are given at the end of the chapter (p. 157).

1   Has over 1 billion followers.
2   States that Jesus was a prophet.
3   Has rules about how animals should be slaughtered.

4   Worships only one God.
5   Prays during worship.
6   Jerusalem is a holy place.
7   Holy book includes the ten commandments.
8   Some branches wear head coverings.
9   Has a sacred language.
10 Holy day is a Sunday.
11 Believes in contributing to the common good.
12 Holy book is the Tanakh (including the Torah).
13 Has five pillars of faith.
14 Believes in loving one's neighbour and acceptance of others.
15 Advocates peace.

(Adapted from EqualiTeach 2018)

When teaching children about diversity it is important to emphasise the similarities as well as the differences that exist between themselves and others, and among families, communities and cultures. Practitioners should therefore be aware of the similarities between major world faiths as well as the diversity that exists within an individual faith. For instance, there are many commonalities between Christianity, Islam and Judaism. However, there is no complete agreement on interpretations of holy books, key beliefs or daily routines within individual faiths, as followers have different interpretations and levels of religious adherence.

FAITH SCHOOLS

Historically, faith and education have been closely linked. The Roman Catholic Church was the first provider of schools, with schools emerging from the late sixth century. After the Reformation, the Church of England began to provide its own schools (Religion Media Centre [RMC] 2018). Education remained closely linked to religious institutions until the nineteenth century, when reforms introduced widespread state-funded schools. Under the Education Act of 1944, half of all Church of England schools became 'voluntary controlled' and were state-funded; the state exercised control over the curriculum, the appointment of teachers and governors, and admissions. A third of Anglican schools and most Roman Catholic schools became 'voluntary aided', which meant that although part of the state system, they retained greater control (RMC 2018).

As Britain became more ethnically diverse, minority faiths started to form their own schools. The first state-funded Islamic school opened in 1998, the first Sikh school in

1999 and the first Hindu school in 2008 (RMC 2018). Faith schools have to teach the national curriculum but have autonomy regarding religious studies. Faith academies, however, do not have to teach the national curriculum. In 2018, there were more than 280 independent faith schools; 20% of these were considered illegal as they were not registered with the Department for Education, which is a legal requirement (RMC 2018).

Supporters of faith schools defend the right to teach children within an environment that reflects a particular religious ethos. Supporters of state-funded faith schools argue they are high achieving schools which foster respect, discipline and care for others. They claim that the obligation to adhere to the national curriculum and to present a range of views regarding moral and social issues prevents extremism or indoctrination (RMC 2018). However, critics argue that faith schools foster religious, ethnic and socio-economic segregation, hindering community cohesion. There are concerns that some faith schools promote an understanding of issues that is at odds with mainstream British values (abortion, homosexuality, the family, evolution, women's rights) (RMC 2018). Furthermore, some illegal faith schools have been found to operate from unsatisfactory premises, staffed by unqualified teachers and endorsing a hard-line perspective of the Jewish, Christian or Muslim faith (RMC 2018).

EXPLORING ANTISEMITISM

Judaism has existed as a faith for over 3,500 years and is thought to be the first monotheistic religion (followers believe in one God only). Judaism started in what is now referred to as the Middle East. Jewish populations are distributed around the world but many regard Israel as their homeland. The Jewish State of Israel was founded in 1948 within the larger area of what was previously known as Palestine. The political decision to create the Jewish State of Israel remains controversial and contributes to the hostility experienced by Jewish people.

Jews, who first arrived in the British Isles in Roman times, have long been considered to be well integrated into UK society, with the Jewish community frequently cited by the government as the benchmark of successful minority integration (Community Security Trust [CST] 2018). Jewish people can expect to lead a full life in the UK, following their religious, cultural, educational and political affiliations and activities (CST 2018); however, they have historically suffered, and continue to encounter persecution and prejudice throughout the UK, Europe and globally.

 **ACTIVITY**

Media coverage

Undertake a media search to examine news items presented about Jewish people. What forms of prejudice are reported? Do the news items contain misconceptions or stereotypical thinking? What impact might such prejudices have for Jewish children and their families today?

Throughout history, anti-Jewish attitudes have taken many manifestations, including religious, nationalist, economic and racial-biological. Jewish people have been held accountable for many events, for example, the development of liberalism, democracy, communism and capitalism, and for inciting various revolutions and wars (CST 2018). During the Second World War, 6 million Jewish people were murdered by the Nazis; the near-destruction of European Jews in the Holocaust has generally rendered open prejudice against Jewish people taboo in public life. Discrimination towards Jewish people is defined as 'Antisemitism'.

The word 'Antisemitism' emerged in the late nineteenth century to describe pseudo-scientific racial discrimination against Jewish people. Now, it describes all forms of discrimination, prejudice or hostility towards Jews (CST 2018). Antisemitic incidents can take several forms, including violent physical attacks on Jewish people or their property, verbal or written abuse, hate mail, Antisemitic leaflets and posters, abuse on social media and negative political discourse. Several definitions of Antisemitism have been created by international bodies to formally recognise it as a form of racism. However, in 2016 the UK Government formally adopted (although not legally binding) the International Holocaust Remembrance Alliance's (IHRA) definition:

> Antisemitism is a certain perception of Jews, which may be expressed as hatred toward Jews. Rhetorical and physical manifestations of Antisemitism are directed toward Jewish or non-Jewish individuals and/or their property, towards Jewish community institutions and religious facilities. (CST 2020)

 **ACTIVITY**

Antisemitism – reflecting upon the atrocities of the Holocaust

Eva Kor, a Jewish survivor of the Holocaust, offers an account of her time in Auschwitz.

Watch the following video clip and consider:

www.bbc.co.uk/ideas/videos/the-holocaust-twin-who-forgave-the-nazis/p0837wjy

1   The immediate and long-term impact of the atrocities on Eva and her sister.
2   How you could start to address the atrocities and racial prejudice of the Holocaust with young children in a sensitive and age-appropriate way.

The strong association of Antisemitism with the Holocaust can lead to the mistaken assumption that Antisemitism is an exclusively far-right, genocidal phenomenon that ended after the Second World War. However, there is widespread concern about increasing Antisemitic hate crimes, across Europe and globally. It has been seen in recent times in the context of terrorist violence that has included targeting of Jewish people and institutions, with fatal attacks having occurred in France (Toulouse and Montauban, 2012, and Porte de Vincennes, 2015), Belgium (Brussels, 2014) and Denmark (Copenhagen, 2015). Antisemitism is identified as being particularly problematic in France, with synagogues and Jewish schools requiring increased security protection (BBC 2018). Over the last few years, France has been subject to a string of Antisemitic incidents and hostility, including the murder of Jewish people, the desecration of Jewish cemeteries, vandalism of Jewish buildings or institutions and malicious commentary on the internet and media. In 2019, more than 100 graves at a Jewish cemetery in the town of Westhoffen, near Strasbourg, were defaced with Nazi swastikas and the number 14 (reference to a 14-word white supremacist slogan) (BBC 2019).

In 2018, the European Union Agency for Fundamental Rights (FRA) published a report based on a survey of 16,395 self-identified Jewish people (aged 16 or over) in 12 EU member states. These member states – Austria, Belgium, Denmark, France, Germany, Hungary, Italy, the Netherlands, Poland, Spain, Sweden and the United Kingdom – are home to over 96% of the EU's Jewish population. Overall, 89% of the Jewish respondents stated that Antisemitism in the country where they live is increasing. More than 85% considered it to be a 'serious' issue; 28% had experienced harassment for being Jewish; 2% had been physically attacked; and 34% had avoided Jewish events because of safety fears. Although Antisemitic content on the internet is the most acute form of Antisemitism (89%), comments are also made in person (18%) or through offensive gestures or inappropriate staring (16%). The report claims that Antisemitic abuse has become so common that 79% of people do not report even the most serious incident to the police or other organisation: 48% believed nothing would change as a result; 43% did not consider the incident to be serious enough; and 22% felt reporting would be inconvenient or cause too much trouble. When asked to describe the perpetrator of the most serious Antisemitic incident experienced, 31% identified the perpetrator as someone they do not know, 30% as someone with Muslim extremist views and 21% as someone with right-wing political views (FRA 2018).

Antisemitism is a growing concern within the UK. The FRA (2018) assert that 75% of British Jews believe Antisemitism to be a 'big problem' in the UK, compared to 48% in the 2012 survey. These fears seem to be justified, as CST recorded 1,805 Antisemitic incidents in 2019 (more than 100 in every month), the highest total ever recorded in the UK (CST 2020); 2019 is the fourth consecutive year that the annual total has increased. Research undertaken by the Pew Research Center (2018) reveals that 23% of British people would not accept a Jewish person in their family and two-thirds of people said they knew 'very little' or 'nothing at all' about Judaism. Although Antisemitism in online social media is the largest single contributor, swastikas and anti-Jewish slogans have been sprayed on Jewish buildings, and Jewish people have been physically assaulted (RMC 2020). The peak in incidents correlate with periods when discourse around Jews and Antisemitism is prominent in the media and politics. In June 2016, the referendum vote to leave the EU strengthened nationalist-nativist narratives that fed hostility against all minority groups. It led to a 29% increase in reported hate crime, with religiously aggravated hate crime reaching 35% – Muslims followed by Jews experienced the sharpest increase (Kallis 2018). In 2018, Antisemitism became a regular feature in UK media, partly due to the allegations of its existence within the Labour Party, and incidents emerging in football (RMC 2020). In 2020, following an investigation into antisemitism by the Equality and Human Rights Commission, the Labour Party was found to have breached the Equality Act 2010 due to serious failings of its leadership to address antisemitism and for the inadequate handling of related complaints (EHRC 2020b).

Children and schools

 **CASE STUDY**

Supporting Jewish children in mainstream education

David and his family are Orthodox Jews. He has recently started at your setting. Some of the other children have begun to single David out and exclude him from friendship groups.

Working with a small group of peers, decide whether David is in either the early years or Key Stage 2 (7–11 years) and:

1   Undertake some research to determine how you would accommodate him with regard to daily routines (food, clothes, personal health care, prayer) and understand some of the key festivals that he and his family are likely to celebrate.
2   Consider the barriers he might face being one of only a few minority ethnic/religious pupils in a mainstream, predominantly secular, early years setting.

There is little published research on how modern forms of Antisemitism affect children and young people, and even less that is focused on teaching and addressing Antisemitism in the classroom (Weller and Foster 2019). Although the Holocaust is a compulsory part of the history curriculum in British secondary schools, there are current calls for the government to consider how issues associated with Antisemitism can be more fully addressed within schools (Ferrari 2020). With increased media coverage and the risk of stereotypical negativity entering into early years settings and primary classrooms, it is important that practitioners play a part in promoting awareness among children of the potential impact of Antisemitism. The UK charity Community Security Trust, which represents the Jewish community on matters of Antisemitism, terrorism and policing, also provides security advice and training for Jewish schools and synagogues. This charity could further support the government to generate age-appropriate materials to promote an understanding of contemporary forms of Antisemitism and the impact of these, and to raise tolerance among non-Jewish communities.

EXPLORING ISLAMOPHOBIA

Islam developed as a world faith over 1,400 years ago. In 2015, the Islamic faith was believed to have 1.8 billion adherents, making up approximately 24% of the world population (Pew Research Center 2017). Followers of Islam are known as Muslims. It is important that Muslims are not viewed as one homogeneous group, as followers of Islam have diverse nationalities, cultures, social class backgrounds, political outlooks and levels of religious observance.

 **ACTIVITY**

What do you know?

Working in a small group, consider and discuss the following questions:

1   What is Islamophobia? What does it look like?
2   Where does Islamophobia stem from?
3   Who does Islamophobia affect?

Islamophobia is a term used to describe a person or society's fear of Islam and/or Muslims, or those who are perceived to be Muslim. The Runnymede Trust's original definition, in 1997, states that the term involves: (1) unfounded hostility towards Islam; (2) practical consequences of such hostility in unfair discrimination against Muslim individuals and communities; (3) exclusion of Muslims from mainstream political and social affairs (Elahi and Khan 2017). Although Elahi and Khan (2017) recommend that 'anti-Muslim racism' be used, the term 'Islamophobia' will be used throughout this chapter as it is more common.

Manifestations of Islamophobia take many forms – at both an institutional and individual level – including: (1) writing and speaking about Muslims as though all Muslims are the same, culturally and morally inferior, sympathetic towards terrorism and/or have nothing in common with non-Muslims; (2) physical and verbal attacks and damage to property; (3) discrimination in terms of employment, housing, health care, the criminal justice system and access to social and cultural spaces, goods and services; (4) the absence of Muslim voices in politics, journalism and culture (Equal-iTeach 2018).

Ever since the 9/11 attack on the World Trade Center in New York (11 September 2001), by an Islamic extremist group, the Muslim community has been under increased scrutiny. According to the Home Office, for the year 2018–19, 47% of all religious hate crimes in the UK, both off- and online, targeted Muslims (RMC 2020). The number of anti-Muslim incidents spikes sharply following terrorist attacks.

 **ACTIVITY**

Media coverage

Undertake a media search to examine news items presented about Islam and Muslim people. What forms of prejudice are reported? Do the news items contain misconceptions or stereotypical thinking? What impact might such prejudices have for Muslim children and their families?

Awan and Zempi (2017) discuss the damaging impact that Islamophobia has on wider society. They assert that Islamophobia isolates Muslims, promoting the notion of 'parallel lives' and self-enclosed communities. The separation of communities means that Muslims and non-Muslims have no or limited experience of each other's daily existence and therefore little opportunity for the emergence of shared values. They claim that the separation of communities on the basis of Islamophobia contributes to the fear, resentment and mistrust of the 'Muslim Other' (Awan and Zempi 2017).

Children and schools

Every time Islamic extremists have carried out a terror attack anywhere in the world, there has been negative media reaction and a rise in Islamophobia (Ahmed 2016). There is a danger that children will assume that all Muslims are terrorists. Due to the adverse, sensationalist media coverage, over 30% of young people believe Muslims are 'taking over England' (Taylor 2015). The prejudiced messages that children see on the television or social media platforms, or hear from their parents, only spur separation and discord (Ahmed 2016). According to Tell MAMA (2017), 11% of Islamophobic incidents happen in educational institutions, with many young Muslims saying abuse is so commonplace it is normalised.

 **CASE STUDY**

Supporting Muslim children in mainstream education

Asma is a practising Muslim, of Pakistani heritage. She has recently started in your class and has expressed a desire to wear a hijab. Some of the other children in the class have started to single her out and are asking many questions.

Working with a small group of peers, decide whether Asma is in either the early years or Key Stage 2 (7–11 years) and:

1   Undertake some research to determine how you would accommodate her with regard to daily routines (food, clothes, personal health care, prayer), and understand some of the key festivals that she and her family are likely to celebrate.
2   Consider the barriers she might face being one of only a few minority ethnic/ religious pupils in a mainstream, primary school that has predominantly white British pupils on roll.

Anti-Muslim racist incidents in schools include physical attacks, threats, destruction of property, verbal abuse, jokes about religious faith, spreading rumours, exclusion and victimisation for wearing a hijab (EqualiTeach 2018). Alongside any physical harm caused, the emotional effects of race and faith-based hate crime include anxiety, isolation, depression, post-traumatic stress, low self-esteem, suicide and poor sense of identity (Durrani et al. 2018; Younus and Mian 2018).

Although Childline has reported a sharp increase in race- and faith-based bullying there is believed to be underreporting of anti-Muslim racism. Some young people do not know how to report hate crimes, while others may be fearful of making the situation worse, or believe that no action will be taken (EqualiTeach 2018). Concerns about racism, together with the underachievement of Muslims learners in mainstream education, have led to many parents either opting for home-schooling (Myers and Bhopal 2017) or enrolling their children in single-faith Islamic schools (Shah 2011). The following factors have been identified as causing some young Muslims to become disengaged from mainstream education: low teacher expectations, a lack of Muslim identity in the ethos of the school and curriculum, restrictions regarding school uniform, racism and anti-Muslim culture (Inman et al. 2014; Myers and Bhopal 2017; Kallis 2018; Shah 2018). Although normally worn around puberty, the number of younger girls wearing the hijab in primary schools is increasing, which often generates racist remarks (Burrows 2017). The prejudice encountered can make it difficult for Muslim children and their families to feel accepted within the non-Muslim communities to which they belong.

Terrorism and the media

Is the word 'terrorism' used more freely when the perpetrator is a Muslim? Religious differences, leading to extremism, have occurred for centuries and exist on the margins of all religions and nationalities. Perpetrators of terrorist attacks, who maintain that they are acting on behalf of a religion or culture, cannot assert they have the backing of the community or faith they represent (EqualiTeach 2018). Unfortunately, media coverage and public discourse have become so preoccupied with affiliating extremism and terrorism to the Muslim population, that it has stigmatised the Muslim identity. To prevent a distorted view of terrorism, it is important that children and young people are made aware of the many acts of terror that have been carried out by individuals and groups of varying religions and nationalities. The Holocaust, one of the most widely known acts of extremism, has already been considered. But there are other examples:

- Between the 1970s and 1990s the Irish Republican Army (IRA), a largely Catholic group who wanted Northern Ireland to join with Ireland and be separate from the UK, carried out a series of killings across Britain and Northern Ireland. Loyalist groups, who were largely Protestant and wanted Northern Ireland to remain part of the UK, reacted by killing Catholics (EqualiTeach 2018).
- In 2011, far-right extremist Anders Breivik killed eight people by detonating a car bomb and shot dead 69 people in Norway (mainly teenagers). Breivik states that his main motive for the attacks was to publicise his manifesto which calls for the deportation of all Muslims from Europe.
- In 2016, Thomas Mair murdered MP Jo Cox. Mair believed that the existence of white people was being threatened. He saw Jo Cox as the enemy as she wanted the UK to remain in Europe and was a defender of immigration. When police searched his house, they found far-right material, including books on the Nazis and white supremacism (EqualiTeach 2018).

- In 2017, radical Islamist Salman Ramadan Abedi detonated a homemade bomb as people were leaving the Manchester Arena following a concert. He killed 22 people and injured 139, more than half of them children and young people.

The way in which terror attacks are reported by the media is one of the main catalysts for Islamophobia. When Islamic terrorist attacks occur, the media often lead with the religion of the attacker, placing the blame upon the religion, rather than the individual who carried out the attack (Driggs 2018). Hamid (2017) claims that anti-Muslim scare stories presented in the media are now so normalised that it is difficult to distinguish between what is true and what is not. Rarely do media stories offer a distinction between extremists and ordinary Muslims and provide accurate knowledge about the faith. Instead, Muslim people are frequently 'othered' and represented as un-British in the UK media (Saeed 2007). However, there are many Muslims who relate more to their British identity than their Islamic faith identity but who still encounter Islamophobia (Platt 2014). Islamophobia experienced by Muslims often serves to strengthen bonds within Muslim communities, reinforcing their faith identity and leading to feelings of alienation, anger and, in extreme cases, radicalisation (Abbas 2019).

RELIGION AND SOCIAL JUSTICE FOR CHILDREN, WOMEN AND LGBTQIA+

While religion can offer protection and guidance, certain practices linked to religious faith or culture may infringe on the rights of children, women and LGBTQIA+ people, putting them at risk of social injustice or harm. Before proceeding with this section it is essential that general conclusions should be tempered, as within any one religion there typically exist various denominations, movements or traditions, with their own distinct institutions, cultures and teachings (Fortune and Enger 2005). Not recognising this would lead to crude stereotypes regarding religious affiliation and the aforementioned social groups.

Children and women

Gender inequality exists globally, with varied effects in different regions. These differences are a result of cultural legacies, historical development, geographic location and the religious norms which predominate in society. The status of women in society is an outcome of the interpretation of religious texts and of the cultural and institutional structure of religious communities (Klingorová and Havlíček 2015). Thus, the influence individual religions have on the status of women is extremely differentiated.

While there have been some positive changes towards equality, most religions today maintain male social dominance within societal structures. Feminists argue that religion oppresses women in many ways; for example: sacred texts with predominantly male gods and prophets, written and interpreted by men; rules in places of worship which segregate women or prevent them from participating fully; religious laws and customs which give women fewer rights than men and regulate women's domestic role; and religious organisations which prevent women from being in positions of leadership. In some countries, women cannot travel without having written permission from a male relative, are not protected by legislation against violence, and are at risk of prosecution or being ostracised if they become pregnant outside of marriage.

Oppressive or harmful practices, embedded in communities' social norms, are often justified on the grounds of religion, culture or tradition (UNICEF 2010). Although children of all religions and cultures may experience violence, girls are more exposed to gender-based violence, including female genital mutilation, female infanticide, breast ironing (flattening of pubescent girls' breasts), child marriage and 'honour'-related violence (UNICEF 2010).

 **ACTIVITY**

Religious faith and safeguarding

Watch the NSPCC video 'Inter-faith overview of safeguarding children'.

https://www.youtube.com/watch?time_continue=2&v=FPSKnDyxbzE&feature=emb_title

What key messages and measures is the NSPCC attempting to promote among faith leaders?

Religious leaders are regarded as being fundamental in combating violence against women and children. In 2006, many religious leaders from around the world adopted the 'Multi-Religious Commitment to Confront Violence against Children' (Kyoto Declaration). The Declaration outlines ways religious communities can work to eliminate violence against children (UNICEF 2010). Religious leaders are asked to consider: what forms of violence are embedded in religious or cultural traditions; what the country's laws are in relation to violence against children; and what has to be done to protect children from violence within the community and at local and national levels.

There is significant discourse regarding the oppression and treatment of Muslim women. Debates about the veil, gender violence and terrorism contribute to stereotypes of Muslim women as oppressed, passive victims, symbolic of Muslim communities' perceived failure to integrate, and as potential extremists (Rashid 2017).

| Hijab | Niqab | Burqa |

Figure 8.1 The hijab, niqab and burqa

Source: Flickr
Hijab: Photo by feriansyah, reproduced under CC BY 2.0 licence. https://www.flickr.com/photos/feri_jagoan/10719143526/
Niqab: Photo by POTIER Jean-Louis, reproduced under CC BY-ND 2.0 licence. https://www.flickr.com/photos/jeanlouispotier/5963722126/
Burqa: Photo by Ninara, reproduced under CC BY 2.0 licence. https://www.flickr.com/photos/ninara/9504181554/

The veil is particularly regarded as problematic, whether it is the suggestion that wearing the niqab (full face veil) should be banned, or whether girls in primary schools should be allowed to wear a hijab (headscarf) (EqualiTeach 2018) (see Figure 8.1). Critics argue that wearing these garments raises security concerns, indicates women's oppression and inferior position in Islam, and demonstrates a lack of integration into British society (Rashid 2017; EqualiTeach 2018). This denies British Muslim women as having any agency. Rather than women and girls being forced to wear them by male family members, Burchardt and Griera (2019) suggest that it may be an individual choice made by the female, dependent on their interpretation of the Quran. Although there may be valid reasons about whether the niqab or burqa should be worn in certain professions (doctors, nursery nurses) or contexts (schools, airports), media portrayal and public debates continue to make Muslim women targets of discrimination (Rashid 2017).

 **ACTIVITY**

Debating religious headwear/clothing

Watch the following YouTube clip and draw upon the article below to generate a debate 'for' and 'against' Muslim women wearing the hijab, niqab or burqa.

www.youtube.com/watch?v=eXzUuKdfnRE

www.glamourmagazine.co.uk/article/women-reveal-why-they-choose-to-wear-a-hijab

While it is essential to address the gendered violence encountered by females, Rashid (2017) argues that media attention given to violence, such as 'honour' killings, has exacerbated Islamophobia. Such crimes are regularly sensationalised, racialised and portrayed as the exclusive practice of Muslims. Rashid (2017) asserts that such crimes are seen as distinct from a spectrum of gender violence committed across wider society, such as domestic violence or child abuse, and that the focus should be rather on the relationship between gendered violence and toxic masculinity, where discussions involve men in general not just Muslim men. Where patriarchy becomes exclusive to Muslim men, it risks reinforcing anti-Muslim stereotypes, which then adversely affect Muslim women (Rashid 2017). Rashid advises that simplistic generalisations should be avoided; voices of women should be centred; and women of faith be viewed as actors in wider society, not just as members of their religious community. Discourse which is restricted to women only in terms of oppression ignores the diversity among women, removes agency from women and perpetuates harmful stereotypes (EqualiTeach 2018).

Lesbian, gay, bisexual, transgender, queer, intersex and asexual (LGBTQIA+)

The relationship between religion and sexual orientation ('homosexuality' will be used as the term to represent all non-heterosexual orientations) is complex, has fluctuated throughout time and differs across individual religions. For centuries, many religions have controlled sexual behaviour through the principle of a legal, sacred marriage service that sanctifies and moralises the complementary roles of men and women. Consequently, theologians began to conceptualise homosexuality as an inversion of natural God-given laws (Forrest 2018).

LGBTQIA+ people of faith often face a double challenge of discrimination – anti-LGBTQIA+ abuse from within the religious group as well as race/religious prejudice from within the LGBTQIA+ community. Stonewall (2018) reports how 51% of Black, Asian and minority ethnic (BAME) LGBT people and 12% of LGBT people of faith have experienced discrimination from others in their local LGBT community. With only 39% believing their faith group to be welcoming of LGB people (and 25% of trans people), many BAME LGBT people, and those of faith, remain closed about their sexual orientation (Stonewall 2018).

Many religious institutions are beginning to re-examine their stance on homosexuality in order to be more inclusive. As children within some religious communities have never had an opportunity to explore aspects of LGBT, they may not realise that it can be possible to both be gay and follow a religion (Stonewall 2019a). Stonewall (2019b) asserts that LGBT people are often underrepresented or misrepresented in mainstream media, with little attention given to the divide between faith and LGBT communities.

LEGISLATION AND EDUCATION POLICY

The Equality Act 2010

As discussed in Chapter 1, this Act places a duty on early years settings and schools to prevent direct and indirect discrimination, harassment and victimisation on the grounds of nine protected characteristics, which include race and religion or belief. The Act requires organisations to contribute to the advancement of equality and good relations, for equality to be reflected in the design of policies and the delivery of services, and for policies to be kept under review (Legislation.gov.uk 2010).

Prevent Duty

From 2015 all schools and registered childcare providers are subject to a duty under the Counter-Terrorism and Security Act 2015 (Section 26), to demonstrate due regard for the need to prevent people from being drawn into terrorism (Department for Education [DfE] 2015).

The Prevent Duty requires teachers, doctors, faith leaders and others to refer any suspicions about people to a Prevent body. Where this body considers that action is required, an individual can be placed on the government's Channel Programme. This is a support plan which may include mentoring.

Critics argue that Prevent disproportionately targets Muslim communities, which contributes to 'demonising' Muslims, making some individuals feel isolated and thus open to radicalisation (BBC 2017). Myers and Bhopal (2017) argue that Prevent may lead to assumptions that Muslim children who attend a single-faith Islamic school or are home educated are at risk of being radicalised. Statistics released by the Home Office (2019a) show that 66% of individuals referred to the Channel Programme were aged 20 years or under and 88% were male, with extremist comments being made in class, within coursework or material shared on social media. Of the 394 individuals who received Channel support in 2017/18, 45% were related to Islamist extremism and 44% to right-wing extremism (Home Office 2019a).

Spiritual, Moral, Social and Cultural Development and Fundamental British Values

The Education Act 2002 requires schools to promote the spiritual, moral, social and cultural development of their pupils. Since 2014, as part of this, maintained schools, academies and independent schools are required to promote fundamental British values of democracy, the rule of law, individual liberty, and mutual respect for and tolerance of those with different faiths and beliefs (DfE 2014b). These values were set out in the Prevent strategy in 2011. Schools must have a clear strategy for embedding these values and show how their work with pupils has been effective.

Religious Education

Religious Education (RE) is mandated by the Education Act 1944 as amended by the Education Reform Act 1988 and the School Standards and Framework Act 1998. RE is compulsory in all state-funded schools but parents have the right to withdraw their child. Although the curriculum is required to reflect Christianity, it also addresses different religions and moral themes. Each local authority has a Local Agreed Syllabus. The Qualifications and Curriculum Authority has produced a non-statutory National Framework for Religious Education, which offers guidelines for teaching the subject at all key stages (excluding pupils in nursery).

Relationships Education, Relationships and Sex Education and Health Education

From September 2020, Relationships Education is compulsory for all primary school pupils, and RSE (and Health Education in England) is compulsory for all pupils in secondary education (DfE 2019d). Parents are able to withdraw pupils from Sex Education but not Relationships or Health Education. The teaching of the subject remains controversial partly due to clashes with the cultural and religious beliefs of some families. However, the focus in primary education should be on teaching 'positive relationships', relating to friends, family and relationships with other children and with adults. LGBT parents are suggested as a diverse family structure that could be reflected in class. When teaching, schools are reminded that the age and religious background of pupils must be taken into account, so that issues are sensitively and appropriately addressed. Faith schools are permitted to teach the relevant faith perspective on relationships as long as a balanced debate takes place.

 **REFLECTION**

Debating controversial issues

Think about what you have read within this chapter to offer a balanced view (arguments for and against) for each of the statements below. Please be professional when entering into discussion and debate.

I   'Schools should place restrictions on the religious clothing and symbols that pupils wear.'
2   'Child practitioners should play a role in combating religious extremism.'
3   'Single-faith schools should be supported in the UK.'
4   'France is right in banning Muslim women from wearing the burqa (full veil).'
5   'Religion leads to the oppression of, and harmful practices towards, females.'

Before attempting to challenge prejudice and extreme views, or to address conflict arising from religious differences, it is essential that a respectful and secure environment is fostered. Safe spaces need to be created within schools and early years settings (DfE 2015) where children and young people can partake in open but guided discussions, supported by knowledgeable, skilled and unbiased practitioners, as views presented can be controversial. It is important that practitioners are proactive and introduce children to sensitive issues, such as Antisemitism and Islamophobia, rather than waiting for them to surface. Although the Education Act 1996 prevents teachers from imparting partisan political views, early years practitioners and teachers have a duty to promote the core principles of the Universal Declaration of Human Rights and the Equality Act (EqualiTeach 2018). Practitioners who encourage children to think beyond media representations and reject misinformation and harmful stereotypes will help foster tolerant and accepting communities.

KEY POINTS

....

- It is crucial that child practitioners reflect upon any personal bias relating to religion/ culture, which may impact on their work with children and families.
- Having a religious faith is central to some people's identity and everyday life.
- It is important to help children recognise the similarities that exist across different religions, as well as the differences that exist within individual religions.
- An understanding of contemporary forms of Antisemitism should be promoted among children and young people.
- Islamophobia often serves to reinforce a sense of marginalisation and risks, radicalising individuals.
- Skilled and unbiased practitioners should create safe spaces where children can discuss controversial issues, going beyond media representations.

....

Answers to 'Whose Religion?' Activity

1. C, I;   2. C, I;   3. I, J;   4. C, I, J;   5. C, I, J;   6. C, I, J;   7. C, I, J;   8. C, I, J;
9. I, J;   10. C;   11. C, I, J;   12. J;   13. I;   14. C, I, J;   15. C, I, J

FURTHER READING

EqualiTeach (2018) *Faith in Us: Educating Young People on Islamophobia.* St Neots: EqualiTeach CIC.

Presents a range of issues linked to Islam and Islamophobia, with useful practical activities that can be undertaken with young children.

European Union Agency for Fundamental Rights (2018) *Experiences and Perceptions of Antisemitism: Second Survey on Discrimination and Hate Crime against Jews in the EU.* Vienna: Fundamental Rights Agency.

This report provides a detailed coverage on Jewish people's experiences with hate crime, discrimination, violence and Antisemitism in the European Union.

USEFUL WEBSITES

BBC BiteSize: www.bbc.co.uk/bitesize/subjects/zxnygk7

RE:Online: www.reonline.org.uk/teaching-resources

Twinkl: www.twinkl.co.uk/resources/home-key-stage-1-subjects/religion

9

ASYLUM SEEKER AND REFUGEE CHILDREN (AND CHILDREN WHO HAVE ENGLISH AS AN ADDITIONAL LANGUAGE)

CONTENTS

CHAPTER OVERVIEW

The key focus of this chapter is to explore the harrowing and complex experiences often encountered by asylum seeker and refugee children. Careful consideration is given to the health and well-being of this marginalised group, and the challenges children may face when settling into new communities and educational settings, including the impact of prejudice. Attention is also given to the way in which children acquire an additional language in early years and school settings, and strategies for supporting this group of children are presented.

This chapter considers:

1   Definitions and trends of displaced people.
2   Legislation and the asylum process in the UK.
3   Health and social well-being of refugee and asylum seeker children.
4   Prejudice towards asylum seekers and refugees, including media representation.
5   Educational challenges for refugee and asylum seeker children and support strategies.
6   How children acquire English as an additional language (EAL).

DEFINITIONS AND TRENDS OF DISPLACED PEOPLE

The UK has a long history of providing asylum and refuge, dating back to the seventeenth and eighteenth centuries, when the French-speaking Huguenots fled France during periods of severe persecution at the hands of the Catholic majority (Gwynn 1985). However, it was the Second World War which led, between 1945 and 1952, to the greatest population movements in Europe, as the Nazi and Soviet regimes and subsequent border changes resulted in a vast number of displaced people, in particular Jews facing persecution from Soviet bloc countries (Haywood 2008; Candappa 2016). In contrast to the past, where large groups of white populations have sought refuge in the UK, today's asylum-seeking and refugee communities originate largely from Africa, Asia and the Middle East. These more visible populations bring with them diverse languages, religions and traditions which have influenced the country's response to asylum seekers and refugees (Candappa 2016).

It is important to distinguish between individuals who have 'migrated' to the UK and those who have come seeking asylum, or who have been granted refugee status (Knowles 2013b). *Economic migrants* are people who move, either temporarily or permanently, from one area or country of residence to another for work, study or seeking a better life (Heslehurst et al. 2018). These individuals will have made a formal application to move from one country to another and arrive with the necessary visas (Knowles 2013b).

People also migrate to flee conflict or persecution for reasons of race, nationality, political or religious beliefs, sexuality, membership of a particular social group, or armed conflict. In 2018, the number of people displaced by conflict and persecution worldwide was estimated to be 70.8 million (Refugee Council 2020). Of these, 25.9 million were refugees, while 41.3 million were internally displaced within their country of origin (Refugee Council 2020). The UK receives only a fraction of the world's refugees.

Asylum seekers are individuals who have fled from their home country, seeking international protection on the grounds of war, persecution and human rights abuses in their home country, and whose claims for refugee status have not yet been determined (United Nations High Commissioner for Refugees [UNHCR] 2019). An *unaccompanied asylum-seeking child* is someone who is under 18 years of age, claiming in their own right and separated from both parents/guardians (Home Office 2019b). A *refugee* is an asylum seeker whose application has been successful and who has been legally recognised as requiring the protection of another country under the 1951 Convention relating to the Status of Refugees (UNHCR 2019).

 **ACTIVITY**

Analysing statistics

Access the most current documents available to examine trends of displaced children. Identify:

1   The number of displaced children, including which countries they originate from and which they seek refuge in.
2   The characteristics of displaced children (age, gender, reasons for fleeing their home country).
3   Their health status upon arrival to countries of refuge.

The following sources may be useful:

Amnesty International UK, the Refugee Council and Save the Children

www.amnesty.org.uk/files/FAMILY%20REUNION/Without%20my%20family%20
report/Without_my_family_report.pdf

The Children's Society

www.childrenssociety.org.uk/what-we-do/our-work/refugee-and-migrant-
children/child-refugee-statistics

United Nations High Commissioner for Refugees

www.unhcr.org/5d08d7ee7.pdf

Many factors influence the decision-making of people in search of safety in another country, including finances, historical or community ties, language and the respect for human rights (Amnesty International [AI] UK et al. 2019). But the decision to leave home is invariably an immediate response to escape danger. In such circumstances, choices are often limited as individuals may not have passports or the resources to travel far, and some members of the family may have been left behind, with their whereabouts unknown (Knowles 2013b). Judgements about the merits of different asylum systems or economies are rarely among the considerations (AI UK et al. 2019). The prime motivation is to seek safety, and the majority of asylum seekers find refuge in countries that neighbour their own as many leave their homes reluctantly and intend to return (AI UK et al. 2019).

 GLOBAL TRENDS 2018–19

- 85% of the world's 25.9 million refugees are hosted by neighbouring countries or those in the immediate region, often in developing countries (AI UK et al. 2019).
- Turkey is the biggest refugee hosting country in the world (Refugee Council 2020).
- The UK is home to 1% of the 25.9 million refugees (Refugee Council 2020).
- The proportion of women and girls in the refugee population is approximately 48% (UNHCR 2019).
- Children represent about half of the refugee population (UNHCR 2019).
- 19,835 unaccompanied children applied for asylum in the 28 countries of the European Union (AI UK et al. 2019).
- The UK received 3,651 applications from unaccompanied children seeking asylum, accounting for 10% of total asylum applications (Refugee Council 2020); 89% of them were boys aged 14–17 (AI UK et al. 2019; Refugee Council 2020).

LEGISLATION AND THE ASYLUM PROCESS

The right to claim asylum in another country is enshrined in international law:

1   *1951 Geneva Convention Relating to the Status of Refugees and the 1967 Protocol ('the Refugee Convention')* – the primary framework of international refugee protection. Asylum seekers must show that they have a justifiable fear of persecution and are unable to seek protection from the authorities in their own country.

2   *1950 European Convention on Human Rights* – a human rights claim can be part of an asylum claim under the Refugee Convention, or it can stand alone. Most claims are based on 'prohibition on torture and inhuman or degrading treatment' (Article 3) or 'right to respect for family life and private life' (Article 8).

3   *European Union Asylum Qualification Directive* – sets common criteria for identifying people in need of international protection and a minimum level of benefits available for those granted this status in EU member states.

Other legislation used to support applications in the UK includes: the 1989 Convention on the Rights of the Child; the European Convention on Human Rights and Human Rights Act 1998; Dublin Regulation 2013; the Borders, Citizenship and Immigration Act 2009; the Children Act 1989; and the Immigration Act 2016.

The asylum process

Asylum claims should be made as soon as an asylum seeker arrives in the UK. The individual is then protected from removal until a decision has been made. During the 'screening interview', the UK Border Agency records the personal details of the applicant and their journey to the UK. This is followed by an 'asylum interview' where the applicant gives their account of the persecution encountered in their own country.

Applicants are held in an Immigration Removal Centre while they await a decision on their asylum claim. Those seeking asylum do not have permission to work in the UK but they can apply to the UK Border Agency for financial support during the review period.

If the claim is successful the applicant gets Refugee Status, which lasts for five years. After five years, if it is still unsafe for the individual to return to their country, they can apply for a legal status of having 'Indefinite Leave to Remain' in the UK. Once an individual is granted protection, they have the right to work, claim benefits and be reunited with their immediate family in the UK. Those who are not granted refugee status must leave (Consonant n.d.; Home Office 2019b).

CASE STUDY

Unaccompanied asylum seeker – 'Farid'

'I'm 10 years old and from Afghanistan. My family were living a peaceful life as Muslims until the Taliban took control and then everyone was in danger. We were scared to leave our homes. The worst day was when my mother was told that our father had been killed. Then Taliban soldiers came in the night and took my brother, who was 13, to join their army. We still don't know where he is.

'My mother, scared that the Taliban would come for me, paid a man to get me to the UK. The journey was terrifying. I walked for days in bad weather, spent most nights with no bed or blanket and had little food. I went on a boat and in trucks. There were lots of violent men. I feared for my life as I saw them beat to death Abed, a boy I'd travelled with.

'When I came to the UK, everything was so different. I felt terrified. I've put in an asylum claim and social services are finding me a special foster family.'

1   What impact on his health/well-being? could the trauma have had on Farid when he experienced his home-country problems, the journey to the UK and the refugee and detention process in his new country?
2   What are some of the challenges Farid may face when settling into a new home and school?
3   What factors could be put into place to support Farid and aid his resilience and recovery?

Asylum seeker children

Human rights violations against children include sexual and gender-based violence (child marriage, female genital mutilation [FGM]), abduction, maiming, attacks against schools, under-age recruitment in armed conflicts, forced domestic servitude, child trafficking, genocide and ethnic cleansing. Persecution and terror form the everyday realities of many children's lives, and some live with ongoing artillery attacks (AI UK et al. 2019).

Many unaccompanied children come from Afghanistan, Eritrea, Iran, Iraq, Sudan, Albania, Ethiopia and Syria (AI UK et al. 2019; Refugee Council 2020). Most will have endured horrifying experiences, and separation from their families affects their well-being. The presence of a child's family has an important effect on their recovery and ability to adapt to the country of asylum (AI UK et al. 2019). However, the UK's rules on the rights of child refugees to support visas for close family to join them are more restrictive than many countries in Europe (AI UK et al. 2019).

Upon arrival to the UK, unaccompanied children must be immediately referred to local authority children's services. Local authorities have duties to safeguard the welfare of all children 'in need' (including unaccompanied children) within their area under the Children Act 1989. Having a chronological age above or below 18 years determines the support they are provided. Children aged under 16 are likely to be placed with a foster parent or in a children's home. A child aged over 16 may be placed in supported or shared accommodation but there should be sufficient supervision by on-site staff to keep young people safe. A local authority should provide support for unaccompanied children after they turn 18 and up to the age of 21 or 24 if they continue in education. However, many unaccompanied children lack documents to establish their birth date. Where the age of a child is in doubt, reference must be made to guidance provided by the Home Office (2019b) on 'Children's asylum claims' (Consonant n.d.; Home Office 2019b).

HEALTH AND SOCIAL WELL-BEING

Asylum seeker and refugee children are not homogeneous – even children who arrive from the same country will have had different socio-economic living conditions and diverse migration histories. Thus, the health status and needs of this group of children vary greatly.

The physical health status of asylum seeker children on arrival is generally good, with some having better health than children in the settled population, although this correlates with their mode of arrival (Renton et al. 2016; Welsh Government 2018). Unaccompanied children who have arrived spontaneously are likely to have undertaken a dangerous journey which increases the possibility of injuries and illnesses (Welsh Government 2018). In contrast, children who have arrived via a government scheme will normally have had access to health care. Common health problems of newly arrived children include accidental injuries, hypothermia, blood-borne viruses, burns, nutrition disorders and reproductive/sexual health issues (Royal College of Paediatrics and Child Health [RCPCH] 2018c; Welsh Government 2018). Overcrowded living conditions and substandard hygiene and sanitation facilities place children at risk for communicable diseases such as diarrhoeal diseases, tuberculosis, cholera, typhus, malaria, measles and hepatitis B and C (RCPCH 2018c; World Health Organization [WHO] 2018b). Children fleeing regions of conflict are likely to have missed child immunisation programmes (RCPCH 2018c). Refugee and asylum seeker children are also prone to dental problems, respiratory and gastrointestinal illnesses, and skin- and soil-transmitted infections (Department of Education and Early Childhood Development [DEECD] 2011; Welsh Government 2018). Poor oral health has been linked to problems with sleeping, eating and speech, which can have long-term impact on a child's development (Renton et al. 2016).

Many asylum seeker and refugee children have a history of violence or abuse and will have witnessed the death or disappearance of friends and family members. It is important for practitioners working with these children to understand the trauma of such adverse childhood experiences on well-being (Welsh Government 2018). Living in refugee camps might have a lasting impact and the journey to safety may have been perilous; deaths among refugees crossing the Mediterranean Sea have increased rapidly (Welsh Government 2018). Children are at risk for sexual exploitation, trafficking and being recruited as child soldiers, and many women will have experienced gender-based violence (All Party Parlimentary Group [APPG] 2017; WHO 2018b). Pregnant asylum seekers and refugees face specific challenges, including higher rates of maternal death, infant mortality, delivery-related complications and low birth weight (Renton et al. 2016; Welsh Government 2018). Women in regions of conflict may not have benefited from antenatal care which can prevent the transmission of sexually transmitted infections, reduce the risk of complications in pregnancy and provide health advice relating to infants and young children (RCPCH 2018c; WHO 2018b).

Exposure to violence and abuse causes mental health and physical injuries in individuals, destroys family life through loss and separation, damages trust in social relations, and can have a lasting impact on life security (British Red Cross 2011). Traumatic events which are unexpected leave people with little or no time to prepare psychologically and can have a devastating impact on long-term well-being. When events are unfamiliar, people cannot draw on previous experiences as coping strategies. However, each child's ability to withstand and recover from traumatic experiences differs, as does their ability to manage daily challenges and disruptions to their lives (British Red Cross 2011), and some children will not present with any significant mental health problems (DEECD 2011). Sometimes trauma can act as motivation for psychological growth as individuals may gain strength from identifying themselves to be survivors (British Red Cross 2011).

Psychological problems are prevalent among asylum seekers and refugees often as a consequence of violent experiences encountered within the home country, particularly internalising disorders (post-traumatic stress disorder [PTSD], depression, phobias) (Jensen et al. 2014; Renton et al. 2016; WHO 2018b). Children may also be grieving for family members and friends who have been killed or left behind, and for the loss of their identity, social status, home, material possessions, cultural and religious belonging and familiar community (British Red Cross 2011). Serious externalising symptoms appear to be no more common in asylum seeker and refugee children than in children from the majority population (WHO 2018b). Behavioural problems tend to be linked to anxiety and flashbacks, with sleep and behaviour disturbances common in younger children (RCPCH 2018c). However, children deemed to be at high risk of acute behavioural difficulties, such as anger, self-harm and suicide, should be referred to Child and Adolescent Mental Health Services as soon as possible (Children's Society 2018).

Once in the UK, some families see rebuilding their lives together as a new beginning whereas others may struggle with having to start again (British Red Cross 2011). This process of cultural transition is defined as 'acculturation' and the accompanying pressures labelled as 'acculturative stress' (Jensen et al. 2014). Stressors during the period of transition to a new country include coping with the impact of past trauma, ongoing separation from relatives, adjusting to a new home, school and environment, learning a new language, finding housing, financial difficulties, having fewer social connections, renegotiating roles and responsibilities within the family structure, and finding ways to continue religious and cultural traditions (British Red Cross 2011). Many asylum seeker and refugee children in the UK live in poverty, often as a result of immigration policies. Such circumstances limit families' access to food, clothing, medicine and quality housing, which are all essential to child health and development (Renton et al. 2016). Overcrowded, poorly ventilated and damp accommodation, and housing insecurity, are linked to a range of illnesses among children (including asthma and bronchitis, tuberculosis, accidental injury and strained relationships) and children's care and development may also be indirectly affected through the impact of their parents'/carers' mental health problems (Renton et al. 2016). In combination with socio-economic deprivation, these parenting difficulties increase the risk for child abuse (WHO 2018b).

Family separation is a significant cause of anxiety that can have debilitating psychological impacts which hamper settlement in a new country. Long-term depression and feelings of powerlessness can stem from the uncertainty regarding the location and condition of a loved one (British Red Cross 2011). Furthermore, the longer the period of separation, the poorer the outcomes can be when the family eventually reunites, as many refugees will have experienced traumatic events which negatively affect their ability to rebuild their relationships in a new context (British Red Cross 2011). The literature on mental health often refers to 'risk' factors and 'protective' factors. The British Red Cross (2011) recommends that the term 'supportive' factors is used instead, as factors that provide asylum seekers and refugees support through difficult experiences cannot protect the events from occurring but do offer some resilience to endure them. Key supportive factors are identified as religious faith, supportive relationships, community connections (own linguistic and religious communities), meaningful activity and routines, and adequate financial/material resources (British Red Cross 2011).

PREJUDICE, SCHOOLS AND THE MEDIA

Compounding the many challenges refugees face is the growing anti-refugee and anti-migrant discourse which can have serious implications for refugees' social well-being as they settle in their new community (Pocock and Chan 2018). Migrants, including asylum seekers and refugees, can be discriminated against for many reasons, including ethnicity, skin colour, religion and having a foreign accent or foreign qualifications (Fernández-Reino 2020). More visible populations are especially pathologised in political rhetoric and media debate, associated with criminal activity, terrorism and a drain on the nation's resources, which has increased far-right extremism (Fernández-Reino 2020). Asylum seekers and refugees are perceived as more deserving of support when they can contribute to the economy, have humanitarian grounds for entry, have evidence of physical or mental health trauma and violence, and are Christian rather than Muslim (Pocock and Chan 2018; Patil and McLaren 2019). Factors increasing prejudice include inflammatory statements made by local politicians and mass media, British National Party activity, overstretched public services, poor-quality housing, high unemployment, little previous settlement by ethnic minorities in an area, high levels of segregation in housing, failure of schools to challenge hostility, and a lack of community relations strategies.

Compared to many other nations, people in the UK tend to be more positive about welcoming refugees and believe that they will integrate successfully into society (Kaur-Ballagan 2020). Eastern and Central European countries tend to have much lower acceptance of those migrating (Pocock and Chan 2018). However, the number of racist incidents in primary and secondary schools across the UK has risen sharply, with 4,590 cases of racial abuse among pupils reported in 2017 resulting in fixed or permanent exclusion (The Guardian 2018):

- 52% teachers had witnessed 'anti-refugee' sentiments in pupils and 24% of pupils did not know what a refugee was (*The Independent* 2019).
- 54% of primary and secondary teachers across the UK believed mass media were contributing to children's negative sentiments (*The Independent* 2019).
- 60% of children believed that 'asylum seekers and immigrants are stealing our jobs' and 35% agreed that 'Muslims are taking over our country' (Equality and Human Rights Commission 2016).

The challenge for early years and primary education practitioners is how to encourage children to value diversity in the shadow of negative messages (Candappa 2016). Pocock and Chan (2018) assert that the first step is to build fact-based critical discourse among children and young people. This can be undertaken through adapting approaches advocated by Philosophy for Children, SAPERE and 'critical media literacy' (McQueeney 2014). However, many teachers do not feel equipped to address racism in schools and avoid conversations about race and religion (Lewis 2016; The Conversation 2017).

ACTIVITY

Syrian refugee boy attacked at school

Watch the following video clip.
  www.bbc.co.uk/news/av/world-48274580/bullied-syrian-teenager-fears-for-his-safety

1   Discuss the possible impact on Jamal.
2   Identify ways practitioners can promote understanding and tolerance towards asylum seekers and refugees.

The UK has a long record of dealing with racial and xenophobic prejudice. In 1965, the British parliament passed the Race Relations Act to protect migrants from South Asia and the Caribbean from discrimination. The UK was one of the first countries to pass anti-discrimination laws and has one of the most favourable anti-discrimination policies in Europe (Fernández-Reino 2020). Xenophobic prejudice reduction interventions, such as legislation, national anti-racism media campaigns, cross-cultural/intergroup contact, cultural diversity training and peer learning, are applied across various settings including schools, health fields and workplaces (Pocock and Chan 2018).

Impact of the media

The subject of immigration, asylum seekers and refugees frequently occupies a prominent place in national and local media coverage. Much reporting is unbalanced, misleading and inflammatory, and there is little counter-information made available to the public (Refugee Media Group in Wales [RMGW] 2004; Blumell et al. 2020). Inaccuracies, which include misrepresentation, confusion of comment conjecture and misuse of statistics, often relate to fear-inducing topics (Runnymede Trust 2011).

ACTIVITY

Media coverage

Undertake a media search to examine news items presented about asylum seekers and refugees. What forms of prejudice are reported? Do the news items contain misconceptions or stereotypical thinking? What impact might such prejudices have for asylum seeker or refugee children and their families?

Hard news reportage has traditionally been marked by a negative discourse of crisis related to the societal impact of asylum. Asylum seekers and refugees are typically positioned as 'outsiders' and portrayed as a 'threat' to society via coverage focused on mass influxes, criminal behaviour, terrorism, economics and welfare state crises, and negative cultural and moral differences regarding Muslims, women and children (under-age marriage, FGM, sexual violence and promiscuity) (RMGW 2004; Joseph Rowntree Foundation [JRF] 2006; Blumell et al. 2020). Anti-foreigner rhetoric was particularly noticeable in the UK media during the Brexit campaign of 2016 (Blumell et al. 2020). Stories often focus on males rather than reporting on the experiences of female asylum seekers. Such narrow discourse hinders the ability of the public to consider immigration within the realms of human rights, social justice, anti-racism or the contribution made by immigrants to the labour market (JRF 2006).

Racially motivated crimes, civil injustice, institutional racism and humanitarian crises relating to asylum seekers and refugees do not appear frequently as news items (JRF 2006). Soft news – articles that report positively, or which seek the views or present the experiences of individual asylum seekers and refugees – are frequently missing from print media (Runnymede Trust 2011; Blumell et al. 2020). In 2012, the Leveson Inquiry concluded that the British press reporting on immigrants, refugees and ethnic minorities was frequently sensational, aggressive and prejudicial (Refugee Council 2012). The media is most dangerous when using excerpts made by politicians and government officials. For example, Theresa May's infamous quote:

> Immigrants are stealing your job, making you poorer and ruining your country. Never mind the facts, just feel angry at foreigners. And make me Conservative leader. (Theresa May cited in Farron 2015)

This imbalanced media discourse of a perpetual crisis over social problems regarding immigrants influences adverse policy changes (JRF 2006) and creates the incentive for the legitimation of prejudice and discrimination (Runnymede Trust 2011). Hostile attitudes are more common among uncritical readers and harassment most likely when inflammatory media images overlap with periods of deprivation and competition for services in limited supply (Runnymede Trust 2011). New forms of media can provide participatory and empowering spaces for asylum seekers, refugees and advocacy agencies but reportage on related issues via these platforms is currently scarce (Blumell et al. 2020).

EDUCATION AND LANGUAGE PROFICIENCY

Achieving a connection to school is a fundamental part of the adjustment of refugee children after resettlement (DEECD 2011). For many children, school provides an important security base outside the home and it can play a pivotal role in restoring normality and order in children's lives (Candappa 2016). Due to the diverse backgrounds of asylum seekers and refugees, it is crucial that schools do not view these children homogeneously; instead, it is important that practitioners develop highly personalised teaching and pastoral strategies (Madziva and Thondhlana 2017). In order to do this as much information as possible should be gathered during the admissions process for new arrivals regarding children's home situations, health and prior education, using an interpreter if necessary.

CASE STUDY

Sisters Rima (age 9) and Yara (age 4) – Syrian refugees

Two sisters have recently started at Windgate Primary. Despite arriving with no English language, Yara has settled in very well. She is making friends and happily practises English words and phrases she is picking up. In contrast, Rima is struggling to adjust. The following describes her experiences:

> Most days I cry because I feel scared. I can't understand the teacher or what I'm supposed to do. Some children say things about me and then run away. This makes me feel upset, so I push and pull them to make them understand. I was good at maths in Syria but now my teacher gives me numbers to colour – it's work for a baby. I hate coming to school. I don't have any friends and the teachers seem annoyed with me. My favourite time is when I go to see Mrs Davies, my EAL teacher. (Rima)

Think carefully about the sisters.

1   What factors might be helping Yara to settle more quickly into her early years setting?
2   How can the early years practitioners continue to support her needs?
3   Why do you think Rima is struggling?
4   What advice would you give to her teacher to: (1) support her in the class with English language; (2) promote friendships; and (3) help her to access the curriculum in a way that is meaningful so that she feels capable.

Asylum seeker and refugee children often settle successfully into early years settings and schools in the UK. However, many children have complex needs and encounter various barriers in their new communities, which may make it challenging for practitioners to offer personalised support for children's learning and social environments. Many asylum seeker and refugee children are new to English on joining school in the UK are dealing with the impact of trauma, and most will have had little formal schooling in their home country (Candappa 2016). Consequently, asylum seeker and

Table 9.1 Asylum seeker and refugee children: challenges and support strategies

Challenges and barriers	Support strategies
• Lack of information regarding pre-migration experiences, home life, medical issues, previous education	• Supporting families with the admissions process
	• Welcome pack for all new arrivals
	• Whole school approach to inclusion
• No/limited English language	• Strong pastoral system, including high levels of support for mental health
• No/disrupted previous schooling	
• Diverse pedagogical practice and school discipline to that experienced in the country of origin	• Ongoing support of a caring adult
	• Peer support/buddy schemes
	• Continuing professional development for practitioners
• Undiagnosed special educational needs	• Better support and resources for refugee and asylum seeker children with special educational needs and minority-language pupils
• Poverty and unstable accommodation	
• Bullying and discrimination	
• Difficulties forming new attachments and making friends	• Information/curriculum resources available in different languages
• Physical, mental health and behavioural difficulties	• Robust anti-racist and anti-bullying policies
• Lack of practitioner awareness of issues affecting refugees and asylum seekers	• Partnerships between schools, parents/carers and specialist agencies
• Difficulties in establishing relationships with parents/carers	• Personalised learning packages
	• Maps of the world pinpointing places the children have visited/lived in
• Insufficient funding for EAL support, educational resources and support from external agencies	• Role play area with everyday objects from a range of cultures
(Jensen et al. 2014; Candappa 2016; UNICEF 2018a; Children's Society 2020c).	(Candappa 2016; UNICEF 2018a, 2018b; Ryf 2018; Children's Society 2020c).

refugee children often face significant personal, social and academic challenges which influence their capacity to settle and thrive. Table 9.1 outlines some of the challenges faced, along with strategies which may support children and their families.

Social and emotional needs

Secure relationships can help to foster familiarity, attachment and identity, key psychological conditions to establishing a sense of belonging to a place (Fullilove 1996). Therefore, losing intimate social connections on migration can be disturbing, and failure to make positive and secure new attachments can be a major cause of stress. The social network established at school is paramount in determining how asylum seeker and refugee children settle and thrive. Fears newly arrived children commonly have about unfamiliar school settings include anxiety about whether they will make new friends, not being able to speak English and that teachers will shout at them for not knowing what to do (Hamilton 2013b). These children, who have so much to adjust to (many of whom will still be healing from traumatic events), may choose not to disclose their past, either as a form of self-preservation or due to the belief that their new community has negative opinions of refugees (Candappa 2016).

It can be an isolating experience for a child when there is no one at school who can understand them. Lack of English language and awareness of local cultures, together with differences in ethnicity, religious beliefs and mode of dress, may expose asylum seeker and refugee children to 'otherness', which can result in low-level bullying and exclusion from their peer group (Candappa 2016). The child's response might be to withdraw and enter a period of silence where they observe, learn and adjust. Other children, however, may find other ways to communicate, such as hostile physical contact with their peers which may result in them being rejected from social circles (Hamilton 2013b). Teachers can help children to build positive relationships by fostering a caring and respectful environment, raising children's awareness about non-verbal methods of communication, and buddying minority-language children with a designated classmate to ease new pupils into the life of the school (Hamilton 2013b; Candappa 2016).

Increased demands on teachers' time, in a performance-driven culture, may make the task of providing the individualised support often required by asylum seeker and refugee children too demanding for some practitioners, especially in school and early years settings where there are high levels of diversity (Hamilton 2013a). Furthermore, stereotypes held by practitioners on the grounds of pre- and post-migratory refugee experiences, ethnicity, gender, socio-economic status, cognitive ability and levels of individual resilience may influence expectations, interactions and the support provided to asylum seeker and refugee children (Rutter 2006; Hamilton 2013b). Where bonds with individual children fail to be established, children's needs risk being ineffectively addressed, and some may become disengaged from their settings.

It is therefore crucial that schools and early years settings create an inclusive culture for asylum seeker and refugee children (one where children's current needs can be catered for in the context of past experiences and in an environment in which they feel safe and secure and they belong), without being singled out as different, even in a positive way (Candappa 2016). Many inclusive strategies are highlighted in Table 9.1 but key to supporting children is a caring ethos, which celebrates cultural, religious and linguistic diversity, where debate is held around social justice and humanitarian issues, and where opportunities are provided for asylum seeker and refugee children to gain confidence, self-esteem, resilience and a sense of agency in taking control of their lives (Candappa 2016; Madziva and Thondhlana 2017).

Language

Developing competence in English language is a fundamental survival need in refugee and asylum seeker children's new lives. It is essential for social interaction, accessing the curriculum, cognitive development and developing confidence, and is the most significant guarantee that pupils will achieve in education and succeed later in life (Department for Education and Skills [DfES] 2003). Consideration should therefore be given to providing nurturing environments in which talk has a central place and where children feel safe to try out their new language without fear of making mistakes (Crosse 2007; Ryf 2018). Realistic expectations are also essential, as insisting on oral responses before children feel confident may lead to high levels of anxiety, which could be detrimental to language learning and relationships. School and early years practitioners should find opportunities to share different languages in settings, as this will help to normalise bilingualism and encourage monolingual children to experience language diversity (Ryf 2018).

Acquiring a language is a complicated procedure which consists of several interconnected pieces: phonology (the sounds of the language); vocabulary (the words of the language); grammar (the way the words are ordered to make sentences); discourse (the way the sentences are put together to explain concepts); and pragmatics (the rules of how to use the language) (Tabors 1997). Although these basic language skills are normally acquired by the time a child is 6 years old (Siraj-Blatchford and Clarke 2000), vocabulary acquisition is a lifelong process. Most minority-language children become 'socially' fluent in a new language in two to three years (basic interpersonal communication skills), but it may take upwards of five years to achieve the more complex structures and vocabulary levels associated with academic proficiency (cognitive academic language) comparable to their English-speaking peers (see Cummins 2001; Ryf 2018).

Consistent development of the first language is significantly more important than the number of hours of second-language tuition received (DEECD 2011), because if a child understands concepts and meanings in their primary language, it is easier for them to transfer this knowledge to a second language (Cummins 2000; Rutter 2006). Children who are 8 to 12 years old when they arrive and have received two to three years of education in their first language before migration, often have the fastest attainment of Cognitive Academic Language when schooling occurs in the second language in the new country (DEECD 2011). However, deficiency ideology has traditionally positioned bilingualism to be a burden on cognitive processes, that is, the continued development and use of the first language will inhibit the learning of a subsequent language (Perregaux 2007). Yet in many countries children successfully learn more than one language from birth. Where deficit perspectives exist, minority-language learners' risk being perceived as having 'no language', 'a special educational need' or 'lacking academic potential'. Sustained use of the first language is central for promoting feelings of positive self-worth and identity and for maintaining family ties, cultural values and traditions (Siraj-Blatchford and Clarke 2000). Practitioners may need to help some parents recognise the importance of the continuing use of the home language in the development of subsequent language/s.

Each child will have their own individual pattern of progress in acquiring a new language. In the UK, the main method of assessment used to identify children's levels of English is the 'Hester Stages' (Hester 1990 cited in Barrs 1991). The Hester Stages consist of four levels of fluency of English (Stage 1 – New to English, through to Stage 4 – A highly fluent user of English in most social and learning contexts), based on speaking, listening, reading and writing. However, the assessment of minority-language learners is problematic. Judgements made from monolingual assessments, based on British middle-class values and norms, can lead to low baseline scores which may not accurately reflect the ability of minority-language children (Siraj-Blatchford and Clarke 2000; Loewen 2004). A more accurate picture of language competency can be acquired through the use of assessments which are contextualised, carried out in regular classrooms, undertaken in the home language as well as the second language, and where children are supported by bilingual staff (Loewen 2004; Crosse 2007).

One of the theoretical supports for inclusive education for minority-language learners originates from Schumann's 'acculturation' theory (1986), that social and psychological contact with the target language group is essential for successful language acquisition to take place. Although the importance of intensive English language support from the outset for migrant children is widely acknowledged, exactly how this should be done remains debated (Candappa 2016). For example, children who are separated from mainstream classes in order to gain English language provision are provided with high-intensity teacher attention and support. However, if withdrawal is prolonged it can impede friendships and exploratory talk with dominant-language peers and can mark children out as being different (Candappa 2016). Therefore, the National Association for Language Development in the Curriculum recommends specialist support within the mainstream classroom wherever possible alongside the class teacher and other children (Ryf 2018).

Minority-language pupils should follow the same programmes of study as English-speaking peers but tasks should be differentiated to allow for additional oral work. Differentiated learning and assessment strategies can help minority-language children to feel included and competent, as many recognise when they are given meaningless tasks to complete (Hamilton 2013a). However, some curriculum areas such as science, history and geography place a high cognitive load on minority-language learners. These subjects are often associated with unfamiliar abstract ideas and require specific or technical language (McKeon 2001). The language used in these subjects is typically 'decontextualised' with few clues in the immediate environment to help derive meaning. The learning context can be enhanced through the employment of visual resources, body language cues and relating learning to children's previous experiences. Focusing on the basic words and phrases a newly arrived child will require (in order to survive the first few weeks in an unfamiliar environment) is also important (Parker-Jenkins et al. 2007). Practitioners who are familiar with a few phrases from children's first languages can use these to assist children during the settling-in period. Focusing on activities which develop listening skills and offer opportunity for repetition of language allows children to listen to the sounds of a new language (Siraj-Blatchford and Clarke 2000). Early years classrooms typically lead to the natural emergence of language and literacy through greater social inter action provided through play and the increased usage of visual images, key words and phrases, which are emphasised to support the language learning of young chil- dren in general (Hamilton 2013a).

Listening to and speaking in an unfamiliar language can be an exhausting and iso- lating experience, and there is a risk of minority-language children being misunder- stood. Older children especially may be reluctant to use language in schools due to fear of criticism, ridicule and being seen to be different (Schumann 1986). It is not uncommon for minority-language learners to say little or nothing at school for up to seven months when they are adjusting to the unfamiliar (Dukes and Smith 2006). Although children may remain silent for a considerable length of time, their com- prehension of the second language is often initially greater than their oral ability (Fumoto et al. 2007). Minority-language pupils who are going through a period of silence, or those who are more reserved by nature, are in danger of being isolated by their monolingual peers and being labelled by practitioners as having specific learn- ing differences (Siraj-Blatchford and Clarke 2000). Careful professional judgements are required, as distinguishing language differences from special educational needs is enormously challenging, with numerous pre- and post-migratory factors potentially disabling asylum seeker and refugee children rather than any underlying condition (Fumoto et al. 2007; DEECD 2011; Ryf 2018).

 REFLECTION

What do you think?

Now that you have come to the end of the chapter, please discuss each statement with a small group of peers. Please be professional during the discussion and identify differ- ent opinions.

1   'Refugees and asylum seekers have usually had similar experiences.'
2   'Refugees and asylum seekers take our jobs.'
3   'Refugees and asylum seekers drain the economy.'
4   'Minority-language children should be discouraged from using their first language in schools and early years settings and instead use as much English as possible.'
5   'Practitioners will not be able to provide personalised care and learning support for asylum seeker and refugee children without the disclosure of their experiences.'

KEY POINTS

- Human rights violations against children include sexual and gender-based violence, domestic servitude, child trafficking and recruitment in armed conflicts.
- The health status of asylum seeker and refugee children varies greatly but internalising psychological disorders are prevalent.
- Racist and religious-based prejudice in schools have increased sharply but many teachers lack the confidence to address such issues.
- School can restore normality and order, but it is important that personalised teaching and pastoral strategies are carefully developed for asylum seeker and refugee children.
- Children usually become 'socially' fluent in a new language in two to three years, but it may take five years or longer to achieve 'cognitive academic language'.
- Consistent development of the first language is crucial to the development of subsequent languages.
- Differentiated learning and assessment can help minority-language children to feel included; expectations should be kept realistically high.

FURTHER READING

Amnesty International UK, the Refugee Council and Save the Children (2019) *Without my Family: The Impact of Family Separation on Child Refugees in the UK.* Available at: https://resourcecentre.savethechildren.net/node/16673/pdf/without-my-family-report-aw-jan2020-lores.pdf

Presents the experiences and needs of unaccompanied asylum seekers and refugee children.

Candappa, M. (2016) Invisibility and Otherness: Asylum seeking and refugee students in the classroom. In Richards, G. and Armstrong, F. (eds) *Teaching and Learning in Diverse and Inclusive Classrooms.* Second edition. pp. 74–86. Abingdon: Routledge.

A comprehensive account of supporting the needs of asylum seeker and refugee children in classrooms in the UK.

Ryf, V. (2018) Including bilingual learners and children with English as an additional language. In Knowles, G. (ed.) *Supporting Inclusive Practice and Ensuring Opportunity is Equal for All.* Third edition. pp. 52–69. Abingdon: Routledge.

Offers a theoretical overview of good practice for EAL/bilingual learners in classrooms, with many practice-based activities.

Welsh Government (2018) *Health and Wellbeing Provision for Refugees and Asylum Seekers.* Available at: https://gov.wales/sites/default/files/publications/2019-03/health-and-wellbeing-provision-for-refugees-and-asylum-seekers_0.pdf

Provides a detailed account of the health status and needs of asylum seeker and refugee families.

USEFUL WEBSITES

Amnesty International UK: www.amnesty.org.uk
British Red Cross: www.redcross.org.uk
Children's Society: www.childrenssociety.org.uk
Refugee Action: www.refugee-action.org.uk
Refugee Council: www.refugeecouncil.org.uk

10

GYPSY, ROMA AND TRAVELLER CHILDREN

CONTENTS

CHAPTER OVERVIEW

This chapter will explore the societal prejudice and inequalities in health and education experienced by Gypsy, Roma and Traveller children, and the cultural discord frequently faced as a result of accessing public services that have been primarily designed for the general population. Consideration is also given to the impact of mass media.

This chapter considers:

1   Terminology used to represent Gypsies, Roma and Travellers.
2   Key elements of Gypsy, Roma and Traveller cultures.
3   Societal prejudice, inequalities and media representation of Gypsies, Roma and Travellers.
4   Health outcomes and inequalities faced by Gypsies, Roma and Travellers.
5   Educational outcomes and experiences encountered by Gypsy, Roma and Traveller children.
6   How practitioners can support Gypsy, Roma and Traveller children and their families in early years settings and schools through critical inclusion.

TERMINOLOGY

Although the term 'Gypsy, Roma and Traveller' is used throughout this chapter it is done so with reservation. Finding an overarching term is problematic as it risks incorrectly portraying multiple and diverse communities as one homogeneous group and it is the reason why this population have not been reduced to the single abbreviation of 'GRT'. The term 'Gypsy, Roma and Traveller' represents three main peoples but each group consists of sub-groups,* with varied histories, occupations and cultural and linguistic backgrounds. In the UK, it is common to differentiate between Gypsies (English Gypsies, Scottish Gypsy/Travellers and Welsh Gypsies), Irish Travellers, and Roma, who have arrived more recently (from the 1990s) from Central and Eastern Europe. The groups are often categorised as a single group because many communities have historically been nomadic.

It is important to acknowledge the contested nature of the terms. Gypsy people have lived in the UK since the sixteenth century. It is thought that the term 'Gypsy' derived from a misunderstanding that Gypsies originated from Egypt, although records and genetic evidence suggest that the Roma first arrived from northern India.

---

* Sub-groups include Gypsies; Travellers of Irish, Scottish or Welsh heritage; Sinti; Bargees/ Boat dwellers; New Age Travellers; migrant Roma populations; and Circus Travellers and Showground Travellers.

While some people find the term 'Gypsy' to be offensive, due to negative connotations often attached to it, other individuals are proud to associate themselves with this term (UK Parliament 2019). The term 'Traveller' overlooks ethnicity and restricts identity to a lifestyle that may no longer be followed as an increasing number of families are now living in housing. The acronym 'GRT' has little meaning to most Gypsies (McFadden et al. 2018); furthermore, reducing diverse communities to a single abbreviation can create and reinforce homogeneous assumptions. Practitioners should consult with individuals and families about the terminology they would like to be used to address them.

 **ACTIVITY**

What do you know?

1   Identify words/phrases commonly used to describe Gypsy, Roma and Traveller people. Are most of these words/phrases positive or negative?
2   What do you know about Gypsy, Roma and Traveller cultures?
3   Have you ever worked with a Gypsy, Roma or Traveller child in a setting? If so, what are the best ways to support them?

KEY ELEMENTS OF GYPSY, ROMA AND TRAVELLER CULTURES

Gypsy, Roma and Traveller people have a rich and diverse history and culture. Despite centuries of enforced assimilation, a major feature of these communities has been their ability to adapt to changing social pressures and economic circumstances, while maintaining a central identity. Nomadism has traditionally been a fundamental part of the Gypsy, Roma and Traveller cultures, with many families still living a travelling lifestyle. Some families live on local authority or privately owned caravan sites or are resident on their own plot of land. However, since the 1984 Criminal Justice and Public Order Act and a reduction of authorised sites, a minority of families have no secure place to stay and are moving between unauthorised encampments. The growth in the urbanisation of many Gypsy, Roma and Traveller families, due to a decline in agricultural work, has resulted in changing needs and skill-sets and the acceptance of more radical ideas. Gypsies, Roma and Travellers now work in a range of trades, for example as landscape gardeners, tarmackers, motor-trade workers and scrap metal dealers, with some entering teaching, finance, and sport, leisure and entertainment industries (Save the Children 2006). This has led to more families living in bricks-and-mortar housing. It is important for practitioners to recognise that Gypsy, Roma and Traveller children who have moved into houses are increasingly developing values and experiences similar to those held by children from the general population.

Community identity is based on deeply rooted cultural traditions and social norms. Although the term 'Gypsy, Roma and Traveller' describes a varied body of communities which have distinct lifestyles and religious and moral beliefs, shared characteristics may include: communal solidarity (the communities tend to be independent and self-sufficient); a high regard for the family unit and family descent; clearly defined familial and gender roles; great value placed on the care and socialisation of children and the care of the elderly and infirm; preference for family-based learning and self-employment; a strict code of cleanliness regarding interior living spaces; commitment to a nomadic lifestyle; and specific customs and rituals regarding birth, marriage and death (Save the Children 2006; Lloyd and McCluskey 2008).

Gypsy, Roma and Traveller people are considered to be adults from the age of 14 and are thus expected to assume adult responsibilities. Consequently, many young people either leave by the age of 14 or do not continue with secondary education (Levinson 2015). Many parents view secondary education as de-skilling their children, as it reduces integration into the family, resulting in the dilution of knowledge of the cultural, economic and practical skills required. From an early age, boys are expected to work alongside their male relatives to develop work-based skills, negotiating abilities and master essential driving skills, to gain financial independence. Alternatively, girls are encouraged to marry young and to carry out domestic and childcare duties in preparation for married life (Derrington 2016). Historically, within Gypsy, Roma and Traveller communities a strong male power base has existed. It is perhaps because of the perceived threat to masculine identities that many men in these communities have been found to be more resistant to change (Levinson and Sparkes 2003). In comparison, some Gypsy and Traveller girls are beginning to question traditional gendered expectations that exist within their communities (Hamilton 2018a).

 **ACTIVITY**

Familial/gender roles and education – Margaret

Watch the YouTube clip about Margaret, an 8-year-old Irish Traveller. Make notes about any gendered expectations and how these might influence the decision Margaret makes about her future role within the community versus opportunities afforded to her within mainstream education.

This Morning (daytime TV show) (1 September 2016): 'The Gypsy kids too embarrassed to get an education'

www.youtube.com/watch?v=3rCGjvtYolE&t=185s

Culture: Enculturation and acculturation

When two cultures coexist, even on the peripheries, interactions of enculturation and acculturation are at play, which render ethnic boundaries permeable, and give rise to self-ascribed and other-ascribed identities. Shepherd and Linn (2015) explain how enculturation and acculturation interact at four different levels both for an individual and sub-groups: (1) Low enculturation (rejection of the heritage culture), combined with high acculturation (acceptance and participation in the new culture), result in *assimilation*, whereby subcultures adopt traits of the dominant culture. (2) High enculturation (maintenance of the heritage culture), combined with low acculturation (rejection of the new culture), result in *separation*, whereby subcultures are separated into ethnic groups. (3) Low enculturation combined with low acculturation result in *marginalisation*, whereby a subculture risks becoming excluded from their heritage culture and new culture. (4) High enculturation combined with high acculturation result in *integration*, whereby subcultures maintain most characteristics of their heritage culture while adopting traits of the dominant culture.

SOCIETAL PREJUDICE, INEQUALITIES AND LIFE CHANCES

Gypsies, Roma and Travellers are the most disadvantaged people in the UK, facing significant inequality in the areas of accommodation, health, education, employment, criminal justice and societal prejudice (Equality and Human Rights Commission [EHRC] 2019b; UK Parliament 2019). Despite some development, there has been a failure by policy-makers to tackle inequalities in a sustained way (UK Parliament 2019). The lack of progress has led to the Ministry of Housing, Communities and Local Government launching a national strategy in 2019, which involves several government departments working together to tackle inequality and improve the lives of Gypsy, Roma and Traveller people in the areas of education, health and social integration.

Gypsy, Roma and Traveller people have historically been persecuted across Europe. Their experience has been characterised by significant discrimination, victimisation and social exclusion, which contributes to the lack of trust many individuals from the communities tend to have in the state and public services. In the sixteenth century, a law was passed in England that allowed the state to imprison or execute anyone that was perceived to be a Gypsy. During the Second World War, approximately hundreds of thousands of the Roma population of Europe was exterminated by the Nazis in an act known as the *Porrajmos* (the 'devouring') – the Gypsy Holocaust (UK Parliament 2019).

Deep-seated prejudice towards Gypsy, Roma and Traveller people remains embedded within UK society. In 2017, the Traveller Movement reported that 91% of Gypsy,

Roma and Traveller people had faced discrimination and 77% had experienced hate speech or a hate crime (Traveller Movement 2017). People openly express negative attitudes and hostility towards Gypsies, Roma and Travellers (44%) more than any other ethnic or social group, including Muslims (22%), transgender people (16%), gay, lesbian and bisexual people (9%), people aged over 70 (4%) and disabled people with a physical impairment (3%) (EHRC 2019b).

For many people, their only information about Gypsies, Roma and Travellers comes from the media. Myths about the communities are based on racist stereotypes, which are often perpetuated by the media, and only serve to reinforce public prejudice. In order to consider the experiences of Gypsy, Roma and Traveller children in early years settings and schools, their encounters have to be understood within the context of their portrayal in the media and in public discourses – groups who are continually marginalised and criticised for not contributing socially and financially to society (Bhopal 2011). The continued stereotype of Gypsies, Roma and Travellers is one of outcasts, as not belonging. Deficit ideology and discriminatory attitudes and practices have been found within education, health services and the police (Commons Select Committee [CSC] 2016).

 **ACTIVITY**

Media coverage

Undertake a media search to examine news items presented about Gypsy, Roma and Traveller people. Are the messages mainly positive or mainly negative? Could these messages lead to misconceptions or stereotypical thinking? What impact might such messages have for these children and their families?

HEALTH OUTCOMES AND INEQUALITIES

UK studies consistently show that Gypsy, Roma and Traveller people have significantly poorer health and lower life expectancy than individuals from the general population, even when compared to other economically disadvantaged groups. Forty-two per cent of English Gypsies are affected by a long-term health condition, as opposed to 18% of the general population, and life expectancy for Gypsy, Roma and Traveller people is 10–12 years less than that of the general population (UK Parliament 2019). Individuals from these communities are at increased risk of disability, anxiety, depression, suicide, diabetes, chest pain and respiratory problems (CSC 2016; McFadden et al. 2018; O'Sullivan et al. 2018). Poor health outcomes for women and children include increased maternal and infant mortality. One in five Gypsy, Roma and Traveller mothers will experience the loss of a child, compared to 1 in 100 in the general population

(UK Parliament 2019). Children from these communities have the poorest health of any ethnic or social group in the UK, with high rates of dental caries, accidental injury and vaccine-preventable diseases. There is often a low uptake of preventative health services, including family planning, antenatal and postnatal care, childhood immunisations and developmental assessments (McFadden et al. 2018).

Reasons why Gypsy, Roma and Traveller people are vulnerable to poorer physical and mental health outcomes include poor-quality accommodation, increased risk of homelessness, insecurity of tenure, limited access to primary health services, low educational achievement, social exclusion, community tension and prejudice from local people (McFadden et al. 2018; EHRC 2019b). As with any other section of society, there is a strong correlation between quality of housing and quality of health, but because of the accommodation experiences of Gypsies, Roma and Travellers, this relationship is intensified. Environmental problems include access to running water, maintaining dry and adequately heated homes and living near pollutants such as industry or heavy traffic.

Barriers to primary health care

Gypsies, Roma and Travellers face various problems in accessing primary health care services. This may result in overreliance on accident and emergency services. Although a mobile lifestyle leads to underutilisation of health care services, poor access is also experienced by settled Gypsy, Roma and Traveller communities. Barriers are underpinned by complex factors, including mistrust of public health services; difficulties in registering with a GP or dentist; poor literacy skills; fear of prejudice and lack of understanding by health care staff of their lifestyle and needs; cultural normalisation of ill-health; and pride in self-reliance (McFadden et al. 2018; EHRC 2019b; UK Parliament 2019). Issues that may not be openly discussed in more traditional communities include mental ill-health, cancer and access to antenatal services. Individuals from these communities may not seek health care until they are at crisis point (EHRC 2019b). A lack of systematic and transferable health records, particularly for mobile groups, can mean that serious conditions are not identified and treated early. Poor-quality care and negative experiences encountered by individuals or their families/friends may lead to a reluctance to engage with services.

As 3 in 4 Gypsies, Roma and Travellers live in non-caravan housing, the UK Parliament (2019) assert that less focus should be given to planning and accommodation issues and more emphasis placed on specialist support for children's education and accessing health services. As the uptake of maternity, early years and child health services can reduce lifetime inequalities and improve health across the life course, early years practitioners play an important part in helping to link these families into mainstream services. McFadden et al. (2018) suggest that trust and engagement can be promoted by: (1) health services working more closely with community organisations (advocates) who understand Gypsy, Roma and Traveller people; (2) making it easier for these people to get health care when they need it (walk-in services and flexible antenatal and GP appointments where children can be immunised); (3) having several family members dealt with at once and being seen each time by the same health professional so that trust can be established.

CASE STUDY

Reluctance to use health care services

Charity is five months pregnant. She is 20 years old and has one child, Tommy, aged three. Tommy is always full of cuts and bruises because he enjoys rough and tumble play with older children on the site. Charity has not yet had any antenatal checks and Tommy has not been for routine health checks or immunisations.

Questions

1   Why might Charity be reluctant to use health care services for herself and Tommy?
2   Identify different services which could provide support to Charity and her young family, and discuss how she could be helped to gain access to these.

EDUCATIONAL OUTCOMES AND EXPERIENCES

Concerns over the engagement and attainment of Gypsy, Roma and Traveller pupils in the UK education system, and a commitment to improve provision for these children, are not new issues; rather they have been acknowledged across a series of government documents since the 1960s.

It is essential not to assume a single view of how Gypsy, Roma and Traveller groups regard mainstream education, nor see the focus of educational concern as a deficit model of their lifestyle and culture, as there can be a sharp distinction of opinions and level of engagement among different communities and within individual families. Gypsy, Roma and Traveller children can and do achieve within education. Across the UK and Europe there are increasing numbers of Gypsies, Roma and Travellers educated at academic and professional levels, economically successful and socially integrated with little or no sacrifice of cultural identity (Department for Children, Schools and Families [DCSF] 2009c).

There is, however, a well-documented and long-standing record of poor educational outcomes for Gypsy, Roma and Traveller children. Absenteeism, underachievement and school drop-out rates are more pronounced than that of any other minority ethnic or social group at every stage of education (Bloomer et al. 2014; Derrington 2016; EHRC 2019b). Gypsy, Roma and Traveller pupils are more likely to be categorised as having special educational needs, excluded because of their behaviour, leave school without formal qualifications and be less likely to make the transition to secondary school (Foster and Norton 2012; Office for National Statistics [ONS] 2014; EHRC 2019b).

In England, 72.5% of white British children achieved a 'good level of development' at foundation stage, higher than Black (69.6%), Bangladeshi (67.1%), Pakistani (64.3%) and Other white (63.9%) children, and children of other ethnicities (66.6%); attainment was lowest for Gypsy, Roma and Traveller children (33.2%) and highest for Indian children (77.3%) (EHRC 2019b). The attainment gap, which first appears in the early years, is one that increases up to the end of statutory school age. At Key Stage 4 (GCSE level), 75.3% of pupils of Chinese heritage gained a strong pass (grade 5 or above) in English and maths, the highest percentage out of all ethnic groups. The worst performing groups were Irish Traveller pupils (9.9%) and white Gypsy/Roma pupils (5.3%) (Gov.UK 2019). There is also a disparity in school exclusion rates. Exclusion rates were highest for Gypsy/Roma pupils (88.0 per 1,000) and Irish Traveller pupils (77.3 per 1,000), compared to 24.2 per 1,000 for white British pupils (EHRC 2019b).

It appears that government policies and initiatives have failed to make sufficient progress for Gypsy, Roma and Traveller children in mainstream education. However, critical thinking is required as to what really serves the interests and requirements of children from these communities as seen from their own needs and perspectives, rather than basing it on the plural values of mainstream society.

Understanding engagement and underachievement

Primary education is generally regarded in a positive light by Gypsies, Roma and Travellers (Wilkin et al. 2009) as many parents want their children to gain a good level of literacy, numeracy and ICT skills. There has, however, historically been a low uptake of early years education among the communities (DCSF 2009c). Many parents prefer not to send their children to school before they reach statutory school age as childcare is usually regarded as the responsibility of the mother (DCSF 2009a). As children progress, the intersectionality of culture, gender, class and religion increasingly clashes with the requirements of mainstream education, making the transition to secondary education uncertain. Factors influencing the engagement and educational attainment of Gypsy, Roma and Traveller pupils include: a lack of understanding in schools of their culture; low teacher expectations and negative attitudes; racism; an irrelevant curriculum; parents who have had negative or limited experiences within education; mobility issues linked to travelling; and parents' fear of exposing their children to the beliefs and practices of mainstream society (drugs, alcohol and sexual relationships for girls) (Cudworth 2008; Wilkin et al. 2009; Foster and Norton 2012; Derrington 2016). Some of these factors will now be considered in more detail.

Cultural discord

Education is valued in the wider sense, with the home and community regarded as the main learning environments. However, Gypsy, Roma and Traveller children are required to operate in an education system where values and practices have been designed to cater primarily for white middle-class pupils from a settled community. The difficulties Gypsy, Roma and Traveller pupils experience are exacerbated by a performance-driven education system that is structured around a statutory curriculum (Cudworth 2008). British law is based on the principle that every child should fully participate in an education system until they reach the compulsory school leaving age of 16 (Education Act 1996). It is a system, rooted in the beliefs and aspirations of a non-Gypsy/Roma/Traveller culture, which values individualistic activity and formal qualifications to acknowledge children's competencies. Such ideology conflicts with Gypsy, Roma and Traveller societies, which have traditionally been oriented towards group needs and survival rather than individual needs and gain (Levinson 2008). Family loyalty, and a desire to be regarded as a full community member, may be of greater importance to some young people than opportunities presented through the education system (Levinson 2015; Hamilton 2018a). Therefore, once a basic level of literacy and numeracy is attained, cultural patterns and traditional employment may take priority over school education, and many young people leave education. Learning that has no obvious connection to the home or community may be regarded as oppositional (Levinson 2008). Thus curriculum relevancy, by offering an alternative curriculum that complements the roles Gypsies, Roma and Travellers traditionally enter, is essential if education is to be continued.

The discord between mainstream schooling and cultural beliefs can lead to confusion, conflict and difficult choices regarding education, career aspirations and wider identities for young people. There is often intolerance of deviating from cultural norms, and young people who remain in education may be ostracised by their family and wider community (Hamilton 2018a). Such disapproval can unnerve parents and children who may be contemplating secondary education. However, it should not be assumed that all Gypsies, Roma and Travellers will feel restricted or in conflict as a gradual shift in attitudes towards education is occurring. Hamilton (2018a) shows how some young learners from these communities are developing resilience and determination in their efforts to deal with the cultural clash caused between home–school interfaces, and questioning some of the gendered beliefs within their community, particularly those which impact on their right to a full education.

Educational policy, together with inclusive education and human rights (all mainstream concepts, constructed by middle-class policy-makers) may present serious tensions and dilemmas. Hamilton (2018a) reports how efforts to keep Gypsy and Traveller children in mainstream education cause them to function in a conflicting dual cultural framework. Even if they remain in education and attain formal qualifications, there is no guarantee they will gain employment within mainstream society, as prejudice towards these communities is deeply entrenched. These young people risk becoming socially excluded from one society or both.

Racism and intra-community conflict

Under the Equality Act 2010, early years settings and schools have a duty to eliminate discrimination and promote equality of opportunity and positive relationships between people from different racial/ethnic backgrounds. The fear of racism is one of the main reasons parents say they keep their children away from mainstream education. Parents' fears may be justified, for as already discussed, there is significant prejudice towards Gypsy, Roma and Traveller communities (EHRC 2019b), with school children often lacking awareness and understanding of these communities (O'Sullivan et al. 2018). White-on-white racism is not as well recognised in comparison to non-white minority racism (Bhopal 2011) and, because of this, Gypsy, Roma and Traveller pupils may suppress their identity in school (Welsh Government 2014). There is a culture of non-reporting of racist incidents as children from these communities are expected to sort out their own problems. Consequently, many Gypsy, Roma and Traveller children deal with prejudice by retaliating physically, sometimes with the encouragement of their parents, which often leads to exclusion (Welsh Government 2014; Derrington 2016). Misconceptions which may be taken into the classroom and playground by practitioners and pupils include:

- 'Gypsy, Roma and Traveller boys are quick to resort to violence if they feel undermined or are subject to name-calling.'
- 'Gypsy, Roma and Traveller parents are not interested in their children's education.'
- 'Gypsies, Roma and Travellers are thieves and criminals.'
- 'Gypsies, Roma and Travellers are all nomadic.'

Poor experiences encountered during childhood, including racism and bullying, can further isolate Gypsy, Roma and Traveller people from mainstream society.

CASE STUDY

Racism in mainstream education – Ben Bennett

By the age of 12, Ben, an English Romany Gypsy, had experienced 11 different schools and been excluded from two. After a group of boys attacked him, leaving him with a broken hand, his parents decided to home-school him. Ben's sister, Anastasia, has also faced persistent racist abuse and been excluded from two schools – at the ages of four and six. Ben told a reporter:

> I'd always get racial backlash for being who I am … People would call me a dirty, filthy gyppo and say, 'My mummy and daddy said I can't play with you because you're a pikey and you'll rob my bike.' Teachers would also say they don't feel comfortable teaching me.

In July, 2018 Ben was presented the 'Diana Award' for his work campaigning and challenging racism and discrimination against young Gypsy, Roma and Traveller people.

Watch the following YouTube clip and read the accompanying news item. Then answer the questions that follow.

www.youtube.com/watch?v=Ld6mli3T3iU

www.aljazeera.com/news/2017/12/gypsy-children-expelled-uk-schools-171229075235572.html

Questions

1   What forms of racism might be present in schools/classrooms? Think about overt and covert forms.
2   What impact could such discrimination have on Gypsy, Roma and Traveller children?
3   What can be done to raise tolerance of Gypsy, Roma and Traveller communities within an early years or primary school setting?

It is essential that early years practitioners, teachers and policy-makers are also aware of the intra-community conflict that some young people who remain in education may be subjected to. Hamilton (2018a) suggests that in an attempt to address discrimination arising from the general population, the complex situation of intra-cultural prejudice is often overlooked. Many young Gypsies and Travellers described how they were jeered or ostracised by family and community members because of engaging in education. Such conflict can create significant confusion, anxiety and hurdles for Gypsy, Roma and Traveller pupils and their families, leading to disengagement and withdrawal from school despite an individual's ambitions and level of attainment.

CASE STUDY

Intra-cultural conflict – Shaunie

Shaunie is an 11-year-old Irish Traveller. She enjoys school and has plans to go to university as she wants to be a child psychologist. However, her parents are concerned that she is too school focused. They think she spends far too long doing her homework rather than helping with the housework and her younger siblings. She has many non-Traveller friends but is not allowed to see them outside of school. She feels lonely as she is not close to the children in her community – they call her 'little school girl' when they see her because of how much she engages with school.

Questions

1   What factors might enable Shaunie to fulfil her aspirations?
2   What factors might prevent Shaunie from continuing in education?
3   How could such conflict impact Shaunie's social and emotional well-being?

Teacher knowledge and expectations

Secure attachment with teachers has been found to positively impact on the attendance and retention of Gypsy, Roma and Traveller children in education (Derrington 2007). Unfortunately, there is a tendency for some schools and teachers to fall into adopting a cultural deficit model that problematises children from these communities. A lack of knowledge of Gypsy, Roma and Traveller cultures, lifestyles, customs and languages can lead to pupils being unable to see their home culture represented or reflected in a positive way in the school curriculum and environment. Low expectations which may be based on misplaced ideas that Gypsy, Roma and Traveller pupils will not stay long in the school, or unchallenged stereotypes, can result in children not reaching their potential.

Most Gypsy, Roma and Traveller children are likely to speak English as their first language in schools and early years settings; however, some may also use Romani or Gaelic words and phrases. Practitioners may not recognise the presence of another language; instead perceiving this as a deficit – as a language delay or disorder rather than as an issue relating to English as an additional language (DCSF 2009a). This may be further compounded because irregular attendance and the low take-up of early years provision mean there is less opportunity for practitioners to get to know individual children, to be able to make a fair assessment. Furthermore, assessment processes used within the early years foundation stage are primarily based on practitioners' judgement and thus are culturally biased. This risks Gypsy, Roma and Traveller children being assessed on skills they do not have, rather than having an appropriate context in which to display the skills they do have (DCSF 2009a).

Children's cultural behaviours are often misunderstood or seen as deviant in a school context (Foster and Norton 2012). Moreover, where bonds with individual pupils fail to be established, teachers risk perceiving Gypsy, Roma and Traveller children homogeneously. Such a view is detrimental as it overlooks the variations between children's cultures, family stability, socio-economic status, cognitive ability and personal resilience. This may prevent teachers from recognising the abilities, pastoral needs and cultural heritage of individual children, resulting in further marginalisation and disengagement from the learning environment.

 ## UNDERSTANDING BEHAVIOUR IN SCHOOLS AND CLASSROOMS

- Gypsy, Roma and Traveller children are used to socialising with adults from their community in different contexts. Their conversational style can be direct and may be perceived as being rude and confrontational.
- Gypsy, Roma and Traveller children often seek peer group approval which may involve 'acting out' or fighting.
- Grouping Gypsy, Roma and Traveller children with other pupils who have low social skills and behavioural issues provides the potential for conflict.
- Cultural norms around masculinity (physical strength, sexual prowess, business skills and practical skills) often result in boys' behaviour being at odds within a school environment.
- A lack of quiet space within the home, parents' literacy skills and cultural/family obligations may mean homework tasks are not completed.

SUPPORT STRATEGIES AND CRITICAL INCLUSION

Over the years, various strategies have been implemented to support and promote the attainment and school engagement of Gypsy, Roma and Traveller pupils. Strategies include:

- supporting families with school admission processes; allowing children to be registered at more than one school; a carefully planned induction for new pupils; a key worker system; a focused transition to secondary school; a flexible, relevant and culturally affirming curriculum; specialist training for staff; distance learning materials; systematic tracking and target setting of children's educational progress;

first-day absence calls; emphasis on social as well as academic needs; promoting attendance of pre-school children at early years settings; teaching children of differing ages in the same class; buddying systems and nurture groups; Traveller Education Service (TES); involving Gypsy, Roma and Traveller parents and the wider community positively in the school; an effective race equality policy, including ethnic monitoring to analyse the impact of school policies and procedures.

Additional strategies include:

- *Attendance*: Under the 1996 Education Act parents can opt to 'educate otherwise' which means elective home education is a popular choice by many families. Schools are required to be open for 190 days (380 sessions), with Gypsy, Roma and Traveller children having to attend 200 sessions a school year to prevent parents from being prosecuted (DCSF 2008).
- *Traveller Education Service*: By the 1970s many local authorities had developed a basic TES in attempts to raise the educational achievement and promote the culture of Traveller children in schools. The regional TES, which consists of peripatetic teachers, classroom assistants and welfare officers, was established in 2013 to work in partnership with children, families, schools and other stakeholder agencies.
- *Outreach services*: Services offered vary across local authorities but often these provide valuable support to mobile families in homes/sites. Developing trusting relationships with families is essential. Families have to be certain that agencies are working in the best interests of their children and see the benefit of the provision in order to engage with it.
- *Gypsy, Roma and Traveller History Month (GRTHM)*: Launched in 2008 by the DCSF, this is celebrated throughout the UK over the month of June. Schools, libraries and museums support the initiative by providing activities and information to share the history, culture and language of the different communities, challenge prejudices and stereotypes and promote community cohesion.

Despite ongoing efforts, children from these communities continue to encounter inequalities, prejudice and conflict. It is crucial to problematise reductionist and stereotypical thinking. Some Gypsies, Roma and Travellers will want to continue with secondary education and beyond, while others may want to remain at home to learn the traditions of their culture; some may wish to study vocational subjects, while others will want to pursue academic subjects; some may want to see their cultural heritage represented in the curriculum, while others may want this to go unnoticed; and some children will only make friends with peers from their community, while others prefer to establish friendships outside their community. Rather than a deficit ideology, which positions Gypsies, Roma and Travellers as 'deviants' and 'underachievers', people from these communities should be acknowledged as equals – individuals who function within cultures and structures that are different, as opposed to better or worse than mainstream culture (Hamilton 2018b). It is important that practitioners take a critical view of supporting Gypsies, Roma and Travellers by:

1   *Promoting social justice* – balancing cultural sensitivity against gender equality;

2   *Adopting critical inclusion* – where addressing difference is carefully considered, limits are acknowledged and what is 'truly inclusive' for individuals questioned;

3   *Deconstructing stereotypes and homogeneous assumptions* – even children from the same family have different needs, experiences, aspirations and support networks;

4   *Understanding complex cultural forces* – the social and emotional impact on individuals who go against cultural norms;

5   *Questioning what legitimate knowledge is* – who can say that mainstream education is in the best interest of all?

 **REFLECTION**

Case study – Johnny

Now that you have come to the end of the chapter, reflect upon all you have learned to advise Johnny's teacher.

Johnny is 5 years old. His teacher describes him as a 'boisterous, over-confident and cheeky boy, who is always fighting with other boys in his class'. She feels that some of his conversations are far too advanced for his age and some of the language he uses inappropriate. He is interested in practical tasks and numbers but anything else and he becomes easily distracted. He seems to have a better relationship with Mr Evans, the male teacher assistant.

Questions

1   Reflecting upon what you have learned from this chapter, what advice would you give to Johnny's teacher?

2   Think back to your early assumptions about the Gypsy, Roma and Traveller cultures. Has your view changed? What key knowledge do you feel you have gained that you will take into practice?

KEY POINTS

- A lack of authorised sites and changing employment is resulting in more Gypsy, Roma and Traveller families living in housing.
- Absenteeism, underachievement and high rates of exclusions and school drop-out rates remain problematic.
- Many parents have negative experiences of accessing education and health care services, and have low levels of literacy.

- Although attitudes are changing, there is generally disapproval among the community regarding secondary school due to a desire to protect cultural values and traditions.
- It is essential that practitioners (1) deconstruct reductionist stereotypical thinking held about Gypsies, Roma and Travellers and (2) consider the impact that going against cultural norms by remaining in education may have on the social and emotional well-being of young people from these communities.

FURTHER READING

Derrington, C. (2016) Supporting Gypsy, Roma and Traveller pupils. In Richards, G. and Armstrong, F. (eds) *Teaching and Learning in Diverse and Inclusive Classrooms*. pp. 41–51. Abingdon: Routledge.
Offers a detailed account of Gypsy, Roma and Traveller cultures and how to support children from these communities in school settings.
McFadden, A., Siebelt, L., Jackson, C., Jones, H., Innes, N., MacGillivray, S. and Atkin, K. (2018) *Enhancing Gypsy, Roma and Traveller Peoples' Trust: Using Maternity and Early Years' Health Services and Dental Health Services as Exemplars of Mainstream Service Provision*. Dundee: University of Dundee. Available at: https://doi.org/10.20933/100001117
Comprehensive overview regarding the health and well-being of pregnant women and new mothers from Gypsy, Roma and Traveller communities, and their experiences of and engagement with health services.

USEFUL WEBSITES

Equality and Human Rights Commission: www.equalityhumanrights.com
Friends, Families and Travellers: www.gypsy-traveller.org
Traveller Movement: www.travellermovement.org.uk
Travellers' Times: www.travellerstimes.org.uk

11

SUPPORTING
'MOST-ABLE' CHILDREN

CONTENTS

CHAPTER OVERVIEW

This chapter focuses on identifying and addressing the needs of children showing signs of being 'most-able'. Consideration is given to exploring the concept of 'intelligence' and how this can be measured, as well as outlining some of the challenges and barriers faced by this group of children. Most-able children seem to have 'dropped off' the focus of policy, making them a particularly marginalised group in schools. Without proper recognition, these children risk underachieving and their needs and experiences in schools and early years settings going unacknowledged.

This chapter considers:

1   Definitions, concepts and dilemmas of categorising most-able children.
2   Concepts of intelligence.
3   How most-able children can be identified.
4   Educational policy for most-able pupils.
5   Challenges and barriers commonly encountered by most-able children.
6   How most-able children can be supported in schools and early years settings.

DEFINITIONS AND CONCEPTS OF INTELLIGENCE

In order to support most-able children, it is first necessary to define what is meant by the term. However, the concept of what it means to be intelligent varies across cultures, countries and even districts within a country. The complexity often involved in supporting the needs of high-ability learners has led to the following international concerns: ensuring that the processes used to determine intelligence and aptitude are based on more than IQ tests; support provision is not elitist and that able children from the most disadvantaged communities have an opportunity to excel; practical talents are valued as much as academic ability; and practitioners have sufficient access to high-quality training (Sutherland 2012).

ACTIVITY

Who are they?

1   What labels are used to describe children who show high ability in one or more areas?
2   What kind of things would make a child stand out as having high potential?
3   Why is labelling children 'most-able' or 'high-ability' problematic?

The terms used to describe children who are capable of high attainment can be highly contentious, and there is no single term or definition which is universally accepted or understood (Montacute 2018). In England, the Department of Education and Ofsted tend to refer to these children as the 'most-able'; in Wales they are referred to as 'more able and talented (MAT)'; in Scotland as the 'highly able'; and in Northern Ireland as 'gifted and talented' and 'exceptionally able'. While it is recognised that it is not ideal, 'most-able' is generally the main term used within this chapter to refer to children who are working, or who have the potential to work, ahead of their age peers, either across the curriculum or in one or more areas (including high ability in a non-academic subject area). Other terms often used to describe these children include 'more able', 'exceptionally able', 'bright', 'high-flyer', 'switched on', 'articulate', 'smart', 'clever', 'genius' and 'high learning potential'.

In the past, schools in England tended to refer to most-able children as 'gifted or talented'. 'Gifted' is generally defined as high intellectual ability which might be identified using intelligence tests (Montgomery 2015). This includes children with a high aptitude for grasping concepts well and quickly in academic subjects such as the sciences, mathematics and languages. 'Talent' is used to refer to individuals who have remarkable skills in a performance area such as music, sport, creative and performing arts, leadership and communication. Comparisons are usually made in relation to age-related learning expectations (Fogarty 2018).

Some labels, such as 'dyslexia' and 'dyscalculia', can be useful as they help to explain a difficulty and target provision and resources (Montgomery 2015). However, labels used to describe high learning potential are often problematic:

- They can trigger misleading stereotypes and unfair or unrealistic expectations.
- They may limit or disguise children's other abilities.
- They may lead to a child only being challenged in what they are already good at.
- People may see the label rather than the holistic needs and abilities of the child.
- They might result in isolating children from their peers.
- Abilities can take months or years to be recognised.
- High ability can be a result of rapid development which ceases to exist once other children's development has caught up, meaning children no longer merit the label.
- Comparative terms are not helpful. For example, at what are they 'more able' and 'more able' than whom?

(Sutherland et al. 2009; Sutherland 2012)

Numerous theories have developed as a result of academics striving to understand the concepts of giftedness and talent. There is some suggestion that high ability is innate. However, studies regarding the early histories of prodigies have demonstrated that significant amounts of nurture and practice are required to achieve 'world class expertise' (Montgomery 2015). Underpinning this chapter is the idea that high ability is just one factor in educational success. Positive and individualistic learning opportunities, support from home and school, along with hard work and practice can see an aptitude be translated into expertise and/or success (Sutherland et al. 2009; Montgomery 2015). It is therefore essential that practitioners see past any labels that have been attached to children. Instead, the focus should be on gathering detailed information about the child, through careful and continuous observation and assessment, in order to maximise a range of appropriately challenging opportunities for learning which will allow a child to blossom.

TYPES OF INTELLIGENCE

There are many broad definitions and conflicting views relating to the concept of 'intelligence'. For the purpose of this chapter, consideration will be given to the following perspectives of intelligence: cognitive intelligence, multiple intelligence and emotional and moral intelligence.

Cognitive intelligence

The first intelligence test, which was created in 1904, by the French psychologist Alfred Binet, was used to identify learners who required specialised educational support (Boronski and Hassan 2015). Binet's test sought to determine children's mental ages by comparing their results against the 'typical' scores of given age groups. This concept of 'mental age' was furthered in 1912 by William Stern, a German psychologist, who divided mental age by chronological age to arrive at a 'mental quotient' (Fletcher and Hattie 2011). American psychologist Lewis Terman later multiplied this by 100 and coined it 'intelligence quotient' (IQ) (Fletcher and Hattie 2011). Individuals who hold a traditional view of intelligence as being purely cognitive often believe that intellect is inherited and therefore fixed (Fogarty 2009).

Standardised IQ test scores follow a normal distribution (or 'bell curve') where the average score is set to 100 and the standard deviation of that score to 15, meaning that 68% of the population will have scores between 85 and 115. Those with scores over 115 are classed as having above-average intelligence and possessing high cognitive abilities. However, the point at which labels such as 'gifted' and 'genius' are assigned can vary. The classification of intelligence presented in Table 11.1 has been adapted from that offered by Carolyn (2019).

Table 11.1 Classification of intelligence

Classification	IQ score	Frequency
Gifted or moderately gifted	130–145	Approximately 2 in every 100
Highly gifted	145–160	Approximately 1 in every 1,000
Exceptionally gifted	160–180	Approximately 1 in every 10,000
Profoundly gifted	180+	Approximately 1 in every 1,000,0000

Table 11.2 Multiple intelligences

Type of intelligence	Signs displayed
Musical	Children may sing or play instruments well, remember melodies and easily recognise when notes are off-key.
Bodily-kinaesthetic	Children are often very active, find it challenging to sit still for prolonged periods, enjoy hands-on activities, are good at sports and possess advanced fine-motor skills.
Linguistic	Children possess a vocabulary larger than is expected for their age, are good at telling and making up stories, and enjoy playing word games.
Logical-mathematical	Children may enjoy playing strategy games such as chess, often ask how things work in order to understand the world more deeply, and are quick at mental arithmetic.
Visual and spatial	Children are good at reading diagrams and maps, enjoy puzzles and jigsaws, build constructions out of materials such as Lego, and are talented at drawing for their age.
Interpersonal	Children who are natural leaders, enjoy being with their peers and are good at offering advice to their friends.
Intrapersonal	Children who have a good understanding of their self. They are independent, can express how they feel, are aware of their strengths and weaknesses, and can learn from mistakes.
Naturalist	Children are aware of their environment, and enjoy exploring the outside world and learning about issues relating to such subjects as biology and astronomy.

(Adapted from Pound 2005; Sutherland 2012)

Multiple intelligences

Howard Gardner (1993) presents an alternative view – multiple intelligence theory. The theory arose from his dissatisfaction with the idea of intelligence as something that could be measured and represented as an IQ score (Pound 2005). Rather than identifying the 'level of intelligence' a person has, he wanted to determine *how people are intelligent*. Gardner identified several types of intelligences (see Table 11.2), which he claimed are present in all individuals to some degree, depending on the extent to which they have been developed by one's background, experiences and opportunities (Pound 2005). It is, however, important to realise that multiple intelligences do not exist in isolation; rather they are interconnected. For example, a talented dancer would require musical, bodily-kinaesthetic and spatial intelligence.

Emotional and moral intelligence

Another dimension of intellect is emotional intelligence. Inspired by Howard Gardner, one of the key theories of emotional intelligence stems from the work of Daniel Goleman (1998 cited in Fogarty 2009). Goleman's definition of emotional intelligence is based on five key elements: self-awareness, which includes confidence and decisiveness; self-regulation, which includes being able to manage one's own emotions; motivation; empathy; and social skills, including leadership (Goleman cited in Fogarty 2009). An extension of emotional intelligence is offered by Robert Coles, who refers to 'moral intelligence'. He asserts that some children show a particular aptitude for becoming more intelligent in their inner selves; these children learn how to better empathise with others, show respect and learn how to deal with complex and sensitive discussions on moral issues in the modern world (Coles cited in Fogarty 2009). This theory is based on how children's values and beliefs are both born and shaped throughout childhood. Learners who are more interested and capable of engaging in social justice, inclusion and diversity education are likely to have higher levels of emotional and moral intelligence.

Helping children to understand intelligence

The way intelligence is viewed can vary significantly among cultures and social groups. In order to encourage children to perceive themselves as able and confident learners, it is important that practitioners do not consider intelligence as being fixed (Sutherland 2012), nor limit the concept to a cognitive view which links intelligence to achievement in curriculum subject areas. Key principles, essential for practitioners to hold if they are to help children to develop a positive view of intelligence, include:

- A belief that intelligence is multifaceted and developmental.
- Awareness of any personal biases, which may favour or negate against certain children and groups of learners.
- Not writing individual children off because of perceived differences and 'deficits' associated with their home-life, culture, challenging behaviours, or special educational needs and disability (SEND).
- Encouraging children not to be afraid of making mistakes, and to reflect and develop from any errors made.
- Praising the effort children put into an activity, rather than just focusing on the end-product.

(Sutherland 2012)

CASE STUDY

Abdul – most-able/highly talented

Abdul is a very lively 6-year-old boy who is popular with his peers. His teacher has struggled to engage him in the academic side of schooling, which disappoints his parents because they are extremely keen for him to do well. Abdul's teacher finds his behaviour challenging as he is unable to sit still; he regularly shouts out answers, goes off task and fidgets with other children, disrupting them. However, he demonstrates an exceptionally high aptitude for performing arts. He picks up lyrics to songs and lines for role-play at an unusually fast pace and his dance moves are impressive for a child of his age. Mr Stone, the music and drama teacher, has suggested to his parents that they enrol him in an academy for children who are highly talented in performing arts. His parents do not seem to be particularly supportive of the idea.

Questions

1   Refer to Gardner's 'multiple intelligences'. Identify the different intelligences Abdul seems to be excelling in.
2   What strategies could the class teacher/school put into place to both support Abdul's talent and help him engage in more academic tasks?
3   What barriers could prevent Abdul from progressing with his talent?

IDENTIFICATION OF 'MOST-ABLE' CHILDREN

In order to meet the needs of most-able children, it is important that they are identified as early as possible, so that an individualised and developmentally appropriate curriculum can be designed (Gross 2015). However, identifying these children can be a complex process, with no universally single accepted way to measure the extent of a child's intelligence or potential (Sutherland et al. 2009; Montacute 2018). Significant debate centres around when to identify learners, whether testing is accurate and what role teachers should have in the identification process (Montacute 2018). It is argued that: identification should be regarded as a continuous and fluid process; evidence be gathered from a variety of settings; children's abilities be presented as profiles; and practitioners recognise that a child's ability to show aptitude and demonstrate skills will be affected by factors such as culture, language and gender (Sutherland et al. 2009).

Testing

Testing is commonly used to identify most-able children. When testing a child's abilities, areas which may be evaluated include cognitive abilities through an IQ test;

academic achievement in reading, writing and mathematics; and memory and processing speed (Potential Plus 2020b). The Cognitive Ability Test (CAT) is the most widely used test in the UK to assess the reasoning abilities of children between 6 and 17 years old and is frequently used by secondary schools to predict GCSE and A-level grades. Some parents may independently seek external assessments through an educational psychologist or by children undertaking the High Learning Potential Assessment developed by Potential Plus UK, which is suitable for children from 4½ years of age, or the Early Years Assessment of Potential for children aged 3–4 years, to give an indication of their child's abilities (Potential Plus 2020b). However, testing can only reveal so much about a child's ability and may only measure a certain type of intelligence (Potential Plus 2017; Montacute 2018). Children's abilities manifest themselves in different ways, in different contexts and at different times (Sutherland et al. 2009). A child might be highly able in one area but struggle in another. Due to the possibility of atypical development, it is essential to go beyond traditional methods of identification and to gain a holistic profile of the child including their educational, social, emotional and psychological needs, as well as achievements outside school (Sutherland et al. 2009).

Observation

Teachers often rely on their own professional judgements of individual children. In order to identify and best support most-able children it is essential that practitioners are proficient in their area of expertise, knowledgeable of children and young people's development, and skilled at observational and assessment processes. The possible presence of teacher bias, and subsequent impact of this, have already been discussed; nevertheless it is paramount that practitioners remain mindful of any unconscious bias that might skew their judgement regarding their perceptions of most-able children. It is therefore important that practitioners strive to build an authentic partnership with parents/carers, have an open mind and listen to information parents have to share on the child's abilities (Sutherland 2012).

Although England no longer publishes official checklists for schools of 'typical behaviours or characteristics' which may be exhibited by most-able children, they are used by other countries of the UK. Checklists focus teacher attention on factors wider than IQ and attainment test scores, and therefore can provide a more holistic perspective on the child's abilities (National Council for Curriculum and Assessment [NCCA] 2007). They are useful informal assessments, particularly within primary schools, but should be triangulated with other data rather than used as a single tool. Training in the use of checklists to identify high ability and underachievement is advisable, and it should be remembered that they act as a guide only. Checklists might be subject focused or general. A general checklist could include characteristics such as:

- Having advanced reasoning, vocabulary and physical skills (the child learns to walk and talk before the typical age-range or learns subjects like mathematics and English at a quicker pace than their peers).
- Possessing very good memories/mastering new skills with few repetitions.
- Having intense curiosity and often asking questions.
- Being sensible and having mature emotions.
- Having flexible and alternative ways of solving problems.
- Preferring higher levels of complexity in play situations or formal tasks.
- Having an early understanding of abstract concepts (death, time).
- Making spontaneous elaboration with new experiences.

(Baby Space 2015; Montgomery 2015)

For examples of checklists see NCCA (2007, pp. 22–23), 'General and subject specific checklists', and Montgomery (2015, pp. 7–10), Chapter 1, 'General checklist'.

POLICY IN THE UK NATIONS

Wales

In 2008, the Welsh Government, in collaboration with the National Association for Able Children in Education Cymru, produced 'Meeting the Challenge – Quality Standards in Education for More Able and Talented (MAT) Pupils'. Meeting the Challenge introduced a consistent approach across all local authorities and schools to addressing the needs of MAT learners, and provided a framework for the development of whole school MAT provision. In 2010, 'A Curriculum for all Learners' provided additional advice.

Scotland

The Scottish Government partly funds the Scottish Network for Able Pupils (SNAP), a progressive organisation which provides specialist support to schools, teachers and parents. Support for highly able students is enshrined in Scottish law in the Additional Support for Learning Act 2004.

Northern Ireland

The National Council for Curriculum and Assessment (NCCA) provides guidance for teachers on the use of differentiation, consideration of early exam entry, and monitoring the progress of 'gifted and talented' and 'exceptionally able' students.

England

- 1999: 'Gifted and Talented' policy introduced within the Excellence in Cities agenda. Schools were required to: (1) identify 5–10% of pupils as gifted and talented and place them on a register; (2) appoint a 'Gifted and Talented' coordinator; and (3) implement a teaching and learning programme for gifted and talented pupils.
- 2002: The National Programme for Gifted and Talented Education was launched to enhance the development of learners between the ages of 4 and 19.
- 2007: A move away from a centralised programme to local activities. The 2002 National programme was outsourced to the Centre for British Teachers' Education Trust and renamed 'Young, Gifted and Talented'.
- 2010: The national programme for gifted and talented abandoned by the Coalition government due to a loss of confidence. Funding was re-routed to help disadvantaged students attend university, and materials transferred to National Archive.
- 2018: 'Future Talent Fund' proposed; organisations to apply for funding to run projects to help schools support gifted students from disadvantaged backgrounds. The initiative was cancelled less than a year after it was announced, to prioritise improvements in the early years.

(Smithers and Robinson 2012; Welsh Government 2015; Koshy et al. 2017; Montacute 2018; Whittaker 2018)

England – current policy

Currently there is no specific national policy or central services for the most-able pupils. Instead, teachers act as gatekeepers of both identification and provisions, with advice provided by Ofsted (English Government Inspectorate Office for Standards in Education) and Potential Plus UK. However, it should be noted that the Ofsted school inspection framework does not specifically identify 'most-able' learners for consideration. Critics argue that a lack of comprehensive national policy affects funding allocation and the quality of provision available to the 'most-able' learners, with standards varying between schools (Koshy et al. 2017). Consequently, many schools do not have good enough provision for this group of pupils, with the early years and primary phase having the highest percentage (50%) of schools with poor provision for the most-able pupils (Potential Plus 2020c), and high-learning-potential students from disadvantaged households continuing to lag behind their more affluent peers (Koshy et al. 2017).

BARRIERS TO LEARNING

Robert Gagné proposed that high learning potential is transformed into giftedness or talent through the interaction of a range of positive environmental facilitators which are present in a child's home and school environment (Gagné cited in Gross 2015). However, environmental supports alone are not enough to scaffold the development of giftedness or talent. Most-able children must also possess certain intrapersonal characteristics; an enjoyment of intellectual challenge and self-acceptance of their ability, without 'dumbing down' for social acceptance, are particularly crucial (Gross 2015). Barriers which may prevent children from developing their high learning potential include dual and multiple exceptionality, interpersonal characteristics, and teacher perceptions and biases.

Dual and multiple exceptionality

'Double or dual' and 'multiple' exceptionality (DME) are terms used to describe children who have a gift or a talent alongside one (or more) SEND. According to Potential Plus (2020d), 5–10% of children with high ability also have SEND. Disabilities that commonly exist alongside high learning potential, include: (1) neurological disorders (autism spectrum, attention deficit, sensory processing, dyspraxia); (2) learning difficulties (dyslexia, dysgraphia, dyscalculia); and (3) sensory and speech impairments (Potential Plus 2020d).

When a child has SEND and high learning potential, they often experience complicated challenges in their lives and may require considerable support to ensure that they do not underachieve (Montgomery 2015). In order to alleviate social, emotional and behavioural difficulties (SEBD) and to support educational attainment, early identification and appropriate intervention strategies in the early years of schooling are paramount. A challenging curriculum, interesting learning opportunities and a skilful and sensitive mentor will help to motivate and support DME children. However, the identification of most-able children with SEND is not always easy. Particularly problematic is identifying high learning potential in pupils with English as an additional language (EAL) and dyslexia (Montgomery 2015).

Factors contributing to the underachievement of DME children include handwriting difficulties, the child's personality, cultural disadvantage and low socio-economic status, funding and resource issues linked to dual or multiple needs, inadequate pedagogy, poor classroom management and an irrelevant curriculum. DME children who are placed in lower sets because of their SEND and not intellectually stimulated can become frustrated, demotivated and develop SEBD. Subsequently, their behaviour and SEND often become the key focus for intervention and the high ability overlooked (Montgomery 2015).

Interpersonal characteristics

Most-able children can be more vulnerable to mental ill-health because of negative aspects of perfectionism. Almost always being able to fulfil expectations as a young child, these children may set unreasonable goals for themselves and suffer high levels of self-criticism and emotional stress when they are unable to achieve their own extreme standards (Fogarty 2018; Potential Plus 2020e). However, in some cases, perfectionism among most-able children has also been found to contribute to high levels of attainment (Christopher and Shewmaker 2010). An environment that nurtures a perfectionist child's resilience, while encouraging them to take risks and to be challenged, is important. Some children may suffer from intense emotions which can result in extreme anxiety and feelings of unfairness, causing them to overreact (Potential Plus 2020e). Consequently, most-able children may experience challenges in forming friendships. This may also be due to them functioning at a higher cognitive and social level to their same-age peers. Being most-able might also single them out as different, making other children (including siblings) jealous, intimidated or unable to relate to them, (Fogarty 2018). Difficulties with social relationships, bullying and being misunderstood may contribute to a sense of isolation (Potential Plus 2020e). Furthermore, some children may have sensory sensitivity causing them to struggle in loud and busy environments, eat certain foods or wear certain clothing (Potential Plus 2020e).

Teacher perceptions and biases

While it is commonplace to refer explicitly to levels of disability linked to a child's delayed cognitive impairment, there may be reluctance by some practitioners to refer to levels of high ability among learners (Gross 2015; Fogarty 2018). This may be due to the belief that most-able learners are already at an advantage, so providing them with additional provision and teacher support is elitist, particularly when there are other children deemed to be more in need of assistance. When a child's ability far exceeds that of their teacher, a complex relationship dynamic may be formed (Fogarty 2018). Some teachers can feel threatened by a child's advanced knowledge or be at a loss as to how to provide for these children if they permit them to 'race ahead' with tasks and materials.

It is not uncommon for teachers to hold unconscious biases with regard to which learners are more likely to be 'high ability' or 'better behaved', on the grounds of gender, language, ethnicity and socio-economic factors (Hamilton 2013a; Montacute 2018). For instance, children who are confident, mature and charismatic are more likely to be identified as high ability compared to children who are more reserved, struggle to articulate their words, have EAL or have challenging behaviour (Sutherland 2012). Most-able children from lower-income backgrounds are especially prone to falling behind in their school years and are unlikely to gain places in the most selective universities and in top professions (Montgomery 2015; Montacute 2018). Even disadvantaged pupils who perform well in primary school are more likely to fall behind at secondary school, with many children from lower-income families reluctant to engage with intervention programmes because it does not 'fit in' with their peer group (Montacute 2018).

Teachers often react differently to male and female learners: boys and girls tend to have their own social dynamics and cultural norms which influence future roles/aspirations, which can all impact on how most-able children are nurtured. Girls are often praised for being articulate, focused, organised, tidy, diligent and cooperative (Hamilton and Jones 2016), whereas boys are identified as being dominant in both class activities and at breaktime, taking control of work areas, play spaces, toys and equipment (NCCA 2007; Legewiea and DiPretea 2012). If work is too easy, boredom in boys usually comes to the attention of a teacher sooner than in girls, with boys more likely to disrupt others, answer out of turn or be labelled as fidgety or having attention deficit hyperactivity disorder (Hamilton and Jones 2016). Boys (as well as some girls) may deliberately underachieve and decide to 'do the minimum' or 'clown around' in order to avoid being teased or bullied for being studious (Sutherland et al. 2009; Hamilton and Roberts 2017). The passivity of some most-able girls may result in them receiving less recognition for their abilities and consequently fewer challenging activities (NCCA 2007).

 **ACTIVITY**

Should calling someone a 'nerd' be a hate crime?

Watch the following YouTube clip and then discuss the questions which follow with a small group of peers.

www.youtube.com/watch?v=bErlrHGUc9g

1   Should labels used to describe most-able children such as 'geek' and 'nerd' be identified as a hate crime?
2   What impact could such labels have on children?
3   How could practitioners help to promote understanding and tolerance regarding the needs of, and issues faced by, most-able children?

SUPPORTING MOST-ABLE CHILDREN

Most-able children who are not sufficiently challenged inside schools and early years settings can become bored and disengaged, leading to underachievement (Muijs and Reynolds 2018). It is therefore vital that both practitioners and parents appropriately support and stretch these children. However, in comparison to other groups of learners who differ from the 'norm', such as SEND, research in this area is limited (Montacute 2018). Some of the strategies identified as being effective in the support of most-able children include accelerated learning, ability grouping, differentiation, and mentoring and cooperative learning.

Accelerated learning

This enables most-able children to be given content that is more advanced, allowing them to move through the curriculum at a quicker pace. 'Grade-based acceleration' involves children skipping forward a school year so that they follow all subjects at a level higher than typical for their age, whereas 'subject-based acceleration' involves children joining classes of older learners for certain subjects only or where they have advanced classes in a subject in addition to their usual lessons (Muijs and Reynolds 2018). Advantages of accelerated learning may include children being more sufficiently challenged so frustration, boredom and disengagement are alleviated; also, children who are also functioning with more advanced social skills than their chronological peers may find it easier to socialise with older children (NCCA 2007; Knowles 2011b). However, as many disadvantages of this strategy have been identified, it is suggested that it only be used in extreme cases for 'exceptionally bright' children. While some children may be functioning at a higher cognitive level, their interpersonal, social and emotional intelligence may not be as well developed, and they may struggle to 'fit in' with older learners, leaving them isolated (NCCA 2007). Furthermore, for some children, outperforming their peers may be a result of faster development during a specific period (Sutherland 2012) and not reflective of the rest of their educational trajectory. Therefore, it must be emphasised that grade-based acceleration can have a detrimental impact on learners (NCCA 2007).

Ability grouping

This is a commonly used strategy as it enables most-able children to receive accelerated learning, through enriched discussion with peers functioning at a similar cognitive level, while remaining within the same year group (NCCA 2007). In primary schools, this is often done by dividing children into tables based on their ability, particularly in settings with single-form entry. In schools with multi-form entry (more than one class per year group), it can take the form of setting and streaming. Setting is where children of comparable abilities are placed into the same class for certain lessons/subjects. In contrast, streaming is where children are allocated to the same ability-based groups for all lessons, regardless of their attainment in each subject. Although ability grouping has been found to have a positive impact on the achievement of most-able children, it can have a negative effect on children in middle and bottom sets due to lower teacher expectations (Muijs and Reynolds 2018). As it can be difficult to identify most-able children with SEND, EAL or from an economically disadvantaged background, some individuals risk being misplaced into low-ability groups and may underachieve as a result of the slower pace of teaching (Montacute 2018). For ability grouping to be effective, it is essential that groups are closely monitored and seen to be flexible. This will determine whether children should be moved between sets, helping to avoid disadvantaging children for prolonged periods of time, if they have been incorrectly placed. However, being positioned in a high-ability group may not necessarily promote a child's self-worth. Some children, placed alongside peers of similar abilities, may compare their own attainment against others and devalue their own achievements if they feel they are not progressing at the same rate. This false perception would not be present in a class of diverse abilities (Muijs and Reynolds 2018).

Differentiation

In most cases, the needs of most-able pupils are best addressed as part of differentiated classroom provision (NCCA 2007). To be effective it is important that practitioners view differentiation in an individualised way, setting work that meets the needs of the individual child. Differentiation may take the form of curriculum compacting, where topics and tasks that have already been learned are replaced with more challenging material. Most-able pupils can thrive when working at a faster pace, as they may not require all steps to be explained. However, there may be occasions when most-able children complete tasks slowly to produce work of greater detail or complexity (NCCA 2007; Sutherland et al. 2009). It might involve an enriched curriculum where activities are adapted so that they go beyond the normal curriculum to promote higher-order thinking (Moltzen 2011). Pupils may engage with the same content or task, but the outcome may be open-ended to allow most-able children to explore and extend their thinking (Sutherland et al. 2009). A practitioner may use different resources which match children's ability when a class is working on the same problem. Some children will not need concrete materials as they may be able to make connections easily. More demanding resources may have dense text, abstract concepts and a complex structure (NCCA 2007). More sophisticated dialogue should also be used with most-able pupils as well as targeted questioning to elicit a range of responses, further develop understanding or introduce alternative ways of approaching tasks (NCCA 2007; Sutherland et al. 2009). Finally, all pupils gain from having agency over their learning, but most-able pupils can especially benefit from being able to select from a range of starting points, materials, subjects or processes and to adapt the work themselves (NCCA 2007; Sutherland et al. 2009).

Mentoring and cooperative learning

Structured mentoring programmes have been found to be particularly enriching for most-able children (Montacute 2018). The mentor might be an expert in a particular area from outside of the school (such as a specialist organisation or university) or older and more experienced children from inside the school. It could also involve summer school or extra-curricular activities which aim to further promote subject knowledge and skills, confidence, motivation, resilience and communication. Children from lower socio-economic backgrounds tend to be less likely to engage in mentoring programmes. Therefore, interventions which target and encourage the involvement of most-able children from disadvantaged backgrounds are necessary in order to close the attainment gap between low-income most-able children and their more affluent most-able peers (Montacute 2018).

Cooperative learning is where most-able children are paired or grouped with lower-ability children. This challenges most-able children to thoroughly comprehend concepts and material in order to teach others. Although it may require them to be patient with peers who take longer to grasp ideas, exposing them to such situations can help them to develop interpersonal, communication and teamwork skills (Muijs and Reynolds 2018). To ensure that there is both group and individual accountability, and that the most-able learner is not left doing all the hard work, each child could be given a particular goal to achieve or task to undertake (Muijs and Reynolds 2018).

 **CASE STUDY**

Rose – most-able/high academic learner

Rose, aged 11 years, is described by her teacher as an 'all-round academically able' child. From a young age, Rose had a thirst for reading, drawing and writing stories. By the time she was 7 years old she had read all but the last level of books in the school's reading scheme. One day, when she returned home with a book that she had read several times, she had an unusual outburst. 'There's no point going to school anymore', she told her mum. 'I'm totally bored with it all.' On discussing the issue with Rose's teacher, her mum was told 'She can't read the last level or there will be nothing left for her in Year 6.' So, Rose began to take her own books, often Harry Potter, to read at school. By the time she reached Year 6 this had progressed to the Lord of the Rings trilogy and she has become known by her peers as the girl who loves to read 'hard books'. Rose, who had enjoyed a close friendship group in lower school, has been teased and bullied throughout Key Stage 2 by girls who used to be her friends.

Questions

1   What strategies could the class teacher/school put into place for Rose to prevent her from becoming disengaged with learning?
2   Why do you think she was treated differently by her peers? What possible impact could this have? And how could her teacher intervene to address the bullying?

REFLECTION

Supporting most-able children: What do you think?

Now that you have come to the end of the chapter, please discuss each statement with a group of peers. Please be professional during the discussion.

1   'By the time these children go to secondary school you have lost them, so priority should be given to funding and resourcing the pre-school and primary phases.'
2   'Disbanding the national programme for highly able students in England is problematic. Without an effective alternative, there is danger of failing a generation of gifted children.'
3   'Additional funding should be given to supporting bright children from poorer households. But what about the rest, particularly those living just above a low income?'
4   'Good schools stretch the most-able children as a normal part of what they do, and these children can be left to 'get on with it' inside inclusive classrooms. Introducing yet another initiative for this group of children simply overburdens teachers.'
5   'Identifying most-able children needs to be based on more than just IQ and test scores. What do you do if a child has a disappointing set of results? Should you drop their 'gifted' label?'

KEY POINTS

- Perceptions of what intelligence is differs widely.
- All four countries of the UK have different approaches to supporting most-able learners.
- Traditional tests used to measure intelligence are contested. High IQ is regarded as a less-than-accurate measure of success, as a range of environmental and personal factors determine whether potential is transformed into giftedness or a talent.
- The needs of most-able children, particularly children from socio-economically disadvantaged families, risk being overlooked in schools and early years settings.
- Most high-ability children can be successfully catered for by differentiated provision inside inclusive classrooms.
- It is essential that supporting 'most-able' learners features within a whole school ethos; that staff have access to continuing professional development; and that close home–school links are fostered.
- As with all children, but particularly essential for this group, they need to be presented with a broad range of stimulating learning experiences which appropriately stretch their abilities.

FURTHER READING

Fogarty, J. (2018) Supporting children who are highly able. In Knowles, G. (ed.) *Supporting Inclusive Practice and Ensuring Opportunity is Equal for All*. Third edition. pp. 70–83. Abingdon: Routledge.

A comprehensive chapter which presents an overview of many important issues relating to supporting highly able children in educational settings.

Montgomery, D. (2015) *Teaching Gifted Children with Special Educational Needs: Supporting Dual and Multiple Exceptionality*. Abingdon: Routledge.

A useful text which presents detailed coverage of issues related to children identified as having both special educational needs and high learning potential.

National Council for Curriculum and Assessment (2007) *Gifted and Talented Pupils: Guidelines for Teachers*. Available at: www.nicurriculum.org.uk/docs/inclusion_and_sen/gifted/Gifted_and_Talented.pdf

A theoretically informative yet practical toolkit for practising teachers which contains case studies and checklists.

USEFUL WEBSITES

Potential Plus UK: www.potentialplusuk.org

Scottish Network for Able Pupils: www.gla.ac.uk/research/az/ablepupils

Sutton Trust: www.suttontrust.com

CONCLUSION
Final Thoughts on Critical Inclusion

There will always be prejudiced individuals who perceive their 'normalised' attitudes and ways of doing as being superior and that these should not be threatened. Cultural and historical events shape discourses and, at the time of writing, social incidents – such as Covid-19 triggering some to apportion blame on certain countries and cultural groups, and police violence against Black people highlighted by the death of George Floyd – have added to the debate regarding societal prejudice and social injustice.

It is essential that early years practitioners and primary school teachers are at the forefront of addressing social justice and diversity issues, to help raise awareness and bring about positive change, particularly for the most marginalised in society. Messages conveyed by politicians and other influential figures, circulated daily through media platforms, shape the beliefs, attitudes and behaviours of parents/carers, practitioners and children. It is imperative to start early, by encouraging children to become critical receivers of social messages, helping them both to critique power relations and the damaging impact of restrictive stereotypes and discriminatory attitudes, and to build skills to manage prejudicial conflict and oppression.

Despite decades of policy and intervention, many individuals remain at the margins of society in the UK. It is therefore essential that a more critical stance to inclusion is adopted. Combating social injustice is not easy; rather it is increasingly known to be an ongoing process that is often fraught with complexities, contradictions, dilemmas, tensions and limits. However, schools and early years settings more likely to make a positive difference to the lives of those most marginalised in society are those which:

- Have the full support of the senior management team in building an inclusive ethos.
- Have effective equality policies, where discriminatory attitudes and practices are challenged.
- Provide social and learning contexts where all individuals feel welcomed and respected and have an opportunity to participate.
- Create safe spaces for open and reflective listening dialogue.

- Provide an appropriately challenging learning environment, where children have opportunities to critically engage with a range of social and diversity issues.
- Ensure that expectations and progress of minority children are in line with other groups and that assessments for all children are fair and free from stereotyping.
- Recognise that social inequalities, knowledge and power relations are disseminated through historical and cultural discourses and everyday social interactions.
- Recognise that children have agency in their lives.
- View change as possible through deconstruction, reflexivity, criticality and empowering the marginalised.

Robinson and Jones Diaz (2006) identify the following as being paramount in approaches to social justice education with children:

- *Criticality and reflexivity* – Ongoing commitment by practitioners to reflect, acknowledge and challenge any personal biases, stereotypical assumptions and beliefs. In order to do this school and early years practitioners will need to realise how their own gendered, social, religious, linguistic and ethnic positioning and discourses may perpetuate the social inequalities that exist within society, to impact on the children and families in their settings, while also recognising that one's views can never be totally objective. Reflexivity, which is developing a critical self-conscious awareness of one's relationships with the Other, is crucial for the delivery of social justice education. Rather than drawing upon a concept of 'tolerance', Robinson and Jones Diaz (2006: 169) assert that a discourse of 'respect' is used instead, as the former is based on a hierarchical power relationship that has limits, whereas the latter is about 'accepting people's rights to choose who they are in the world that sit equally beside different ways of being, knowing and doing'.
- *Promoting theoretical understandings* – Incorporating critical theories of childhood and diversity (such as a feminist poststructuralist perspective) is crucial for delivering social justice education effectively. Modernist discourses do not address children's agency or consider the complex intersection of social identity (intersectionality). Children must be given opportunities to examine, experience and critique different versions of reality. Children are aware of the normalising discourses that exist within society and often regulate their own behaviours and those of others accordingly. Some social injustice issues (sexuality, transgender, death, violence, mental illness) are often not addressed with children as practitioners may consider children to be too young to understand and deal with 'adult themes'. This protection is normally aimed

at maintaining children's 'innocence'. Yet in a globalised planet with progressively diverse communications technologies which have entered children's worlds, children have increased access to 'adult information'.

- *Fostering children's critical thinking* – Traditionally, diversity approaches with children have relied heavily on superficial approaches and colourful resources at the expense of fostering children's critical thinking. If children are to understand their own prejudices and societal injustices, they need to be aware of how power relations, restrictive binaries, stereotypes and inequalities are constructed within historically and culturally social discourses. At the start of this book two strategies were presented for helping children to engage in more critical debate – Philosophy for Children (Chapter 1, pp. 22–23) and critical media literacy (Chapter 2, p.34).

- *The danger of ignoring perceived absences* – The belief that there is no need to address aspects of diversity which are not part of the setting/community that practitioners are catering for. Assumed absences can result in perpetuating further invisibility and marginalisation of minority groups; some of these children and families may be unknowingly present (low income, refugees, sexuality, gender diverse). In homogeneous schools and early years settings, where the absence of social and cultural diversity fails to give children experiences of difference, detrimental stereotypes can manifest. This error has long been acknowledged, documented in the Macpherson Report 1999, following the racially motivated murder of Stephen Lawrence in 1993.

If marginalised children and families are to be supported and empowered, then practitioners must disrupt the normalising discourses and contradictions around social justice that operate in everyday interactions and practices. However, this must be undertaken by knowledgeable, committed and skilled practitioners who pay careful consideration to the cultural and religious background of children, to ensure that controversial social topics are appropriately handled. Coverage of social justice and diversity topics, which draw upon some of the principles outlined within this section – inside initial training programmes as well as continued professional development for early years practitioners and primary school teachers – is vital to the effective delivery of inclusion and diversity education.

REFERENCES

Abbas, T. (2019) *Islamophobia and Radicalisation.* Oxford: Oxford University Press.

Adoption UK (2017) *Adoption UK's Schools & Exclusions Report.* Available at: www.adoptionuk.org/Handlers/Download.ashx?IDMF=e6616ae3-7b0a-449c-b037-070a92428495

Adoption UK (2018) *Bridging the Gap: Giving Adopted Children an Equal Chance in School.* Available at: www.basw.co.uk/system/files/resources/bridging-the-gap.pdf

Ahmad, S., Barrett, J., Beaini, A.Y., Bouman, W.B., Davies, A., Greener, H.M., Lenihan, P., Lorimer, S., Murjan, S., Richards, C., Seal, L.J. and Stradins, L. (2013) Gender dysphoria services: A guide for general practitioners and other healthcare staff. *Sexual and Relationship Theory*, 28(3): 172–85. Available at: www.academia.edu/29590091/Gender_dysphoria_services_a_guide_for_general_practitioners_and_other_healthcare_staff

Ahmed, B. (2016) How Islamophobia impacts Muslim children. *Islamic Horizons*, July–August, pp. 34–5. Available at: https://issuu.com/isnacreative/docs/ih_jul-aug_16/35

Al Jazeera (2019) *UK media's portrayal of Muslims 'misleading and negative': Study.* Available at: www.aljazeera.com/news/2019/07/uk-media-portrayal-muslims-misleading-negative-study-190708104550539.html

All Party Parliamentary Group (2017) *Refugees Welcome? The Experience of New Refugees in the UK: A report by the All Party Parliamentary Group on Refugees.* Available at: https://www.refugeecouncil.org.uk/wp-content/uploads/2019/03/APPG_on_Refugees_-_Refugees_Welcome_report.pdf

Allport, G. (1954) *The Nature of Prejudice.* Reading, MA: Addison-Wesley.

American Psychiatric Association (2013) *Diagnostic and Statistical Manual of Mental Disorders (DSM-5).* Available at: www.psychiatry.org/psychiatrists/practice/dsm

Amnesty International UK, the Refugee Council and Save the Children (2019) *Without my Family: The Impact of Family Separation on Child Refugees in the UK.* Available at: https://resourcecentre.savethechildren.net/node/16673/pdf/without-my-family-report-aw-jan2020-lores.pdf

Anderson, D. (2013) *Reaching Out and Bringing In.* Bloomington, IN: WestBow Press.

Anti-Bullying Alliance (2011) *Bullying of Children with Disabilities and Special Educational Needs in Schools: Briefing Paper for Parents on the Views and Experiences of Other Parents, Carers and Families.* Available at: https://contact.org.uk/media/395239/reports_and_research_bullying_of_children_with_disabilities_2011_parents_briefing.pdf

Anti-Bullying Alliance (2014) *Tackling Disablist Language Based Bullying in School: A Teacher's Guide (SEN and Disability: Developing Effective Anti-Bullying Practice).* Available at: www.anti-bullyingalliance.org.uk/sites/default/files/field/attachment/tackling-disablist-language-based-bullying-in-school-final.pdf

Anti-Bullying Alliance (2017) *Prevalence of bullying.* Available at: www.anti-bullyingalliance.org.uk/tools-information/all-about-bullying/prevalence-and-impact/prevalence-bullying

Argent, K. (2017) Resources. In Cronin, M., Argent K. and Collett, C. (eds) *Poverty and Inclusion in Early Years Education.* pp. 127–50. Abingdon: Routledge.

Awan, I. and Zempi, I. (2017) Impacts of anti-Muslim hate crime. In Elahi, F. and Khan, O. (eds) *Islamophobia: Still a Challenge for Us All.* pp. 37–9. London: Runnymede Trust.

Baby Space (2015) *Gifted children.* Available at: www.babyspace.uk.com/en/gifted-children

Banks, J. (2016) *Cultural Diversity and Education.* Sixth edition. Abingdon: Routledge.

Banse, R., Gawronski, B., Rebetez, C., Gutt, H. and Morton, J.B. (2010) The development of spontaneous gender stereotyping in childhood: Relations to stereotype knowledge and stereotype flexibility. *Developmental Science*, 13 (2), 298–30.

Barber, S. (2012) Time to stop stigmatising mental health problems at school. *The Guardian.* Available at: https://www.theguardian.com/teacher-network/teacher-blog/2012/apr/14/mental-health-stigma-school

Barrs, M. (1991) *Patterns of Learning: The Primary Language Record and the National Curriculum.* London: CLPE.

Bartlett, S. and Burton, D. (2007) *Introduction to Education Studies.* Second edition. London: Sage.

Bartlett, S. and Burton. D. (2016) The influence of gender in the classroom. In Richards, G. and Armstrong, F. (eds) *Teaching and Learning in Diverse and Inclusive Classrooms.* pp. 54–64. Abingdon: Routledge.

BBC (2017) *Reality check. What is the Prevent strategy?* Available at: www.bbc.co.uk/news/election-2017-40151991

BBC (2018) *Anti-Semitism pervades European life, says EU report.* Available at: www.bbc.co.uk/news/world-europe-46439194

BBC (2019) *France anti-Semitism: Jewish graves defaced with Nazi swastikas.* Available at: www.bbc.co.uk/news/world-europe-50657066

BBC (2020) *Quaden Bayles: Australian boy in bullying video receives global support.* Available at: www.bbc.co.uk/news/world-australia-51582696

BBC News (2009) *The Burning Times.* Available at: http://news.bbc.co.uk/1/hi/magazine/8334055.stm

BBC News (2017) *Disabled children hate crime reports increasing.* 15 October 2017. Available at: www.bbc.co.uk/news/uk-41600137

BBC News (2019) *Children as young as 11 placed in unregulated care homes*. Available at: www.bbc.co.uk/news/uk-49734338

BBC News (2020) *BAME foster care shortage in two-thirds of English councils*. Available at: www.bbc.co.uk/news/uk-england-leeds-51136569

Become (2019) *I Wish You Knew*. Available at: www.becomecharity.org.uk/media/1838/i-wish-you-knew.pdf

Bei, Z. (2019) *Intersectionality and inclusion*. Available at: www.allfie.org.uk/news/inclusion-now/inclusion-now-54/intersectionality-inclusion/

Bem, S. (1981) Gender schema theory: A cognitive account of sex typing. *Psychological Review*, 88, 325–64.

Bem, S.L. (1983) Gender schema theory and its implications for child development: Raising gender-aschematic children in a gender schematic society. *Signs*, 8 (4), 598–616.

Benoist, F. (2018) Supporting and including children from low-income families. In Knowles, G. (ed.) *Supporting Inclusive Practice and Ensuring Opportunity is Equal for All*. Third edition. pp. 153–68. Abingdon: Routledge.

Bhopal, K. (2011) 'This is a school, it's not a site': Teachers' attitudes towards Gypsy and Traveller pupils in school in England, UK. *British Educational Research Journal*, 37 (3), 465–83.

Bloom, A. (2014) *Playing to type*. Available at: www.tes.co.uk/article.aspx?storycode=6420270

Bloomer, F., Hamilton, J. and Potter, M. (2014) Challenges and barriers in primary school education: The experiences of Traveller children and young people in Northern Ireland. *Education Citizenship and Social Justice*, 9 (1), 3–18.

Blumell, L.E., Bunce, M., Cooper, G. and McDowell, C. (2020) Refugee and asylum news coverage in UK print and online media. *Journalism Studies*, 21 (2), 162–79.

Bond (Disability and Development Group) (2017) *Stigma, Disability and Development*. London: Bond.

Booth, T. and Ainscow, M. (2011) *Index for Inclusion: Developing Learning and Participation in Schools*. Bristol: Centre for Studies on Inclusive Education.

Boronski, T. and Hassan, N. (2015) *Sociology of Education*. London: Sage.

Borsay, A. (2012) *Disabled Children and Special Education, 1944–1981*. A presentation delivered at the Department for Education, 26 November 2012. Available at: www.historyandpolicy.org/docs/dfe-anne-borsay-text.pdf

Bourdieu, P. (1984) *Distinction: A Social Critique of the Judgement of Taste*. London: Routledge.

Bowman, J. and West, K. (2018) Prime and prejudice: Brief stereotypical media representations can increase prejudicial attitudes and behaviour towards people with schizophrenia. *Journal of Community and Applied Social Psychology*, 29 (3), 167–77.

Brighton and Hove City Council Education Team (2018) *Trans Inclusion Schools Toolkit.* Available at: https://mermaidsuk.org.uk/wp-content/uploads/2019/12/AllsortsYouthProject-Trans-Inclusion-Schools-Toolkit-Sept-18.pdf

British Association for Adoption and Fostering (2020) *What are the different types of fostering?* Available at: https://corambaaf.org.uk/fostering-adoption/fostering/fostering-me

British Red Cross (2011) *Voices of Strength and Pain.* London: British Red Cross.

Bronfenbrenner, U. (1979) *The Ecology of Human Development: Experiments by Nature and Design.* Cambridge, MA: President and Fellows of Harvard College.

Brown, B. (2001) *Combating Discrimination: Persona Dolls in Action.* Stoke-on-Trent: Trentham Books.

Bryant, L. (2020) *Pierre Bourdieu.* Available at: www.historylearningsite.co.uk/sociology/education-and-sociology/pierre-bourdieu/

Burchardt, M. and Griera, M. (2019) To see or not to see: Explaining intolerance against the 'Burqa' in European public space. *Ethnic and Racial Studies,* 5 (42), 726–44.

Burke, P. (1996) *Gender Shock.* New York: Anchor Books.

Burrows, T. (2017) Muslim campaigner calls for hijabs to be banned in primary schools as new survey shows one in five allow them as part of uniform. *Mail Online.* Available at: www.dailymail.co.uk/news/article-4848100/Girls-young-five-allowed-wear-hijabs.html

Burton, M. (2014) Children and young people's mental health. In Burton, M., Pavord, E. and Williams, B. (eds) *Children and Adolescent Mental Health.* pp. 1–38. London: Sage.

Bussey, K. and Bandura, A. (1999) Social cognitive theory of gender development and differentiation. *Psychological Review,* 106, 676–713.

Bussey, K. and Bandura, A. (2004) Social cognitive theory of gender development and functioning. In Eagly, A.H., Beall, A.E. and Sternberg, R.J. (eds) *The Psychology of Gender.* pp. 92–119. New York: Guilford Press.

Buttle UK (2019) *Child poverty in UK in 2019.* Available at: www.buttleuk.org/news/child-poverty-in-uk-in-2019

Bywaters, P. and Brady, G. (2019) *Inequalities in child welfare intervention rates.* Available at: www.nuffieldfoundation.org/project/inequalities-in-child-welfare-intervention-rates

Candappa, M. (2016) Invisibility and Otherness: Asylum seeking and refugee students in the classroom. In Richards, G. and Armstrong, F. (eds) *Teaching and Learning in Diverse and Inclusive Classrooms.* Second edition. pp. 74–86. Abingdon: Routledge.

Carolyn, K. (2019) *What is highly gifted? Exceptionally gifted? Profoundly gifted? And what does it mean?* Available at: www.hoagiesgifted.org/highly_profoundly.htm

Centre for Studies on Inclusive Education (2018a) *CSIE strategy 2016–2019*. Available at: www.csie.org.uk/about/strategy.shtml

Centre for Studies on Inclusive Education (2018b) *About inclusion*. Available at: www.csie.org.uk/inclusion/

Chand, R., Nel, E. and Pelc, S. (2017) Preface. In Chand, R., Nel, E. and Pelc, S. (eds) *Societies, Social Inequalities and Marginalization: Marginal Regions in the 21st Century*. pp v–vi. Cham, Switzerland: Springer.

Charity Commission (2001) *The Promotion of Social Inclusion*. Available at: https://assets.publishing.service.gov.uk/government/uploads/system/uploads/attachment_data/file/359358/socinc.pdf

Chatzitheochari, S., Parsons, S. and Platt, L. (2016) Doubly disadvantaged? Bullying experiences among disabled children and young people in England. *Sociology*, 50 (4), 695–713.

Cheung, R. (2018) *International Comparisons of Health and Wellbeing in Early Childhood*. London: Nuffield Trust.

Child Poverty Action Group (2019) *Child Poverty Facts and Figures*. Available at: https://cpag.org.uk/child-poverty/child-poverty-facts-and-figures#footnoteref2_qrkhtuf

Child Poverty Action Group (2020a) *The Causes of Poverty*. Available at: https://cpag.org.uk/child-poverty/causes-poverty

Child Poverty Action Group (2020b) *Who Is at Risk of Poverty?* Available at: https://cpag.org.uk/child-poverty/who-risk-poverty

Child Poverty Action Group (2020c) *Measuring Poverty*. Available at: https://cpag.org.uk/child-poverty/measuring-poverty

Child Poverty Action Group (2020d) *Recent History of UK Child Poverty*. Available at: https://cpag.org.uk/recent-history-uk-child-poverty

Child Poverty Action Group (2020e) *The Effects of Poverty*. Available at: https://cpag.org.uk/child-poverty/effects-poverty

Child Rights International Network (2018) *Discrimination and the media*. Available at: https://archive.crin.org/en/guides/advocacy/challenging-discrimination/discrimination-and-media.html

Children 1st (2018) *Poverty and Adverse Childhood Experiences (ACEs)*. Available at: www.children1st.org.uk/who-we-are/news/blog/poverty-and-adverse-childhood-experiences-aces/

Children's Commissioner (2018a) *Life in Likes: Children's Commissioner Report into Social Media Use among 8–12 Year Olds*. Available at: www.childrenscommissioner.gov.uk/wp-content/uploads/2018/01/Childrens-Commissioner-for-England-Life-in-Likes-3.pdf

Children's Commissioner (2018b) *Stability Index 2018: Overview & Findings*. London: Children's Commissioner for England.

Children's Commissioner (2019) *Far Less than They Deserve: Children with Learning Disabilities or Autism Living in Mental Health Hospitals.* Available at: www.childrenscommissioner.gov.uk/wp-content/uploads/2019/05/CCO-far-less-than-they-deserve-2019.pdf

The Children's Society (2018) *Distress Signals: Unaccompanied Young People's Struggle for Mental Health Support.* Available at: www.childrenssociety.org.uk/sites/default/files/distress-signals-report_.pdf

The Children's Society (2020a) *What are the effects of child poverty?* Available at: www.childrenssociety.org.uk/what-we-do/our-work/ending-child-poverty/what-are-the-effects-of-child-poverty

The Children's Society (2020b) *The Children's Society reacts to new child poverty statistics.* Available at: www.childrenssociety.org.uk/news-and-blogs/press-releases/the-childrens-society-reacts-to-new-child-poverty-statistics

The Children's Society (2020c) *Education and Schools.* Available at: https://www.childrenssociety.org.uk/youngcarer/refugee-toolkit/education-and-school

Christopher, M. and Shewmaker, J. (2010) The relationship of perfectionism to affective variable in gifted and highly able children. *Gifted Children Today,* 33 (3), 20–30.

Claridge, T. (2015) *Bourdieu on social capital – theory of capital.* Available at: https://www.socialcapitalresearch.com/author/tristan-claridge/

Clough, P. (2006) Routes to inclusion. In Clough, P. and Corbett, J. (eds) *Theories of Inclusive Education.* pp. 1–34. London: Paul Chapman.

Collett, C. (2017) Social, cultural and economic capital. In Cronin, M., Argent, K. and Collett, C. (eds) *Poverty and Inclusion in Early Years Education.* pp. 57–77. Oxon: Routledge.

Commons Select Committee (2016) *Tackling Inequalities Faced by Gypsy, Roma and Traveller Communities.* Available at: https://old.parliament.uk/business/committees/committees-a-z/commons-select/women-and-equalities-committee/news-parliament-2015/gypsy-roma-and-traveller-communities-inquiry-launch-16-17/

The Communication Trust (2014) *Youth Justice Programme.* Available at: www.thecommunicationtrust.org.uk/projects/youth-justice/

Community Security Trust (2018) *Antisemitic Discourse in Britain 2018.* Available at: https://cst.org.uk/public/data/file/6/0/Antisemitic%20Discourse%20Report%202018%20WEB.pdf

Community Security Trust (2020) *Antisemitic Incidents 2019.* Available at: https://cst.org.uk/public/data/file/9/0/IncidentsReport2019.pdf

Conkbayir, M. and Pascal, C. (2014) *Early Childhood Theories and Contemporary Issues: An Introduction.* London: Bloomsbury.

Consonant (n.d.) *The asylum process made simple.* Available at: https://legal.consonant.org.uk/campaigns/the-asylum-process-made-simple/

Contact (2019) *Dealing with Bullying: Information for Parents of Disabled Children.* Available at: www.contact.org.uk/media/1546238/dealing_with_bullying.pdf

Contact (2020) *Research.* Available at: https://contact.org.uk/get-involved/campaigns-research/research/

The Conversation (2017) *How to challenge racism in British schools.* Available at: https://theconversation.com/how-to-challenge-racism-in-british-schools-78153

Coram (2017) *Black, Asian and mixed ethnicities in adoption and fostering: An interview with CoramBAAF consultant Savita de Sousa.* Available at: https://corambaaf.org.uk/-interview-corambaaf-consultant-savita-de-sousa

Coram (2020) *Children waiting for adoption.* Available at: www.coramadoption.org.uk/adoption-process/children-waiting-adoption

Coram Voice (2015) *Children & Young People's Views on Being in Care: A Literature Review.* Available at: https://coramvoice.org.uk/sites/default/files/Children's%20views%20lit%20review%20FINAL.pdf

Cottle, S. (2006) *Mediatized Conflict.* Buckingham: Open University Press.

Crenshaw, K. (1989) *Demarginalizing the Intersection of Race and Sex: A Black Feminist Critique of Antidiscrimination Doctrine, Feminist Theory and Antiracist Politics.* University of Chicago Legal Forum, Vol. 1989, Iss. 1, Article 8. Available at: http://chicagounbound.uchicago.edu/uclf/vol1989/iss1/8

Cronin, M. (2017) Why do we need to think about poverty and social exclusion? In Cronin, M., Argent, K. and Collett, C. (eds) *Poverty and inclusion in early years education.* pp. 11–33. Oxon: Routledge.

Crosse, K. (2007) *Introducing English as an Additional Language to Young Children.* London: Chapman Publishing.

Crowley, K. (2017) *Child Development: A Practical Development.* London: Sage.

Cudworth, D. (2008) There is a little bit more than just delivering the stuff: Policy, pedagogy and the education of Gypsy/Traveller children. *Critical Social Policy,* 28 (3), 361–77.

Cummins, J. (2000) *Negotiating Identities: Education for Empowerment in a Diverse Society.* Second edition. Los Angeles: California Association for Bilingual Education.

Cummins, J. (2001) Knowledge, power, and identity in teaching English as a second language. In Genesee, F. (ed.) *Educating Second Language Children: The Whole Child, the Whole Curriculum, the Whole Community.* Ninth edition. pp. 33–58. Cambridge: Cambridge University Press.

Danby, G. and Hamilton, P. (2016) Addressing the 'elephant in the room': The role of the primary school practitioner in supporting children's mental well-being. *Pastoral Care in Education,* 34 (2), 90–103.

Daniels, M. (2017) *Defining Marginalised; DFID's Leave No One Behind Agenda.* Available at: www.ukaiddirect.org/wp-content/uploads/2017/03/Defining-marginalised.pdf

Danon, L.M. and Kramer, A. (2017) Between concealing and revealing intersexed bodies: Parental strategies. *Qualitative Health Research*, 27 (10), 1562–74.

Department for Children, Schools and Families (2008) *Attendance Advice: Gypsy, Roma and Traveller Children.* Available at: www.lancsngfl.ac.uk/projects/ema/download/file/Attendance-advice-gypsy-roma-traveller-children.pdf

Department for Children, Schools and Families (2009a) *Building Futures: Developing Trust. A Focus on Provision for Children from Gypsy, Roma and Traveller Backgrounds in the Early Years Foundation Stage.* Available at: www.foundationyears.org.uk/wp-content/uploads/ 2011/10/Developing_Trust.pdf

Department for Children, Schools and Families (2009b) *Improving the Educational Attainment of Children in Care (Looked After Children).* Available at: www.brent.gov.uk/media/972015/Improving%20the%20educational%20attainment%20of%20looked%20after%20children.pdf

Department for Children, Schools and Families (2009c) *Moving forward together: Raising Gypsy, Roma and Traveller achievement.* Available at: https://core.ac.uk/reader/4150794

Department for Communities and Local Government (2007) *Getting the Message Across: Using Media to Reduce Racial Prejudice and Discrimination.* London: Communities and Local Government Publications.

Department for Education (2013) *£100 million to support the education of children in care.* Available at: www.gov.uk/government/news/100-million-to-support-the-education-of-children-in-care

Department for Education (2014a) *The Equality Act 2010 and Schools: Departmental Advice for School Leaders, School Staff, Governing Bodies and Local Authorities.* Available at: https://assets.publishing.service.gov.uk/government/uploads/system/uploads/attachment_data/file/315587/Equality_Act_Advice_Final.pdf

Department for Education (2014b) *Promoting Fundamental British Values as Part of SMSC in Schools: Departmental Advice for Maintained Schools.* Available at: https://assets.publishing.service.gov.uk/government/uploads/system/uploads/attachment_data/file/380595/SMSC_Guidance_Maintained_Schools.pdf

Department for Education (2015) *The Prevent Duty: Departmental Advice for Schools and Childcare Providers.* Available at: https://assets.publishing.service.gov.uk/government/uploads/system/uploads/attachment_data/file/439598/prevent-duty-departmental-advice-v6.pdf

Department for Education (2017) *Outcomes for Children Looked After by Local Authorities in England, 31 March 2016. SFR 12/2017.* Available at: https://assets.publishing.service.gov.uk/government/uploads/system/uploads/attachment_data/file/602087/SFR12_2017_Text.pdf

Department for Education (2018) *Promoting the Education of Looked After Children and Previously Looked After Children: Statutory Guidance for Local Authorities.* Available at:

https://assets.publishing.service.gov.uk/government/uploads/system/uploads/attachment_data/file/683556/Promoting_the_education_of_looked-after_children_and_previously_looked-after_children.pdf

Department for Education (2019a) *Relationships Education, Relationships and Sex Education (RSE) and Health Education.* Available at: https://assets.publishing.service.gov.uk/government/uploads/system/uploads/attachment_data/file/805781/Relationships_Education__Relationships_and_Sex_Education__RSE__and_Health_Education.pdf

Department for Education (2019b) *Special Educational Needs in England: January 2019.* Available at: https://assets.publishing.service.gov.uk/government/uploads/system/uploads/attachment_data/file/814244/SEN_2019_Text.docx.pdf

Department for Education (2019c) *Phonics Screening Check and Key Stage 1 Assessments in England, 2019.* Available at: https://assets.publishing.service.gov.uk/government/uploads/system/uploads/attachment_data/file/851296/Phonics_screening_check_and_key_stage_1_assessments_in_England_2019.pdf

Department for Education (2019d) *National Curriculum Assessments at Key Stage 2 in England, 2019 (revised).* Available at: https://assets.publishing.service.gov.uk/government/uploads/system/uploads/attachment_data/file/851798/KS2_Revised_publication_text_2019_v3.pdf

Department for Education (2019e) *National Statistics: Children Looked After in England (including Adoption), year ending 31 March 2019.* Available at: https://assets.publishing.service.gov.uk/government/uploads/system/uploads/attachment_data/file/850306/Children_looked_after_in_England_2019_Text.pdf

Department for Education and Department of Health (2015) *Special Educational Needs and Disability Code of Practice: 0 to 25 Years Statutory Guidance for Organisations which Work with and Support Children and Young People Who Have Special Educational Needs or Disabilities.* Available at: https://assets.publishing.service.gov.uk/government/uploads/system/uploads/attachment_data/file/398815/SEND_Code_of_Practice_January_2015.pdf

Department for Education and Skills (2003) *Aiming High: Raising Achievement of Minority Ethnic Pupils.* London: Department for Education and Skills.

Department of Education and Early Childhood Development (2011) *Refugee Status Report: A Report on How Refugee Children and Young People in Victoria are Faring.* Available at: www.education.vic.gov.au/Documents/about/research/refugeestatusreport.pdf

Department of Health (2015) *Future in Mind: Promoting, Protecting and Improving our Children and Young People's Mental Health and Wellbeing.* London: NHS England Publication Gateway.

Department of Health and Department for Education (2017) *Transforming Children and Young People's Mental Health Provision: A Green Paper.* Available at: https://

assets.publishing.service.gov.uk/government/uploads/system/uploads/attachment_data/file/728892/government-response-to-consultation-on-transforming-children-and-young-peoples-mental-health.pdf

Department of Health and Social Care and Department for Education (2018) *Government Response to the Consultation on Transforming Children and Young People's Mental Health Provision: A Green Paper and Next Steps.* Available at: https://assets.publishing.service.gov.uk/government/uploads/system/uploads/attachment_data/file/728892/government-response-to-consultation-on-transforming-children-and-young-peoples-mental-health.pdf

Department for Work and Pensions (2019) *Workless Households and Educational Attainment Statutory Indicators.* London: HMSO.

Derrington, C. (2007) Fight, flight and playing white: An examination of coping strategies adopted by Gypsy Traveller adolescents in English secondary schools. *International Journal of Educational Research*, 46 (6), 357–67.

Derrington, C. (2016) Supporting Gypsy, Roma and Traveller pupils. In Richards, G. and Armstrong, F. (eds) *Teaching and Learning in Diverse and Inclusive Classrooms.* pp. 41–51. Abingdon: Routledge.

Devarakonda, C. (2013) *Diversity and Inclusion in Early Childhood.* London: Sage.

Di Masi, D. and Santi, M. (2016) Learning democratic thinking: A curriculum to philosophy for children as citizens. *Journal of Curriculum Studies*, 48 (1), 136–50.

Disabled Living Foundation (2017) *Key facts.* Available at: www.dlf.org.uk/content/key-facts

Dovidio, J., Hewstone, M., Glick, P. and Esses, V. (2013) Prejudice, stereotyping and discrimination: Theoretical and empirical overview. In Dovidio, J., Hewstone, M., Glick, P. and Esses, V. (eds) *Prejudice, Stereotyping and Discrimination.* pp. 3–28. London: Sage.

Driggs, J. (2018) *Islamophobia in the United Kingdom: A critical global perspective. California State University.* Available at: https://digitalcommons.csumb.edu/cgi/viewcontent.cgi?article=1250&context=caps_thes_all

Dsdfamilies (2020) *About us.* Available at: www.dsdfamilies.org/charity

Duignan, B. (2020) *Judith Butler.* Available at: www.britannica.com/biography/Judith-Butler

Dukes, C. and Smith, M. (2006) *A Practical Guide to Pre-School Inclusion.* London: Paul Chapman.

Durrani, K., Hankir, A. and Carrick, F. (2018) History and principles of Islam and Islamophobia. In Moffic, H., Peteet, J., Hankir, A. and Awaad, R. (eds) *Islamophobia and Psychiatry.* pp. 321–34. New York: Springer.

Ecclestone, K. (2014) *Stop this educational madness: It's time to resist calls for more mental-health interventions in education.* Available at: www.spiked-online.com/newsite/article/stop-this-educational-madness/15382#.VmtXUGcrGM8

Ecclestone, K. (2015) *Well-being programmes in schools might be doing children more harm than good.* Available at: https://theconversation.com/well-being-programmes-in-schools-might-be-doing-children-more-harm-than-good-36573

Ekins, A. and Grimes, P. (2009) *Inclusion: Developing an Effective Whole School Approach.* Maidenhead: Open University Press.

Ekornes, S., Hauge, T.E. and Lund, I. (2012) Teachers as mental health promoters: A study of teachers' understanding of the concept of mental health. *International Journal of Mental Health Promotion*, 14 (7), 289–310.

Elahi, F. and Khan, O. (2017) Introduction: What is Islamophobia? In Elahi, F. and Khan, O. (eds) *Islamophobia: Still a Challenge for Us All.* pp. 5–12. London: Runnymede Trust.

EqualiTeach (2018) *Faith in Us: Educating Young People on Islamophobia.* St Neots: EqualiTeach CIC.

Equality and Human Rights Commission Scotland (2013) *Gypsy Travellers in Scotland: A Resource for the Media.* Available at: www.equalityhumanrights.com/sites/default/files/gt_media_guide_final.pdf

Equality and Human Rights Commission (2016) *England's Most Disadvantaged Groups: Migrants, Refugees and Asylum Seekers.* Available at: www.equalityhumanrights.com/sites/default/files/is-england-fairer-2016-most-disadvantaged-groups-migrants-refugees-asylum-seekers.pdf

Equality and Human Rights Commission (2019a) *Convention on the Rights of the Child.* Available at: www.equalityhumanrights.com/en/our-human-rights-work/monitoring-and-promoting-un-treaties/convention-rights-child

Equality and Human Rights Commission (2019b) *The State of Equality and Human Rights 2018.* Available at: www.equalityhumanrights.com/sites/default/files/is-britain-fairer-accessible.pdf

Equality and Human Rights Commission (2020a) *Public Sector Equality Duty.* Available at: www.equalityhumanrights.com/en/advice-and-guidance/public-sector-equality-duty

Equality and Human rights Commission (2020b). *Investigation into antisemitism in the Labour Party finds unlawful acts of discrimination and harassment.* Available at: https://www.equalityhumanrights.com/en/our-work/news/investigation-antisemitism-labour-party-finds-unlawful-acts-discrimination-and-harassment

European Union Agency for Fundamental Rights (FRA) (2018) *Experiences and Perceptions of Antisemitism: Second Survey on Discrimination and Hate Crime against Jews in the EU.* Available at: https://fra.europa.eu/en/publication/2018/experiences-and-perceptions-antisemitism-second-survey-discrimination-and-hate

Family Futures (2020) *Dispelling myths around 'harder to place' children.* Available at: www.familyfutures.co.uk/dispelling-myths-around-harder-to-place-children/

Farron, T. (2015) *It's Theresa May – not immigrants – who's really damaging Britain*. Available at: www.politics.co.uk/blogs/2015/10/06/it-s-theresa-may-not-immigrants-who-is-really-damaging-brita

Fast, A. and Olson, K. (2018) Gender development in transgender preschool children. *Child Development*, 89 (2), 620–37.

Featherstone, S. and Bayley, R. (2010) *The Cleverness of Boys*. London: A&C Black Publications.

Felitti, M.D., Anda, R.F., Nordenberg, M.D., Williamson, D.F, Spitz, A.M., Edwards, V., Koss, M.P. and Marks, J.S. (1998) Relationship of childhood abuse and household dysfunction to many of the leading causes of death in adults: The Adverse Childhood Experiences (ACE) Study. *American Journal of Preventative Medicine*, 14 (4), 245–58.

Fernández-Reino, M. (2020) *Migrants and minorities: Britain's pride and prejudice*. Available at: www.politics.co.uk/comment-analysis/2020/01/30/migrants-and-minorities-britain-s-pride-and-prejudice

Ferrari, N. (2020) Ofsted chief reveals teaching of anti-semitism is 'under review'. *Leading Britain's Conversation*. Available at: www.lbc.co.uk/radio/presenters/nick-ferrari/ofsted-chief-teaching-anti-semitism-under-review/

Fine, C. (2010) *Delusions of Gender: The Real Science Behind Sex Differences*. London: Icon Books.

Fine, C. (2017) *Testosterone Rex*. London: Icon Books.

Fine, C. and Rush, E. (2018) 'Why does all the girls have to buy pink stuff?' The ethics and science of the gendered toy marketing debate. *Journal of Business Ethics*, 149 (4), 769–84.

First4Adoption (2020) *Contact in adoption: Making sense of the past*. Available at: www.first4adoption.org.uk/being-an-adoptive-parent/what-does-it-take-to-be-an-adoptive-parent/birth-family-contact-adoption/

Fisher, P. A. (2015) Review: Adoption, fostering, and the needs of looked-after and adopted children. *Child and Adolescent Mental Health*, 20 (1), 5–12.

Fletcher, R.B. and Hattie, J. (2011) *Intelligence and Intelligence Testing*. Abingdon: Routledge.

Fogarty, J. (2018) Supporting children who are highly able. In Knowles, G. (ed.) *Supporting Inclusive Practice and Ensuring Opportunity is Equal for All*. Third edition. pp. 70–83. Abingdon: Routledge.

Fogarty, R. (2009) *Brain-Compatible Classrooms*. Third edition. London: Sage.

Forrest, S. (2018) Sexualities, identities and equal rights. In Cole, M. (ed.) *Education, Equality and Human Rights*. Fourth edition. pp. 130–56. Abingdon: Routledge.

Fortune, M. and Enger, C. (2005) Violence against women and the role of religion. *Applied Research Forum*, pp. 1–7. Available at: https://vawnet.org/sites/default/files/materials/files/2016-09/AR_VAWReligion_0.pdf

Foster, B. and Norton, P. (2012) Educational equality for Gypsy, Roma and Traveller children and young people in the UK. *Equal Rights Review*, 8, 85–112.

Francis, B., Skelton, C., Carrington, B., Hutchings, M., Read, B. and Hall, I. (2008) A perfect match? Pupils' and teachers' views of the impact of matching educators and learners by gender. *Research Papers in Education*, 23 (1), 21–36.

Frederickson, N. and Cline, T. (2015) *Special Educational Needs, Inclusion and Diversity.* Third edition. Maidenhead: Open University Press.

Fullilove, M.T. (1996) Psychiatric implications of displacement: Contributions from the psychology of place. *American Journal of Psychiatry*, 153 (2), 1516–23.

Fumoto, H., Hargreaves, D.J. and Maxwell, S. (2007) Teachers' perceptions of their relationships with children who speak English as an additional language in early childhood settings. *Early Childhood Research*, 5 (2), 135–53.

Gardner, H. (1993) *Frames of Mind*. Second edition. London: Fontana.

Gender Identity Development Service (2020) *Referrals to GIDS, 2014–15 to 2018–19.* Available at: https://gids.nhs.uk/number-referrals

Gibson, S. (2009) Inclusion versus neo-liberalism: Empowering the 'Other'. In Gibson, S. and Haynes, J. (eds) *Perspectives on Participation and Inclusion.* pp. 11–26. London: Continuum.

Glazzard, J., Potter, M. and Stones, S. (2019) *Meeting the Mental Health Needs of Young Children 0–5 Years*. St Albans: Critical Publishing.

Goffman, E. (1963) *Stigma: Notes on the Management of Spoiled Identity*. Englewood Cliffs, NJ: Prentice-Hall.

Gould, G. (2008) *Mental health history: Taking over the asylum*. Available at: www.hsj. co.uk/home/mental-health-history-taking-over-the-asylum/1136349.article

Gov.UK (2019) *GCSE English and maths results*. Available at: www.ethnicity-facts-figures.service.gov.uk/education-skills-and-training/11-to-16-years-old/a-to-c-in-english-and-maths-gcse-attainment-for-children-aged-14-to-16-key-stage-4/latest#by-ethnicity

Griffin, H. (2018) *Gender Equality in Primary Schools: A Guide for Teachers*. London: Jessica Kingsley.

Griffiths, J. (2015) Dealing with DSD. *Midwives*, 18, 48–50.

Gross, M.U.M. (2015) Characteristics of able gifted highly gifted exceptionally gifted and profoundly gifted learners. In Vidergor, H.E. and Harris, C.R. (eds) *Applied Practice for Educators of Gifted and Able Learners*. pp. 3–24. Leiden: Brill.

Grossman, A.H. and D'Augelli, A.R. (2007) Transgender youth and life-threatening behaviors. *Suicide and Life-Threatening Behaviour*, 37 (5), 527–37.

The Guardian (2015) *Adoption and fostering: Finding homes for hard to place children.* Available at: www.theguardian.com/social-care-network/2015/mar/03/fostering-adoption-hard-to-place-children

The Guardian (2018) *Record number of UK children excluded for racist bullying.* Available at: www.theguardian.com/education/2018/nov/30/record-number-of-uk-children-excluded-for-racist-bullying

Gurian, M. (2011) *Boys and Girls Learn Differently!* Second edition. San Francisco: Jossey-Bass.

Gwynn, R. (1985) *England's first refugees.* Available at: www.historytoday.com/archive/englands-first-refugees

Halim, M.L., Ruble, D.N., Tamis-LeMonda, C.S., Zosuls, K.M., Lurye, L.E. and Greulich, F.K. (2014) Pink frilly dresses and the avoidance of all things 'girly': Children's appearance rigidity and cognitive theories of gender development. *Developmental Psychology*, 50 (4), 1091–101.

Hall, S. (1978) *Policing the Crises.* London: Constable.

Hamid, S. (2017) Introduction. In Hamid, S. (ed.) *Young British Muslims.* pp. 1–14. Abingdon: Routledge.

Hamilton, P. (2013a) It's not all about academic achievement: Supporting the social and emotional needs of migrant worker children. *Pastoral Care in Education: An International Journal of Personal, Social and Emotional Development*, 31 (2), 173–90.

Hamilton, P. (2013b) Including migrant worker children in the learning and social context of the rural primary school. *Education 3–13: International Journal of Primary, Elementary and Early Years Education*, 41 (2), 202–17.

Hamilton, P. (2013c) Fostering effective and sustainable home–school relations with migrant worker parents: A new story to tell? *International Studies in Sociology of Education*, 24 (4), 298–317.

Hamilton, P. (2018a) School books or wedding dresses? Examining the cultural dissonance experienced by young Gypsy/Traveller women in secondary education. *Gender and Education*, 30 (7), 829–45.

Hamilton, P. (2018b) Engaging Gypsy and Traveller pupils in secondary education in Wales: Tensions and dilemmas of addressing difference. *International Studies in Sociology of Education*, 27 (1), 4–22.

Hamilton, P. and Forgacs-Pritchard, K. (2020) The complex tapestry of relationships which surround adoptive families: A case study. *Education 3–13: International Journal of Primary, Elementary and Early Years Education*. Published online 17 March 2020.

Hamilton, P. and Jones, L. (2016) Illuminating the 'boy problem' from children's and teachers' perspectives: A pilot study. *Education 3–13: International Journal of Primary, Elementary and Early Years Education*, 44 (3), 241–54.

Hamilton, P. and Roberts, B. (2017) 'Man-up, go and get an ice-pack.' Gendered stereotypes and binaries within the primary classroom: A thing of the past? *Education 3–13: International Journal of Primary, Elementary and Early Years Education*, 45 (1), 122–34.

Harber, C. (2014) *Education and International Development: Theory, Practice and Issues.* Oxford: Symposium Books.

Hardy, R. (2018) *The toxic trio: What social workers need to know. Working with domestic abuse, substance use and mental ill health.* Available at: www.communitycare. co.uk/2018/03/05/toxic-trio-social-workers-need-know/

Haslam, S.A. and Dovidio, J.F. (2010) Prejudice. In Levine, J.M. and Hogg, M.A. (eds) *Encyclopedia of Group Processes and Intergroup Relations.* pp. 655–60. Thousand Oaks, CA: Sage.

Haynes, J. (2019) More Birmingham schools suspend No Outsiders LGBT lessons under pressure: Protests over the teaching of equalities at city primary schools restart amid homophobia claims. *Birmingham Post*, 20 March.

Haywood, J. (2008) *The Great Migrations: From the Earliest Humans to the Age of Globalisation.* London: Quercus.

Health and Social Care Information Centre (2018) *Mental Health of Children and Young People in England: A Summary.* Available at: https://files.digital.nhs.uk/A6/EA7D58/MHCYP%202017%20Summary.pdf

Herrnstein, R. and Murray, C. (1996) *The Bell Curve: Intelligence and Class Structure in American Life.* New York: Free Press Paperbacks.

Heslehurst, N., Brown, H., Pemu, A., Coleman, H. and Rankin, J. (2018) Perinatal health outcomes and care among asylum seekers and refugees: A systematic review of systematic reviews. *BMC Medicine*, 16, 89.

Historic England (2020a) *Mental deficiency between the wars – life in the colony.* Available at: https://historicengland.org.uk/research/inclusive-heritage/disability-history/1914-1945/mental-deficiency-between-the-wars/

Historic England (2020b) *Back to the community – Disability equality, rights and inclusion.* Available at: https://historicengland.org.uk/research/inclusive-heritage/disability-history/1945-to-the-present-day/back-to-the-community/

HM Government (1989) *Children Act 1989.* Available at: www.legislation.gov.uk/ukpga/1989/41/contents

HM Government (2002) *Adoption Act 2002.* Available at: www.legislation.gov.uk/ukpga/2002/38/contents

HM Government (2011) *Equality Act 2010 Guidance: Guidance on Matters to be Taken into Account in Determining Questions Relating to the Definition of Disability.* Available at: https://assets.publishing.service.gov.uk/government/uploads/system/uploads/attachment_data/file/570382/Equality_Act_2010-disability_definition.pdf

HM Government (2017) *Children and Social Work Act.* Available at: www.legislation.gov.uk/ukpga/2017/16/contents/enacted

Holmstrom, R. (2013a) When family life breaks down: Fostering and children in care. In Knowles, G. and Holmstrom, R. (eds) *Understanding Family Diversity and Home–School Relations.* pp. 120–33. Abingdon: Routledge.

Holmstrom, R. (2013b) Families and adoption. In Knowles, G. and Holmstrom, R. (eds) *Understanding Family Diversity and Home–School Relations*. pp. 134–49. Abingdon: Routledge.

Home Office (2019a) *Hate Crime, England and Wales 2018/9*. Available at: https://assets.publishing.service.gov.uk/government/uploads/system/uploads/attachment_data/file/839172/hate-crime-1819-hosb2419.pdf

Home Office (2019b) *Guidance Document: Children's Asylum Claims*. Available at: https://assets.publishing.service.gov.uk/government/uploads/system/uploads/attachment_data/file/825735/children_s-asylum-claims-v3.0ext.pdf

Hopkins, E. (2014) The impact of new media technology on children's learning and wellbeing. In Curtis, W., Ward, S., Sharp, J. and Hankin, L. (eds) *Education Studies: An Issues-based Approach*. pp. 202–16. London: Sage.

Howard, C., Burton, M. and Levermore, D. (2020) *Children's Mental Health and Emotional Wellbeing in Primary School: A Whole School Approach*. London: Sage.

Iacobucci, G. (2017) UK poverty has 'devastating' effect on children's health, doctors warn. *BMJ*, 357: j2285.

The Independent (2017) *Hate crimes against disabled children rise 150% in two years*. Available at: www.independent.co.uk/news/uk/home-news/hate-crimes-disabled-children-rise-150-per-cent-two-years-a8002261.html

The Independent (2019) *Almost one in four British children do not know what a refugee is, survey says*. Available at: www.independent.co.uk/news/uk/refugee-asylum-uk-children-immigration-red-cross-survey-a8958936.html

Independent Press Standards Organisation (2019) *Editors' Code of Practice*. Available at: www.ipso.co.uk/editors-code-of-practice/

Ingleby, E. (2013) *Early Childhood Studies: A Social Science Perspective*. London: Bloomsbury.

Inglis, G. (2016) *The stigma of poverty*. Available at: https://povertyalliance.wordpress.com/2016/10/19/the-stigma-of-poverty/#

Inman, S., McCormack, P. and Walker, S. (2014) Wearing your own culture: Perceptions of Islamophobia in England. In Sedmark, M., Medarić, Z. and Walker, S. (eds) *Children's Voices: Studies of Interethnic Conflict and Violence in European Schools*. pp. 124–41. Abingdon: Routledge.

Intersex Human Rights Australia (2013) *Intersex population figures*. Available at: https://ihra.org.au/16601/intersex-numbers/

Ipsos MORI (2011) *How much does religion matter?* Available at: www.ipsos.com/ipsos-mori/en-uk/how-much-does-religion-matter

Jarrett, T. (2011) *The Equality Act 2010 and Positive Action*. Available at: https://researchbriefings.files.parliament.uk/documents/SN06093/SN06093.pdf

Jensen, T.K., Skårdalsmo, E.M.B. and Fjermestad, K.W. (2014) Development of mental health problems: A follow-up study of unaccompanied refugee minors. *Child Adolescent Psychiatry Mental Health*, 8, 29.

Jones, A. (2018) Looked after children, fostering and adoption. In Knowles, G. (ed.) *Supporting Inclusive Practice and Ensuring Opportunity is Equal for All*. Third edition. pp. 140–52. Abingdon: Routledge.

Joseph Rowntree Foundation (2006) *What's new about new immigrants in twenty-first century Britain?* Available at: www.jrf.org.uk/report/whats-new-about-new-immigrants-twenty-first-century-britain

Joseph Rowntree Foundation (2016) *Special Educational Needs and Their Links to Poverty.* York: Joseph Rowntree Foundation.

Joseph Rowntree Foundation (2020) *UK Poverty 2019/20.* York: Joseph Rowntree Foundation.

Kallen, E. (2004) *Social Inequality and Social Injustice: A Human Rights Perspective.* Basingstoke: Palgrave Macmillan.

Kallis, A. (2018) Islamophobia in the UK: National report 2017. In Bayrakli, E. and Hafez, F. (eds) *European Islamophobia Report 2017*. Ankara: SETA. Available at: www.islamophobiaeurope.com/wp-content/uploads/2018/07/EIR_2017.pdf

Kallman, D. (2017) Integrating disability: Boomerang effects when using positive media exemplars to reduce disability prejudice. *International Journal of Disability, Development and Education*, 64 (6), 644–62.

Karniol, R. (2011) The color of children's gender stereotype. *Sex Roles*, 65, 119–32.

Kaur-Ballagan, K. (2020) *World Refugee Day.* Available at: www.ipsos.com/ipsos-mori/en-uk/world-refugee-day

Kilvington, J. and Wood, A. (2016) *Gender, Sex and Children's Play.* London: Bloomsbury.

Klingorová, K. and Havlíček, T. (2015) Religion and gender inequality: The status of women in the societies of world religions. *Moravian Geographical Reports*, 23 (2), 2–11.

Knowles, G. (2011a) Looked-after children, children in care. In Knowles, G. and Lander, V. (eds) *Diversity, Equality and Achievement in Education*. pp. 125–39. London: Sage.

Knowles, G. (2011b) Children who are gifted and talented. In Knowles, G. (ed.) *Supporting Inclusive Practice. Second edition*. pp. 63–78. Abingdon: Routledge.

Knowles, G. (2013a) Families living in poverty. In Knowles, G. and Holmstrom, R. (eds) *Understanding Family Diversity and Home–School Relations*. pp. 150–64. Abingdon: Routledge.

Knowles, G. (2013b) Immigrant, refugee and asylum seeker families. In Knowles, G. and Holmstrom, R. (eds) *Understanding Family Diversity and Home–School Relations*. pp. 57–72. Abingdon: Routledge.

Knowles, G. (2018a) What it means to have a disability or special educational need. In Knowles, G. (ed.) *Supporting Inclusive Practice and Ensuring Opportunity is Equal for All*. Third edition. pp. 84–95. Abingdon: Routledge.

Knowles, G. (2018b) Gender and inclusion. In Knowles, G. (ed.) *Supporting Inclusive Practice and Ensuring Opportunity is Equal for All*. Third edition. pp. 22–36. Abingdon: Routledge.

Knowles, G. and Lander, V. (2011) *Diversity, Equality and Achievement in Education.* London: Sage.

Kohlberg, L.A. (1966) A cognitive-developmental analysis of children's sex role concepts and attitudes. In Maccoby, E.E. (ed.) *The Development of Sex Differences.* pp. 82–173. Stanford, CA: Stanford University Press.

Koshy, V., Portman-Smith, C. and Casey, R. (2017) England policy in gifted education: Current problems and promising directions. *Gifted Child Today,* 44 (2), 75–80.

Leadley-Meade, Z. (2018) Working with lesbian, gay and bisexual children and families in schools. In Knowles, G. (ed.) *Supporting Inclusive Practice and Ensuring Opportunity is Equal for All.* Third edition. pp. 37–51. Abingdon: Routledge.

Legewiea, J. and DiPretea, T. (2012) School context and the gender gap in educational achievement. *American Sociological Review,* 77 (3), 463–85.

Legislation.gov.uk (2010) *Equality Act 2010.* Available at: www.legislation.gov.uk/ukpga/2010/15/contents

The Lesbian, Gay, Bisexual and Transgender Community Center (2020). *What is LGBTQ?* Available at: https://gaycenter.org/about/lgbtq/

Levinson, M. (2008) Not just content, but style: Gypsy children traversing boundaries. *Research in Comparative and International Education,* 3 (3), 235–49.

Levinson, M. (2015) What's the plan? What plan? Changing aspirations among Gypsy youngsters, and implications for future cultural identities and group membership. *British Journal of Sociology of Education,* 36 (8), 1149–69.

Levinson, M. and Sparkes, A. (2003) Gypsy masculinities and the school–home interface: Exploring contradictions and tensions. *British Journal of Sociology of Education,* 24 (5), 587–603.

Lewis, G. (2016) *Incidents of racism in schools up post-Brexit.* Available at: www.sec-ed.co.uk/news/incidents-of-racism-in-schools-up-post-brexit

Liu, Q. (2017) *Executive Summary – Breaking the Binary: Exploring the Role of Media Representation of Trans People in Constructing a Safer and More Inclusive Social Environment.* Available at: www.allabouttrans.org.uk/wp-content/uploads/2017/06/Executive-summary-Breaking-the-Binary.pdf

Lloyd, G. and McCluskey, G. (2008) Education and Gypsies/Travellers: Contradictions and significant silences. *International Journal of Inclusive Education,* 12 (4), 331–45.

Local Government Association (2016) *Healthy Futures: Supporting and Promoting the Health Needs of Looked After Children.* Available at: www.local.gov.uk/sites/default/files/documents/healthy-futures-supportin-9cf.pdf

Loewen, S. (2004) Second language concerns for refugee children. In Hamilton, R. and Moore, D. (eds) *Educational Interventions for Refugee Children.* pp. 35–52. London: Routledge Falmer.

Loreman, T., Deppeler, J. and Harvey, D. (2010) *Inclusive Education, Supporting Diversity in the Classroom*. Second edition. Abingdon: Routledge.

Madziva, R. and Thondhlana, J. (2017) Provision of quality education in the context of Syrian refugee children in the UK: Opportunities and challenges. *Compare: A Journal of Comparative and International Education*, 47 (6), 942–61.

Mangin, M. (2018) Supporting transgender and gender-expansive children in school: School policies and practices can profoundly affect children whose gender identity differs from their sex assigned at birth. *Phi Delta Kappan*, 100 (2), 16–21.

Marchbank, J. and Letherby, G. (2014) *Introduction to Gender: Social Science Perspectives*. Abingdon: Routledge.

Martin, B. (2011) *Children at Play: Learning Gender in the Early Years*. Stoke-on-Trent: Trentham Books.

Mayor, S. (2017) UK children have 'alarming gap' in health between rich and poor, report finds. *BMJ*, 356: j377.

McFadden, A., Siebelt, L., Jackson, C., Jones, H., Innes, N., MacGillivray, S. and Atkin, K. (2018) *Enhancing Gypsy, Roma and Traveller Peoples' Trust: Using Maternity and Early Years' Health Services and Dental Health Services as Exemplars of Mainstream Service Provision*. Dundee: University of Dundee. Available at: https://doi.org/10.20933/100001117

McKeon, D. (2001) Language, culture and schooling. In Genesee, F. (ed.) *Educating Second Language Children: The Whole Child, the Whole Curriculum, the Whole Community*. Ninth edition. pp. 15–32. Cambridge: Cambridge University Press.

McQueeney, K. (2014) Disrupting Islamophobia: Teaching the social construction of terrorism in the mass media. *International Journal of Teaching and Learning in Higher Education*, 2 (26), 297–309.

Meakings, S., Ottaway, O., Coffey, A., Palmer, C., Doughty, J. and Shelton, K. (2018) The support needs and experiences of newly formed adoptive families: Findings from the Wales Adoption Study. *Adoption & Fostering*, 42 (1), 58–75.

Mencap (2020) *Children, research and statistics*. Available at: www.mencap.org.uk/learning-disability-explained/research-and-statistics/children-research-and-statistics

Mental Health First Aid (2016) *Adult MHFA Manual*. London: Mental Health First Aid England.

Mental Health Foundation (2016) *Children and young people*. Available at: www.mentalhealth.org.uk/a-to-z/c/children-and-young-people

Mental Health Foundation (2018) *Mental Health Foundation Manifesto 2018*. Available at: www.mentalhealth.org.uk/publications/health-inequalities-manifesto-2018

Mermaids (2019) *When it's hardest to speak*. Available at: www.mermaidsuk.org.uk/when-its-hardest-to-speak.-speak.html

Moltzen, R. (2011) Inclusive education and gifted and talented provision. In Richards, G. and Armstrong, F. (eds) *Teaching and Learning in Diverse and Inclusive Classrooms: Key Issues for New Teachers.* pp. 102–12. Abingdon: Routledge.

Montacute, R. (2018) *Potential for Success: Fulfilling the Promise of Highly Able Students in Secondary Schools.* London: The Sutton Trust.

Montgomery, D. (2015) *Teaching Gifted Children with Special Educational Needs: Supporting Dual and Multiple Exceptionality.* Abingdon: Routledge.

Morgan, E. and Taylor, Y. (2019) Dangerous education: The occupational hazards of 'transgender education'. *Sociology,* 53 (1), 19–35.

Morgenroth, T. and Ryan, M.K. (2018) Gender Trouble in Social Psychology: How Can Butler's Work Inform Experimental Social Psychologists' Conceptualization of Gender? *Fronters in Psychology.* Available at: https://doi.org/10.3389/fpsyg.2018.01320

Muijs, D. and Reynolds, D. (2018) *Effective Teaching: Evidence and Practice.* Fourth edition. London: Sage.

Mukolo, A., Heflinger, C.A. and Wallston, K.A. (2010) The stigma of childhood mental disorders: A conceptual framework. *Journal of the American Academy of Child and Adolescent Psychiatry,* 49 (2), 92–103.

Myers, M. and Bhopal, K. (2017) Muslims, home education and risk in British society. *British Journal of Sociology of Education,* 39 (2), 212–26.

NASDAQ (2020) *The 5 largest economies in the world and their growth in 2020.* Available at: www.nasdaq.com/articles/the-5-largest-economies-in-the-world-and-their-growth-in-2020-2020-01-22

National Association of Virtual School Heads (2018) *The Virtual School Handbook 2018–19.* Available at: https://navsh.org.uk/wp-content/uploads/2018/11/NAVSH-The-Virtual-School-Handbook-2018.pdf

National Council for Curriculum and Assessment (2007) *Gifted and Talented Pupils: Guidelines for Teachers.* Available at: www.nicurriculum.org.uk/docs/inclusion_and_sen/gifted/Gifted_and_Talented.pdf

National Society for the Prevention of Cruelty to Children (2014) *Promoting the Wellbeing of Children in Care: Messages from Research.* Available at: http://clok.uclan.ac.uk/14634/1/promoting-wellbeing-children-in-care-messages-from-research.pdf

National Society for the Prevention of Cruelty to Children (2015) *Achieving Emotional Wellbeing for Looked After Children.* Available at: https://learning.nspcc.org.uk/media/1122/achieving-emotional-wellbeing-for-looked-after-children.pdf

National Society for the Prevention of Cruelty to Children (2019) *Statistics Briefing: Looked After Children.* Available at: https://learning.nspcc.org.uk/media/1622/statistics-briefing-looked-after-children.pdf

NHS Health Scotland (2019) *Adverse Childhood Experiences*. Available at: www.
    healthscotland.scot/media/2676/adverse-childhood-experiences-in-context-
    aug2019-english.pdf

Norwich, B. (2013) *Addressing Tensions and Dilemmas in Inclusive Education*.
    Abingdon: Routledge.

Nussbaum, M. (1999) The Professor of Parody. *The New Republic Online*. Available at:
    https://newrepublic.com/article/150687/professor-parody

Nutbrown, C. and Clough, P. (2013) *Inclusion in the Early Years*. Second edition.
    London: Sage.

Oakley, A. (1975) *Sex, Gender and Society*. London: Temple Smith.

Ofcom (2018) *Representation and portrayal on BBC television: Thematic Review*.
    Available at: https://www.ofcom.org.uk/__data/assets/pdf_file/0022/124078/report-
    bbc-representation-portrayal.pdf

Office for National Statistics (2014) *2011 Census analysis: What does the 2011 Census
    tell us about the characteristics of Gypsy and Irish Travellers in England and Wales.
    Statistical release*. Available at: www.ons.gov.uk/ons/rel/census/2011-census-
    analysis/what-does-the-2011-census-tell-us-about-the-characteristics-of-gypsy-or-
    irish-travellers-in-england-and-wales-/index.html

Office for National Statistics (2016) *The National Statistics Socio-economic Classification
    (NS-SEC) 2010*. Available at: www.ons.gov.uk/methodology/classifications
    andstandards/otherclassifications/thenationalstatisticssocioeconomic
    classificationnssecrebasedonsoc2010

Office for National Statistics (2017) *UK drops in European child mortality rankings*.
    Available at: www.ons.gov.uk/peoplepopulationandcommunity/health
    andsocialcare/childhealth/articles/ukdropsineuropeanchildmortalityrankings/
    2017-10-13

Office for National Statistics (2019) *Persistent poverty in the UK and EU: 2017.
    Comparisons of persistent poverty between UK and other EU countries*. Available at:
    www.ons.gov.uk/peoplepopulationandcommunity/personalandhouseholdfinances/
    incomeandwealth/articles/persistentpovertyintheukandeu/2017

Ofsted (2009) *Care and Prejudice: A Report of Children's Experience by the Children's
    Rights Director for England*. Available at: https://dera.ioe.ac.uk/179/7/Care%20
    and%20prejudice_Redacted.pdf

Ofsted (2019) *Fostering in England 2018 to 2019: Main findings 2019*. Available at:
    www.gov.uk/government/publications/fostering-in-england-1-april-2018-to-31-
    march-2019/fostering-in-england-2018-to-2019-main-findings#foster-carers

O'Reilly, M., Svirydzenka, N., Adams, S. and Dogra, N. (2018) Review of mental health
    promotion intervention in schools. *Social Psychiatric Epidemiology*, 53, 647–62.

Organisation Intersex International UK (2012) *What is intersex?* Available at:
    http://oiiuk.org/546/welcome/

O'Sullivan, C., Maguire, J., Hayes, N., O'Sullivan, S., Corcoran, L. and McKenna, G. (2018) The wonder project: An early years arts education project with Traveller mothers and their children. *European Early Childhood Education Research Journal*, 26 (5), 780–806.

OutLife (2018) *What is intersex?* Available at: www.outlife.org.uk/what-is-intersex

Parker-Jenkins, M., Hewitt, D., Brownhill, S. and Sanders, T. (2007) *Aiming High: Raising Attainment of Pupils from Culturally Diverse Backgrounds*. London: Paul Chapman.

Patil, T.V. and McLaren, H.J. (2019) Australian media and Islamophobia: Representations of asylum seeker children. *Religions*, 10 (9), 501.

Pelc, S. (2017) *Marginality and Marginalization*. In Chand, R., Nel, E. and Pelc, S. (eds) *Societies, Social Inequalities and Marginalization: Marginal Regions in the 21st Century*. pp. 13–28. Cham, Switzerland: Springer.

Percy Commission (1957) *Report of the Royal Commission on the Law Relating to Mental Illness and Mental Deficiency (1954–1957)*. London: HMSO.

Perregaux, C. (2007) Developing an early passion for languages. *Children in Europe*, 12, 10–11.

Pew Research Center (2017) *Why Muslims are the world's fastest-growing religious group*. Available at: www.pewresearch.org/fact-tank/2017/04/06/why-muslims-are-the-worlds-fastest-growing-religious-group/

Pew Research Center (2018) *Being Christian in Western Europe*. Available at: http:// assets.pewresearch.org/wp-content/uploads/sites/11/2018/05/14165352/Being-Christian-in-Western-Europe-FOR-WEB1.pdf

Pinney, A. (2017) *SEN Data Bulletin: What Can We Learn from National Data on Children and Young People with Special Educational Needs (SEN)?* Available at: https:// councilfordisabledchildren.org.uk/sites/default/files/field/attachemnt/SEN%20 data%20bulletin.pdf

Platt, L. (2014) Is there assimilation in minority groups' national, ethnic and religious identity? *Ethnic and Racial Studies*, 37 (1), 46–70.

Pocock, N. and Chan, C. (2018) *Refugees, racism and xenophobia: What works to reduce discrimination?* Available at: https://ourworld.unu.edu/en/refugees-racism-and-xenophobia-what-works-to-reduce-discrimination

Potential Plus (2017) *Frequently asked questions about high learning potential*. Available at: www.potentialplusuk.org/wp-content/uploads/2017/02/Frequently-Asked-Questions-170209.pdf

Potential Plus (2020a) *Do you embrace 'geek' and 'nerd'?* Available at: www. potentialplusuk.org/index.php/2020/02/10/do-you-embrace-geek-and-nerd/

Potential Plus (2020b) *High Learning Potential Assessment for Children*. Available at: www.potentialplusuk.org/index.php/families/assessments-for-children/

Potential Plus (2020c) *Ofsted Reporting of Provision for the Most Able Pupils: Comparison of Analyses of Ofsted Reports Published in June 2018 and June 2019*. Available at:

www.potentialplusuk.org/wp-content/uploads/2020/03/Ofsted-Reporting-of-Provision-for-the-Most-Able-Pupils.pdf

Potential Plus (2020d) *Dual or multiple exceptionality*. Available at: www.potentialplusuk.org/index.php/families/dual-or-multiple-exceptionality/

Potential Plus (2020e) *Common difficulties experienced by children with high learning potential*. Available at: www.potentialplusuk.org/index.php/families/common-difficulties/

Pound, L. (2005) *How Children Learn*. London: Practical Pre-school Books.

Pound, L. (2009) *How Children Learn 3: Contemporary Thinking and Theorists*. London: Practical Pre-school Books.

Prever, M. (2006) *Mental Health in Schools*. London: Paul Chapman Publishing.

Psychologists Against Austerity (2015) *The Psychological Impact of Austerity: A Briefing Paper*. Available at: https://repository.uel.ac.uk/download/bfa6d36a930832f3d06a2785523c79daab2bfaaa2525dd8701f84f0f8ebddd3b/11123876/paa-briefing-paper.pdf

Public Health England (2019) *Chapter 1: Education and children's social care*. Available at: www.gov.uk/government/publications/people-with-learning-disabilities-in-england/chapter-1-education-and-childrens-social-care-updates

Rashid, N. (2017) 'Everyone is a feminist when it comes to Muslim women': Gender and Islamophobia. In Elahi, F. and Khan, O. (eds) *Islamophobia: Still a Challenge for Us All*. pp. 61–4. London: Runnymede Trust.

Refugee Council (2012) *Leveson Inquiry: Submission of Evidence*. Available at: http://levesoninquiry.org.uk/wp-content/uploads/2012/03/Submission-by-Refugee-Council.pdf

Refugee Council (2020) *Facts about separated children*. Available at: www.refugeecouncil.org.uk/information/refugee-asylum-facts/separated-children-facts/

Refugee Media Group in Wales (2004) *Let's talk to the media*. Available at: https://oxfamilibrary.openrepository.com/bitstream/handle/10546/112342/let's-talk-media-refugee-community-practitioners-011204-en.pdf;jsessionid=768B43581EA73460FA3F425E2D271B19?sequence=1

Religion Media Centre (2018) *Faith schools in the UK*. Available at: https://religionmediacentre.org.uk/factsheets/faith-schools-in-the-uk/

Religion Media Centre (2020) *Antisemitism on the rise*. Available at: https://religionmediacentre.org.uk/factsheets/antisemitism/

Renton, Z., Hamblin, E. and Clements, K. (2016) *Delivering the Healthy Child Programme for Young Refugee and Migrant Children*. Available at: www.ncb.org.uk/sites/default/files/field/attachment/delivering_hcp_for_young_refugee_and_migrant_children.pdf

Retief, M. and Letšosa, R. (2018) Models of disability: A brief overview. *HTS Teologiese Studies / Theological Studies*, 74 (1), a4738.

Richards, G. (2016) 'I feel confident about teaching, but SEN scares me': Moving from anxiety to confidence. In Richard, G. and Armstrong, F. (eds) *Teaching and Learning in Diverse and Inclusive Classrooms*. pp. 87–99. Abingdon: Routledge.

Rieser, R. (2018) Achieving disability equality: The continuing struggle. In Cole, M. (ed.) *Education, Equality and Human Rights*. Fourth edition. pp. 192–229. Abingdon: Routledge.

Rigby, E. and Starbuck, L. (2018) Public health for paediatricians: Engaging young people from marginalised groups. *Archives of Disease in Childhood: Education and Practice*, 103, 207–10.

Robinson, K. and Jones Diaz, C. (2006) *Diversity and Difference in Early Childhood Education: Issues for Theory and Practice*. Maidenhead: Open University Press.

Rodgers, A. and Wilmot, E. (2011) *Inclusion and Diversity in the Early Years*. London: Practical Pre-school Books.

Roffey, S. (2016) Building a case for the whole-child, whole school wellbeing in challenging contexts. *Educational and Child Psychology*, 33 (2), 30–2.

Royal College of Paediatrics and Child Health (2018a) *United Nations Special Rapporteur on Extreme Poverty and Human Rights – Consultation Response*. Available at: www.rcpch.ac.uk/resources/united-nations-special-rapporteur-extreme-poverty-human-rights-consultation-response

Royal College of Paediatrics and Child Health (2018b) *Visit by the United Nations Special Rapporteur on Extreme Poverty and Human Rights to the United Kingdom of Great Britain and Northern Ireland from 5 to 16 November 2018. Response Submitted by the Royal College of Paediatrics and Child Health*. Available at: www.ohchr.org/Documents/Issues/EPoverty/UnitedKingdom/2018/Academics/RoyalCollege_of_Paediatrics_and_ChildHealth.pdf

Royal College of Paediatrics and Child Health (2018c) *Refugee and Unaccompanied Asylum Seeking Children and Young People – Guidance for Paediatricians*. Available at: www.rcpch.ac.uk/sites/default/files/generated-pdf/document/Refugee-and-unaccompanied-asylum-seeking-children-and-young-people—guidance-for-paediatricians.pdf

Runnymede Trust (2011) *Submission to the Leveson Inquiry: Culture, Practice and Ethics of the Press, December 2011*. Available at: www.runnymedetrust.org/uploads/LevesonInquiryresponsefinal.pdf

Rutter, J. (2006) *Refugee Children in the UK*. Maidenhead: Open University Press.

Rutter, M. (1987) Psychosocial resilience and protective mechanisms. *American Journal of Orthopsychiatry*, 57 (3), 316–31.

Ryf, V. (2018) Including bilingual learners and children with English as an additional language. In Knowles, G. (ed.) *Supporting Inclusive Practice and Ensuring Opportunity is Equal for All*. Third edition. pp. 52–69. Abingdon: Routledge.

Ryle, R. (2015) *Questioning Gender: A Sociological Exploration*. Second edition. London: Sage.

Sadler, K., Vizard, T., Ford, T., Goodman, A., Goodman, R. and McManus, S. (2018) *Mental health of children and young people in England, 2017: Trends and characteristics*. Available at: https://dera.ioe.ac.uk//32622/1/MHCYP%202017%20 Summary.pdf

Saeed, A. (2007) Media, racism and Islamophobia: The representation of Islam and Muslims in the media. *Sociology Compass*, 1 (2), 443–62.

Sameti, M., Esfahani, R. and Haghighi, H. (2012) Theories of poverty: A comparative analysis. *Kuwait Chapter of Arabian Journal of Business and Management Review*, 1 (6), 45–56.

Save the Children (2006) *Working Towards Inclusive Practice Play and Learning Activities: Play and Learning Activities for Early Years Settings that Reflect Gypsy/Roma and Traveller Culture*. London: Save the Children.

Save the Children (2015) *Ready to Read: Closing the Gap in Early Language Skills so that Every Child in England Can Read Well*. London: Save the Children.

Save the Children (2016) *The Lost Boys: How Boys are Falling Behind in Their Early Years*. London: Save the Children.

Save the Children (2018) *Early learning gap between children in and out of poverty widens in half of areas across England*. Available at: www.savethechildren.org. uk/news/media-centre/press-releases/early-learning-gap-between-children-in-and-out-of-poverty-widens

Save the Children (2019a) *How Are You Meant to Help? Parents' Perspectives on Supporting their Children's Learning*. London: Save the Children.

Save the Children (2019b) *Research Briefing: Barriers to Early Learning among Low Income Families in the UK*. London: Save the Children.

Save the Children (2020) *UN Convention on the Rights of the Child: An international agreement for child rights*. Available at: www.savethechildren.org.uk/what-we-do/ childrens-rights/united-nations-convention-of-the-rights-of-the-child

Scheff, T. (1966) *Being Mentally Ill: A Sociological Theory*. Third edition. Chicago: Aldine Publishers.

Schiappa, E., Gregg, P. and Hewes, D. (2005) The Parasocial Contact Hypothesis. *Communication Monographs*, 72 (1), 92–115.

Schumann, J.H. (1986) Research on the acculturation model for second language acquisition. *Journal of Multilingual and Multicultural Development*, 7 (5), 379–92.

Science Museum (2020) *Mental health and illness*. Available at: http://broughttolife. sciencemuseum.org.uk/broughttolife/themes/menalhealthandillness

Scottish Government (2015) *What Works to Reduce Prejudice and Discrimination? A Review of the Evidence*. Available at: www.gov.scot/binaries/content/documents/ govscot/publications/research-and-analysis/2015/10/works-reduce-prejudice-discrimination-review-evidence/documents/works-reduce-prejudice-discrimination-review-evidence/works-reduce-prejudice-discrimination-review-evidence/govscot%3Adocument/00487370.pdf

Selwyn, J. and Meakings, S. (2018) *Beyond the Adoption Order (Wales): Discord and Disruption in Adoptive Families*. Available at: https://gov.wales/sites/default/files/publications/2019-06/beyond- the-adoption-order-wales-discord-and-disruption-in-adoptive-families.pdf

Shah, S. (2011) Muslim schools in secular societies: Persistence or resistance! *British Journal of Religious Education*, 34 (1), 51–65.

Shah, S. (2018) 'I am a Muslim first...': Challenges of Muslimness and the UK state schools. *Leadership and Policy in Schools*, 18 (3), 341–56.

Sharples, A. and Page-Gould, E. (2016) *How to avoid picking up prejudice from the media*. Available at: https://greatergood.berkeley.edu/article/item/how_to_avoid_picking_up_prejudice_from_media

Sharples, H. (2017) Widening inclusion for gay women foster carers: A literature review of the sociological, psychological and economic implications. *Practice*, 29 (1), 37–53.

Shaw, B., Bernardes, E., Trethewey, A. and Menzies, L. (2016) *Special educational needs and their links to poverty*. Joseph Rowntree Foundation. Available at: www.jrf.org.uk/report/special-educational-needs-and-their-links-poverty

Shelter (2019) *A child becomes homeless in Britain every eight minutes*. Available at: https://england.shelter.org.uk/media/press_releases/articles/a_child_becomes_homeless_in_britain_every_eight_minutes

Shepherd T. and Linn, D. (2015) *Behaviour and Classroom Management in the Multicultural Classroom*. London: Sage.

Sherif, M., Harvey, O.J., White, B.J., Hood, W.R. and Sherif, C.W. (1961) *Intergroup Conflict and Cooperation: The Robbers Cave Experiment*. Norman, OK: University of Oklahoma Book Exchange.

Siddiqui, N., Gorard, S. and See, B.H. (2017) *Non-cognitive impacts of philosophy for children: Project Report*. School of Education, Durham University, Durham. Available at: www.dur.ac.uk/education/research/groups/?mode=projectid=738

Simon, K. (2018) *Different types of media bias*. Available at: www.profolus.com/topics/different-types-of-media-bias/

Siraj-Blatchford, I. and Clarke, P. (2000) *Supporting Identity, Diversity and Language in the Early Years*. Maidenhead: Open University Press.

Skelton, C. (2002) The 'feminisation of schooling' or 're-masculinising' primary education? *International Studies in Sociology of Education*, 12 (1), 77–96.

Smith, C. (2013) Using personal dolls to learn empathy, unlearn prejudice. *International Journal of Diversity in Education*, 12 (3), 23–32.

Smith, E. (2012) *Key Issues in Education and Social Justice*. London: Sage.

Smith, M. and Chambers, K. (2016) Half a million unseen, half a million unheard: Inclusion for gender identity and sexual identity. In Richards, G. and Armstrong, F. (eds) *Teaching and Learning in Diverse and Inclusive Classrooms: Key Issues for New Teachers*. pp. 19–29. Abingdon: Routledge.

Smithers, A. and Robinson, P. (2012) *Educating the Highly Able*. London: The Sutton Trust.

Social Metrics Commission (2018) *A New Measure of Poverty for the UK*. London: Social Metrics Commission.

Solomon, D.T., Niec, L.N. and Schoonover, C.E. (2017) The impact of foster parent training on parenting skills and child disruptive behaviour: A meta-analysis. *Child Maltreatment*, 22 (1), 3–13.

Soylemez, A.S. (2010) A study on how social gender identity is constructed in EFL coursebooks. *Procedia – Social and Behavioral Sciences*, 9 (1), 747–52.

Spinner, L., Cameron, L. and Calogero, R. (2018) Peer toy play as a gateway to children's gender flexibility: The effect of (counter) stereotypic portrayals of peers in children's magazines. *Sex Roles*, 79, 314–28.

Stobbs, P., Andrews, E. and Revels, J. (2014) Inclusion and entitlement in the early years for disabled young children and young children with special educational needs. In Pugh, G. and Duffy, B. (eds) *Contemporary Issues in the Early Years*. pp. 199–216. London: Sage.

Stonewall (2017) *School Report: The Experiences of Lesbian, Gay, Bi and Trans Young People in Britain's Schools in 2017*. Available at: www.stonewall.org.uk/system/files/the_school_report_2017.pdf

Stonewall (2018) *LGBT in Britain: Home and Communities*. London: Stonewall.

Stonewall (2019a) *Faith and LGBT inclusion*. Available at: www.stonewall.org.uk/node/133006

Stonewall (2019b) *Why we need more representation of LGBT people of faith in popular culture*. Available at: www.stonewall.org.uk/about-us/news/why-we-need-more-representation-lgbt-people-faith-popular-culture

Sutherland, M. (2012) *Gifted and Talented in the Early Years: Practical Activities for Children Aged 3 to 6*. Second edition. London: Sage.

Sutherland, M., Stack, N. and Smith, C. (2009) *Guidance for Addressing the Needs of Highly Able Pupils (Manual)*. Glasgow: Scottish Network for Able Pupils.

Sweeting, H., Maycock, M.W., Walker, L. and Hunt, K. (2017) Public challenge and endorsement of sex category ambiguity in online debate: The sooner people stop thinking that gender is a matter of choice the better. *Sociology of Health and Illness*, 39 (3), 380–96.

Tabors, P.O. (1997) *One Child, Two Languages: A Guide for Preschool Educators of Children Learning English as a Second Language*. Seventh edition. Baltimore: Paul Brookes.

Tajfel, H. (1969) Cognitive aspects of prejudice. *Journal of Social Issues*, 25 (4), 79–97.

Tajfel, H. (1970) Experiments in intergroup discrimination. *Scientific American*, 223, 96–102.

Taylor, M. (2015) Racist and anti-immigration views held by children revealed in schools study. *The Guardian*. Available at: www.theguardian.com/education/ 2015/may/19/most-children-think-immigrants-are-stealing-jobs-schools-study-shows

Taylor-Robinson, D., Lai, E.T.C., Wickham, S., Rose, T., Norman, P., Bambra, C., Whitehead, M. and Barr, B. (2019) Assessing the impact of rising child poverty on the unprecedented rise in infant mortality in England, 2000–2017: Time trend analysis. *BMJ Open*, 9 (10), 1–6.

Tell MAMA (2017) *A Constructed Threat: Identity, Prejudice and the Impact of Anti-Muslim Hatred.* London: Faith Matters.

TES (2005) *A history of special needs 2005.* Available at: www.tes.com/news/ history-special-needs

Time to Change (2012) *Children and Young People's Programme Development: Summary of Research and Insights.* Available at: www.time-to-change.org.uk/sites/default/ files/TTC%20CYP%20Report%20FINAL.pdf

Time to Change (2017) *Less mental health discrimination and a 'sea change' in public attitudes during the last 10 years of Time to Change.* Available at: www.time-to-change.org.uk/news/less-mental-health-discrimination-and-sea-change-public-attitudes-during-ten-years-time-change

Topping, K. (2012) Conceptions of inclusion: Widening ideas. In Boyle, C. and Topping, K. (eds) *What Works in Inclusion?* pp. 9–19. Maidenhead: Open University Press.

Traveller Movement (2017) *The Last Acceptable Form of Racism? The Pervasive Discrimination and Prejudice Experienced by Gypsy, Roma and Traveller Communities.* Available at: www.travellermovement.org.uk/phocadownload/ userupload/reports/last-acceptable-form-of-racism-traveller-movement-report.pdf

UK AID (2010) *Guidance Note: A DFID Practice Paper.* Available at: https://assets. publishing.service.gov.uk/government/uploads/system/uploads/attachment_data/ file/67664/edu-chi-disabil-guid-note.pdf

UK Intersex Association (2011) *UKIA's recommendations to the medical professions for the assessment and treatment of Intersex conditions.* Available at: www.ukia.co.uk/ ukia/ukia-recommend.html

UK Parliament (2019) *Tackling Inequalities Faced by Gypsy, Roma and Traveller Communities.* Available at: https://publications.parliament.uk/pa/cm201719/ cmselect/cmwomeq/360/full-report.html#heading-6

UNESCO (1994) *The Salamanca Statement and Framework for Action on Special Needs Education*. Available at: https://www.right-to-education.org/sites/right-to-education.org/files/resource-attachments/Salamanca_Statement_1994.pdf

UNESCO (2000) *Dakar Framework for Action – Education for All: Meeting Our Collective Commitments*. World Forum on Education, Dakar, Senegal, 26–28 April 2000, UNESCO, Paris.

UNICEF (2010) *From Commitment to Action: What Religious Communities Can Do to Eliminate Violence against Children*. Available at: https://www.unicef.org/media/files/What_Religious_Communities_can_do_to_Eliminate_Violence_against_Children__(UNICEF_Religions_for_Peace_Guide).pdf

UNICEF (2018a) *Education for Refugee and Asylum Seeking Children: Access and Equality in England, Scotland and Wales*. Available at: https://www.unicef.org.uk/wp-content/uploads/2018/09/Access-to-Education-report-PDF.pdf

UNICEF (2018b) *UK Policy Position: Access to Education for Refugee Children*. Available at: https://downloads.unicef.org.uk/wp-content/uploads/2018/09/UNICEF-UK-POLICY-POSITION-England-2.pdf

UNICEF UK (2020) *A summary of the UN Convention on the Rights of the Child*. Available at: https://www.unicef.org.uk/wp-content/uploads/2019/10/UNCRC_summary-1_1.pdf

United Nations (1995) *Report of the World Summit for Social Development, A/CONF.166.9*. New York: United Nations Publications.

United Nations (2020) *Ending poverty*. Available at: www.un.org/en/sections/issues-depth/poverty/

United Nations Free and Equal (2017) *Intersex Fact Sheet*. Available at: www.unfe.org/wp-content/uploads/2017/05/UNFE-Intersex.pdf

United Nations High Commissioner for Refugees (2019) *Global Trends: Forced Displacement in 2018*. Available at: www.unhcr.org/5d08d7ee7.pdf

Valentine, G. and McDonald, I. (2004) *Understanding Prejudice: Attitudes towards Minorities*. London: Stonewall.

Weale, S. (2019) *Children in low-income families suffer shame and social exclusion*. Available at: www.theguardian.com/society/2019/apr/02/children-in-low-income-families-suffer-shame-and-social-exclusion

Wearmouth, J. (2017) *Special Educational Needs and Disabilities in Schools: A Critical Introduction*. London: Bloomsbury.

Weller, P. and Foster, I. (2019) *Classroom Challenges for Teaching about and Addressing anti-Semitism in the OSCE Region*. Derby: University of Derby Available at: https://derby.openrepository.com/bitstream/handle/10545/623753/2019-04-11%20Finalised%20additional%20detail%20PGW%20ReportUniversity ofDerby%20disclaimer%20cleared.pdf?sequence=1andisAllowed=y

Welsh Government (2014) *Gypsy and Traveller Education: Engaging Families – A Research Report.* Cardiff: Welsh Government.

Welsh Government (2015) *Review to Identify More Able and Talented Provision Across Wales.* Available at: https://gov.wales/sites/default/files/publications/2018-02/review-to-identify-more-able-and-talented-provision-across-wales.pdf

Welsh Government (2018) *Health and Wellbeing Provision for Refugees and Asylum Seekers.* Available at: https://gov.wales/sites/default/files/publications/2019-03/health-and-wellbeing-provision-for-refugees-and-asylum-seekers_0.pdf

Welsh Government (2019) *The Additional Learning Needs (ALN) Transformation Programme: Frequently Asked Questions (FAQs).* Available at: https://gov.wales/sites/default/files/publications/2019-02/aln-frequently-asked-questions-2_0.pdf

Whittaker, F. (2018) *£18m 'future talent fund' cancelled less than a year after it was announced.* Available at: https://schoolsweek.co.uk/18m-future-talent-fund-cancelled-less-than-a-year-after-it-was-announced/

Wickham, S., Anwar, E., Barr, B., Law, C. and Taylor-Robinson, D. (2016) Poverty and child health in the UK: Using evidence for action. *Archives of Disease in Childhood,* 101 (8), 1–7.

Wilkin, A., Derrington, C. and Foster, B. (2009) *Improving the Outcomes for Gypsy, Roma and Traveller Pupils: Literature Review (DCSF Research Report RR077).* London: Department for Children, Schools and Families.

Wilson, W. J. (1987) *The Truly Disadvantaged.* Chicago: University of Chicago Press.

Wilson, W. J. (1996) *When Work Disappears.* New York: Viking.

Women and Equalities Committee (2016) *Transgender Equality: First Report of Session 2015–16.* London: House of Commons.

Wong, W.I. and Hines, M. (2015) Effects of gender color-coding on toddlers' gender-typical toy play. *Archives of Sexual Behaviour,* 44, 1233–42

Wood, L. (2012) *Media representation of disabled people.* Available at: www.disabilityplanet.co.uk/critical-analysis.html

World Bank (2020) *Disability inclusion.* Available at: www.worldbank.org/en/topic/disability

World Health Organization (2014) *Mental health: A state of well-being.* Available at: http://origin.who.int/features/factfiles/mental_health/en/

World Health Organization (2018a) *International Classification of Diseases ICD-11.* Available at: https://icd.who.int/en

World Health Organization (2018b) *Health of Refugee and Migrant Children: Technical Guidance.* Available at: www.euro.who.int/__data/assets/pdf_file/0011/388361/tc-health-children-eng.pdf?ua=1

World Health Organization (2020) *Disabilities.* Available at: www.who.int/topics/disabilities/en/

World Professional Association for Transgender Health (2020) *Statement in response to calls for banning evidence-based supportive health interventions for transgender and gender-diverse youth.* Available at: www.wpath.org/media/cms/Documents/ Public%20Policies/2020/FINAL%20Joint%20Statement%20Opposing%20Anti%20 Trans%20Legislation%20Jan%2028%202020.pdf?_t=1580243903

Yarrow, A. and Fane, J. (2018) *The Sociology of Early Childhood: Young Children's Lives and Worlds.* Abingdon: Routledge.

YMCA (2017) *More Than Words.* Available at: www.ymca.org.uk/wp-content/ uploads/2017/10/More-Than-Words-v1.0-Report.pdf

Young Minds (2018) *Addressing Adversity.* Available at: https://youngminds.org.uk/ media/2715/ym-addressing-adversity-book-web-2.pdf

Younus, S. and Mian, A. (2018) Children, adolescents, and Islamophobia. In Moffic, H., Peteet, J., Hankir, A. and Awaad, R. (eds) *Islamophobia and Psychiatry.* pp. 321– 34. New York: Springer.

Zeleke, W., Koester, L. and Lock, G. (2018) Parents' understanding of adopted children's ways of being, belonging and becoming. *Journal of Child and Family Studies,* 27, 1428–39. Available at: https://doi.org/10.1007/s10826-017-0995-y

INDEX